The Liberalization of
American Protestantism

The Liberalization of

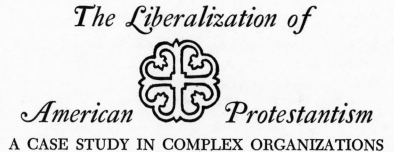

American Protestantism

A CASE STUDY IN COMPLEX ORGANIZATIONS

Henry J. Pratt

WAYNE STATE UNIVERSITY

Wayne State University Press   Detroit   1972

Published simultaneously in Canada
by the Copp Clark Publishing Company
517 Wellington Street, West
Toronto 2B, Canada.

Library of Congress Cataloging in Publication Data
Pratt, Henry J   1934–
    The liberalization of American Protestantism.
    Bibliography: p. 293
    1. National Council of the Churches of Christ in the United States of
America. 2. Christianity and politics. I. Title.
BX6.N2P7   286'.6'73   74–38837
ISBN 0–8143–1475–9

For My Parents

Contents

Preface 9

1 Introduction 13

PART 1 / STRATEGIES

2 The Impact of the 1950 Merger 25
3 The "Active Minority" among Member Churches 46
4 Liberalism versus Conservatism 63
5 The National Lay Committee Controversy 84

PART 2 / RESOURCES

6 Liberal Trends in the Council's Staff 109
7 Local Councils of Churches 122

PART 3 / ACTIVISM

8 Prelude to Activism 141
9 Continuity and Change in Racial Attitudes 158
10 James Forman and the "Black Manifesto" 188
11 The NCC and National Educational Policy 207
12 The Problem of Internal Cohesion 234
13 Conclusion: Toward a Theory of
Interest Group Activism 261

Notes 281
Bibliography 293
Index 300

Preface

Some question may be raised about the scope of this work. The term *liberalization* in the main title connotes the increasingly self-conscious progressivism with which the National Council of the Churches of Christ (NCC), the organization of interdenominational Protestantism in the United States, has attended to the political dimensions of its stands on moral and social issues. I am fully conscious that the council has for many years been accorded a reputation as being "liberal," but I shall undertake to show that this liberalism prior to 1960 was typically imbued with an individualist bias, which ruled out most overt interventions in the process of government, whereas after this date there was an increasing acceptance of "positive government." In using the term *complex organizations*, I have in mind the fact that to properly grasp the council's behavior, it must be viewed as an organization, not internally solidified and monolithic, but rather comprised of largely autonomous subunits—united on some issues, divided on others—out of whose competition, discussions, and mutual accommodations policy eventually emerges.

The NCC's concern with the sphere of foreign policy, though alluded to from time to time, is not to be analyzed in depth. My reason for this is that the council's interest in foreign policy matters has not aroused the concern that has typified the reaction to its domestic political involvement, and thus does not have the same importance in contributing to diversity of opinion among its constituents. I should point out, however, that the council's approach to foreign policy matters is not at variance with its basic perspective on domestic issues; both reflect a liberal outlook, the sources of which are probed at length in this work.

I should like to acknowledge the time and interest of several people who went out of their way to be helpful. Long before I contemplated this particular work, my senior professors at Columbia University, Wallace S. Sayre and David B. Truman, called my attention to interdenominational Protestantism as a subject worthy of greater attention from political scientists. Grants awarded by the Faculty Research Fund at Emory University enabled me in 1965 to conduct a mail survey of political predispositions among local church-council secretaries, and two years later to spend a summer in New York so that I could do research at NCC headquarters. Clarence M. Stone and Jack W. Hopkins, both former colleagues at Emory, have expressed warm interest in the project at all stages. A special word of gratitude is due Edgar Litt of the University of Connecticut, who, more than any other person, was responsible for my setting forth.

Executives in the NCC were most helpful in interrupting their busy schedules to answer questions and ferret out information I requested. Eugene Carson Blake, now the executive secretary of the World Council of Churches, kindly consented to talk with me about his role in the NCC from the mid-1950s through the mid-1960s. H. Conrad Hoyer of the NCC Office for Councils of Churches allowed me to use the office's local state-councils' mailing lists for my survey. Constant Jacquet of the council's Department of Research and Dean M. Kelley of the Department of Religious Liberty were of particular help. It goes without saying that I, and not those mentioned here, am accountable for what appears in the text.

A word of appreciation is due my typist, Charlotte Harris, for her excellence of workmanship and unflagging good cheer. Finally I would like to pay tribute to the meticulous, creative and informed work of my Wayne State University Press editor, Aletta Biersack. Miss Biersack proved herself a most able copyeditor and beyond this demonstrated an ability to make pertinent and extremely worthwhile suggestions about the content of the manuscript. I have no doubt that it is a better piece of work as a result of her efforts.

H. J. P.
Detroit, Michigan
1971

I. Introduction

Observers of the National Council of Churches may disagree on many points, but it is difficult to imagine that any would take issue with the statement that as it begins the decade of the 1970s, the organization has a pronounced liberal orientation on both domestic and foreign issues. The term *liberal* is used here not in the classical European sense, but in its current American usage, as connoting four main attitudes: (1) satisfaction with the economic policies and directions of the modern welfare state and acceptance of them as a given; (2) affirmation of America's world responsibilities and support of international cooperation; (3) the shunning of ideological or doctrinaire commitment in either economic or political matters; and (4) belief in the First, Fifth, and Fourteenth Amendments as embodiments of civil liberties essential to a free society.[1]

Consistent with this outlook the council has directed its energies toward solving a variety of interrelated and mutually reinforcing social problems. Best known is its commitment to the goal of racial justice and equal opportunity for black people, as reflected in its promotion of civil rights legislation and demands for vigorous enforcement of laws designed to promote equal opportunity. The organization has also concerned itself with the problems of hunger and poverty, both in this country and abroad, advocating, for example, massive increases in funds for the Federal Food Stamp Program and for nonmilitary foreign aid.

Wanting to end needless suffering and redirect national resources to urgent domestic needs, the council has voiced opposition to American involvement in the Vietnam War. It has also cooperated with a number of Jewish and Roman Catholic leaders in criticizing the American tendency to seek purely military solutions to the problem of achieving world order.

One would find the council's progressive stands less worthy of attention if the organization were small in size or consistently liberal at the grass roots level. Yet this is in fact anything but the case. The NCC is a broadly inclusive federation composed of 33 Protestant and Eastern Orthodox denominations, whose combined membership is 43 million. Moreover, a disproportionate number of its rank-and-file constituents are situated in the South and Midwest, regions not noted for having consistently liberal views. Not surprisingly, the council has been subjected to vigorous criticism by churchmen opposed to its progressive stands, and cutbacks in programs in 1969 and 1970 have been attributed in part to restiveness among former donors. Yet the fact remains that it has managed to avoid any significant member-body defections in recent years and has shown no evidence of abandoning its social activism.

The organization's recent demand for more vigorous national programs to combat domestic and world problems is all the more arresting in view of its earlier, deeply rooted opposition to any enlargement of national government power. The shift from a moderate to a liberal perspective on these issues is remarkable. Was it caused by internal and bureaucratic or by external and politico-historical factors? Do similar organizations undergo parallel shifts for similar reasons? It is the intriguing question of why a large, federated interest group should make such significant deviations from its historically moderate position that moved the author to undertake this exploration of the development of the National Council of Churches.

YEARS PRIOR TO ACTIVISM

Although it adopted its present name in 1950, the National Council of Churches of Christ was actually established in 1908, when its parent body, the Federal Council of Churches of Christ in America (FCC), came into existence. The FCC emerged out of the confluence of two powerful ideals in late nineteenth-century American Protestantism: those of social service and and interdenominational cooperation. In bringing these two concepts together and giving them institutional form, the founders hoped that the evangelistic efforts of the Protestant churches would find new relevance. They believed that the churches would lead American society toward "Progress" and "The Ideal Society" by "Moral Principle" and "Moral Force." The solution to society's ills lay in "Christianizing the social order," transmuting present institutions based on the premise of human greed into ones rooted in love and cooperation. The conciliation of industrial disputes, research directed at weighing the conflicting claims of labor and capital, the arbitration of international conflicts, all these were viewed as part of a coherent approach to achieving a more cooperative and "Christlike" world. No one regarded it as utopian or naïve when in 1912 the Reverend Edward A. Steiner, an FCC leader, anticipated the coming of "not only the Holy Land of Holy Men, but a Holy Earth . . . a Holy United States bringing down the Holy City from Heaven decked as a bride for her bridegroom." [2]

As the years passed it became increasingly evident that such visions as Steiner's were not to find their worldy embodiment, and the council was obliged gradually to accept pragmatic objectives, even though it never officially denied the need to prepare the way for the establishment of the Kingdom of God on Earth. It had identified itself with a set of practical goals as early as its 1908 founding convention, when delegates voted approval of the "Social Ideals of the Churches" (commonly referred to in later years as the "Social Creed"). The document put the *main line* Protestant churches (such higher status, doctrinally traditional denominations as Presbyterian, Protestant Episcopal, Methodist, and so on, as contrasted to such lower-status, less traditional, and more fundamentalist churches as the Church of God and the Salvation Army) on record in support of the aspirations of American labor. This particularly involved the abolition of child labor, protection of the worker against the consequences of disease, injury, and death, reduction of the work week, and the payment of a "living wage as

a minimum in every industry." In view of Protestantism's traditional pietism and acceptance of the rural virtues, the "Social
Creed" marked a significant turning point in its approach to the
issues of industrialization.

It is important to bear in mind, however, that the adoption
of a set of reform goals did not essentially alter the view that
moral and spiritual progress is most fully achieved when government intervention is held to a minimum. As was characteristic
of most groups embodying the spirit of "reform," the council
emphasized "education" and "voluntary service"—not lobbying
or political pressure—as the proper method of pursuing its objectives. Its basic theory of human nature, expressed in biblical
and theological terms, embodied the notion that the concepts of
sin and human depravity, traditional in Protestantism, should
be redefined as reflections of defective social institutions rather
than individual frailty. Council leaders believed, moreover, that
it was both unnecessary and unwise to involve government in
the effort to reform society, since government actions always
involved an element of coercion. The majority preference for
voluntarism was in no way reduced when a few churchmen
sought to rationalize government intervention on humanitarian
grounds. The council was deeply committed to the notion that
"only cooperative action has moral quality." [3] Man, created in
the image of God, was regarded as essentially good: but his
goodness could only be manifested if the reform strategies
chosen minimized the use of coercion.

Council leaders experienced no sense of inconsistency when
they combined this nonpolitical, voluntaristic approach to domestic questions with active efforts to influence the United
States Government's foreign policy. In 1912 they established
the Commission on Peace and Arbitration (later to be renamed
the Commission on International Justice and Goodwill), which
went on record in favor of the Hague Convention in its outlawing of war and its calling upon nations to submit international disputes to arbitration. A few years later the council
demanded the United States' participation in the League of
Nations ("this truly Christian social order"), and in the 1930s
it called for creation of an international police force to achieve
world order.

The Great Depression, with its massive social dislocations and economic privations, necessitated some change of strategies involving domestic problems. Without becoming directly involved in partisan politics, council leaders made it plain that they approved of the essential thrust of Franklin D. Roosevelt's New Deal. In the "Revised Social Creed," adopted in 1932, they went on record as favoring national economic planning and "social control of the credit and monetary systems," both policies implying a need for enlarging the sphere of government action.

Yet this shift in approach did not qualify the older notion that appeals to enlightened self-interest and moral instincts were preferable in achieving reform objectives. Though FCC leaders were generally sympathetic to the New Deal, they were unwilling to become active participants in the progressive coalition composed of labor and secular liberals that sought in the 1930s and 1940s to provide mass support for FDR's domestic program. Some "Christian realists" called for a more fundamental reassessment. The publication in 1932 of Reinhold Niebuhr's *Moral Man and Immoral Society* did not go unnoticed, especially those sections in which Niebuhr analyzed the strength of human pride and sin manifested in groups and the inadequacy of moral strength alone as a means of achieving social justice. Council leaders read with interest his indictment of the weaknesses of the Social Gospel (with which the council had become identified) and his stress on the need for deliberately exercising group power to achieve proximate political ends.[4] Yet Niebuhr's remained a minority approach in main line Protestant circles, and his thinking did not undercut the council's abiding confidence in voluntary action. In 1940, F. Ernest Johnson, a high official in the organization, published *The Social Gospel Revisited*, which was in part a rebuttal to Niebuhr. In it Johnson voiced his endorsement of the New Deal, choosing to picture it as essentially a noncoercive exercise of national authority. He insisted that "Little by little, though sometimes with a startling suddenness, mankind is learning that the essential divinity of man is a 'first principle' not a derivative."[5]

As an organization committed to the goals of reform and social justice, the council could not resist entirely those liberals and progressives who by the 1940s were advocating government intervention as necessary to the achievement of humanitarian goals. Toward the end of World War II the FCC joined other national groups in calling for the establishment of a permanent Fair Employment Practices Commission (FEPC) under national government auspices. With its creation in 1946 of the Commission on Church and Economic Life, under the leadership of a distinguished expert on labor problems, Cameron P. Hall, and a prominent liberal layman, Charles P. Taft (brother of the U.S. senator from Ohio), the council implicitly accepted the limited welfare-state system established in the Roosevelt years; and it even began to press for further government action in certain policy areas.

Yet this change in outlook on the part of a few council activists failed to attract significant grass roots support, and was even opposed by many leading national churchmen. As the lines of opposition over policy became delineated, with conservatives countering New Deal-Fair Deal liberals, it was increasingly the liberals who found themselves on the defensive. In the early 1950s, following the Federal Council's merger with eleven other interdenominational Protestant bodies, the organization adopted a cautious policy with regard to national legislative issues and considered seriously (even when it refused to adopt) conservative proposals. It accorded semiofficial recognition to the National Lay Committee, a group of conservative business and professional people. While not abandoning the quest for social reform, it tended to reassert its voluntaristic strategy as the best means of achieving this end.

Increasingly in the '50s the council's policy statements were confined to the expression of abstract moral principles, while avoiding the troublesome matter of implementation. They expressed "concern" over issues, rather than recommending any concrete course of action. Evaluating this situation early in 1960, Peter Day, the editor of a leading denominational publication, acknowledged that over the past decade the council had made an important contribution in challenging outworn American shibboleths in the area of foreign policy, especially by censuring the United States' unwillingness to discuss "peace" or to consider the recognition of Red China. But by and large he found the NCC's performance disappointing:

> The unique contribution of the NCC to the American Christian scene is its bigness. But bigness as Haldane has pointed out in his famous essay, "On Being the Right Size," is a limitation. A horse is too big to fly. An elephant is too big to jump. A brontosaurus is too big to survive. In the area of prophecy, the glibness of the NCC has already taken its toll. The Federal Council in its day (1908–50) could sound like Isaiah. The National Council of Churches sounds more like Ezekiel.[6]

The author suggested that considering the problems in American life crying out for attention, the organization's statements were distinguished by their irrelevancy:

> Since its inception ten years ago, the NCC has issued twenty "pronouncements." Beginning with a lifeless theological generalization, they go on to confess the sins of lay members of the constituent churches, dividing delicately between the "some," the "many" and the "all." They then wind up with a bold proposal for solving the problems of the year before last. These forty-nine pages of hierarchical wisdom lead one to the despairing cry, "How could so many mean so little by so much." [7]

The explanation for the council's caution is to be found partly in the pronouncedly conservative, probusiness attitudes that prevailed among most rank-and-file churchmen in the '50s. Numerous contemporaneous works documented and commented on these attitudes. Gibson H. Winter deplored *The Suburban Captivity of the Churches,* while Martin E. Marty questioned whether William H. Whyte's widely read indictment of conformity, *The Organization Man,* might not better be retitled "The Denominational Man." [8] The president of the NCC, he noted, found it necessary in 1955 to warn the churches against the threat to organized religion posed by "America's humanistic nationalism," whose adherents reduced God to "a combination of whipping boy, servant and even a useful ally in dealing with religious people whose actions otherwise might get in their way." [9]

In his critique of Protestant complacency, *The Noise of*

Solemn Assemblies, sociologist Peter L. Berger concluded that "organized religion is irrelevant to the major social forces which are operative and determinative in American society; it does not affect them, and it relates to them in an overwhelmingly passive way." [10] The churches' approach to the social world, Berger asserted,

> is one of affirming the *status quo* and of seeking to harmonize whatever forces tend to disturb it. Thus, again speaking of middle class Protestantism, one is opposed to conflict and in favor of peace on the social scene. The important point to grasp here is that this bias toward harmony operates regardless of what the situation may be. In situations of industrial conflict one will advocate the re-establishment of peace. . . . In situations of racial conflict the same tendency will prevail . . . the system of racial segregation or discrimination receives the designation of peace, while the forces which seek to disrupt the system become seen as disturbers of that peace. [11]

Berger contended that the problem was not that the churches had no impact on politics or public affairs, but that they had allowed themselves to become compromised by the public whose favor they curried; as a result, the churches constituted a de facto religious establishment. He even charged that they had sold out to the bourgeois ethic and had seen to it that the middle class clergy were "normally on the side of the cops." "Americanism," he concluded, had become a state religion in the U.S.; the churches, in exchange for the comfortable status accorded them, had acquiesced in this constitutional heresy. [12]

Though Berger's assertions may have been overstated, the general thrust of his analysis was supported by the results of precise, empirical investigations published in social science journals and monographs. There was concrete data showing that Protestant Americans typically had a conservative outlook on political matters and were inclined to oppose the churches' speaking out on strongly controversial issues. Whereas the political attitudes of American Jews were found to be liberal in bias, [13] Gerhard Lenski documented a right-of-center tendency among white Protestants, as measured both by party affiliation (support for the Republicans among voters in a northern sample) and by issue preferences. Though more progressive tendencies have been shown to exist among main line Protestant clergymen in specialized ministries (campus chaplains, for example) and among those serving in low-income or minority group congregations,[14] Lenski reported that among white middle class congregations "the voting behavior [of pastors] . . . is indistinguishable from that of the middle class portion of the laity." [15] Most Protestant ministers, it should be observed, have churches of this latter type.

ACTIVISM

In light of the council's voluntaristic traditions and the status quo sentiments of its rank and file, only a rash person would have predicted in 1960 that the following decade would differ in any manner from previous ones in terms of strategies for achieving major goals. The organization would presumably continue to do research, issue reports on social problems, and "educate" constituents. Since national attention was focusing on the race question and there was some sentiment among members that the NCC should "do something" to show concern, one might have predicted further statements on civil rights (paralleling those of earlier years), followed perhaps by testimony before a congressional committee, but little beyond that. It would have seemed most unlikely that a platform of achieving social justice through increased government intervention and coercion would have been adopted. Despite occasional "papers" on the part of a few council leaders, the organization's coolness toward increases in government power had persisted for over half a century, and would have been expected to survive the then current national unrest.

Why, then, did the NCC and local and state councils take unprecedented steps in the field of social action during the 1960s? How is one to account for the leaders' breaking sharply with the long-standing "educational strategy" to become enmeshed in the domestic controversy involved in securing legislation to enlarge the powers of an activist government? Why did they throw themselves into the campaign to enact civil rights legislation? What factors caused their attempts to secure national policies beneficial to migrant labor, American Indians, and the urban poor? How did they find themselves among the leading participants in the enactment of the Elementary and Secondary Education Act (1965) and in the organization of minority group neighborhoods in cities throughout the country? What led Saul Alinsky, a radical organizer and not a Christian himself, to finally suggest that in the 1960s "the churches are taking the leadership in social change," a role that had been played by labor unions in the 1930s, and that "churches are now the big dominant force in civil rights?" [16] These are the questions to which the present study addresses itself.

The fundamental change in NCC perspective brings one to the further question of whether parallel shifts in attitudes toward government intervention have occurred in comparable voluntary organizations in this country. Though the increasing acceptance of "positive government" among reform-oriented groups in the twentieth century has been noted by most analysts, there have been few attempts to account for this development as a general phenomenon. Instead, most studies confine themselves to a single organization or social movement.

The question of whether one can approach a theory of reform group reorientation by comparing the development of such bodies as the American Federation of Labor, the American Civil Liberties Union, and the National Association for the Advancement of Colored People to that of the National Council of Churches is fundamental to the study of interest group behavior. At the conclusion of this study, therefore, we shall turn our attention to the way that all four organizations have reoriented their outlooks on the issue of government intervention as one means of achieving their respective goals.

part 1

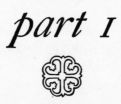

STRATEGIES

2. The Impact of the 1950 Merger

*I*t seems appropriate to begin discussion of the National Council of Churches by focusing attention on formal elements of structure, while postponing for the moment the more complex matter of accounting for the organization's increasingly activist stance relative to national policy issues. In the course of the discussion, however, we shall have occasion to move beyond mere description of organizational components in an effort to determine just how the various units came to assume their present place in the federation, and then to suggest how the arrangement finally arrived at influenced organizational goals and policy. No account that fails to consider the merger and its implications can be entirely successful in explaining the NCC activities of the 1950s and '60s. Although the histories of all federating agencies are interesting, they are peripheral to the concerns of this study. Only the FCC will be discussed, because it was the senior partner of the NCC confederation.

PRELUDE TO MERGER

In the 1920s and early '30s the FCC had acquired a controversial reputation, and this was a factor that tended to forestall close collaboration with other Protestant bodies. This reputation grew from pronouncements that were a logical extension

of the 1908 mandate but that many constituents had nevertheless not anticipated. A few examples will illustrate the actions arousing concern. As early as 1919 the council, in a major
policy statement entitled "The Church and Social Reconstruc-
tion," went on record in favor of "a coordinated nationwide employment service," extension of unemployment benefits to cover
joblessness arising from ill health, accident, and old age, and
in 1922 (in a joint statement with leading Roman Catholic and
Jewish groups) it condemned the twelve-hour workday in the
steel industry. In the early '20s the organization issued another
joint statement with its Roman Catholic and Jewish counterparts, attacking the open shop movement, then being actively
promoted by industrialists, for infringing on the basic rights
of organized labor. For its part in the statement it was denounced by the Ohio Chamber of Commerce as a "Communist"
agency. This charge was to be repeated in other contexts, as
when a few years later Congressman Arthur M. Free introduced a resolution in the House of Representatives describing
the FCC as a Communist organization aiming to establish a
church-state and the American Legion proposed a congressional
investigation.

The council's Research Department, created to gather objective information on social issues, was a particular target of
such attacks. When in 1925 it issued a report that surveyed
Prohibition in a factual, objective manner, Protestant "drys"
charged that the council was deserting Prohibition and the
controversy raged for months. There were also attacks on the
FCC's peace program by congressmen and officials of the Army
and Navy Departments. In 1935 the chief of naval operations
charged the council with Communist collaboration.

In 1932 the council formally amended its 1908 "Social
Creed" in a statement entitled "Revised Social Ideals," which
advocated social planning and social control of credit, social
security legislation, reduction in labor hours, the right of workers to organize for collective bargaining, abolition of child labor,
and economic justice for the farmer through price control of
farm products. Though justified by its leaders as a logical extension of avowed principles, the "revised ideals" in no way

diminished the council's controversial image among conservative church members.

In October 1932, President Franklin D. Roosevelt declared in a Detroit speech that he was "as radical as the Federal Council"; and in an address to its twenty-fifth anniversary celebration a year later, he equated the ideals of the church and the government. As one might have expected, the FCC was sympathetic to most of FDR's programs. Protestant intellectuals closely identifying with the FCC wrote books defending the New Deal with all the ardor of the young New Dealers in Washington. Chief among these were Benson Y. Landis's *The Third American Revolution* (1933) and F. Ernest Johnson's *Economics and the Good Life* (1934). The council's official publications, the *Federal Council Bulletin,* edited by Samuel McCrea Cavert, and *Information Service,* edited by Johnson, broadcast their support. A common theme was that the council deserved some of the credit for preparing the soil in which the New Deal was taking root.

So long as it continued to stress progressive reforms, the council's image in the nation and among its Protestant constituents, a majority of which had Republican bias, would remain controversial. But council leaders chose not to remain at the head of the progressive phalanx once the New Deal became an established fact. In the last analysis the organization was the voice of the Protestant churches, not a reform pressure group. As the Great Depression deepened, Protestantism's complacency because of its comfortable status in earlier years gave way to acute anxiety over sharp losses in church membership and doubts as to whether the traditional ecclesiastical answers had much relevancy for a nation suffering from economic despair and shock. At this juncture the council elected to minimize its reformist image, leaving reform to the New Deal, and to address itself to the problems of declining rank-and-file support within its constituent bodies.

The groundwork for this major change had already been laid. In 1928 a committee report, *Annual Report* of the Federal Council of Churches, had suggested that "evangelizing the unchurched, cultivating the devotional life, Christian education and Christian social action" should define the council's priorities. While social action was thus not absent from the list, its last place on it was no accident. In 1932 the Committee on Evangelism was elevated in status and a Committee on Worship was authorized. These moves marked the beginning of a trend. The following year the council proclaimed that

> Evangelism is coming into its own. It is not an outworn word. The word has indicated its primacy by the fact that the most conservative of our communions has adopted the word as best fitted to describe the work of the church for the souls of men. [1]

Traditionally the FCC had defined the possession of personal religious faith and a concern for social justice as mutually reinforcing, but its new emphasis on "personal religion" implied their sharp distinction as categories.

In the mid-1930s the National Preaching Mission was launched to appeal to member churches that were experiencing a loss of numbers during the depression. Between 1930 and 1940 the United States population increased 7.3 percent, but during roughly the same period (1926 to 1936) an analysis of the *Census of Religious Bodies* reveals that 15 of the 22 FCC constituent denominations for which figures are given suffered membership decline. In aggregate terms, combined membership in the 22 churches fell from 18,311,000 in 1926 to 16,997,000 in 1936, a drop of 7.7 percent. Some of the churches that had been most loyal in their support of the council experienced the sharpest losses. The Methodist Episcopal Church, for example, lost 14 percent in a decade, and the Religious Society of Friends (Quakers), 17 percent. The Preaching Mission was accorded top priority by council leaders in order to increase church memberships, and it proved effective in attracting large audiences.

The shift in emphasis from New Deal liberalism to "personal religion" is also reflected in the content of the official publication, the *Federal Council Bulletin*. Subsequent to 1934 important social legislation that came up before Congress was typically ignored or minimized. The *Bulletin*, for example, did not so much as mention the Social Security Act of 1935 until its issue of May 1936, nearly a year after enactment. Controversial social issues, when mentioned at all in the 1935 to 1937 period, were often discussed as though they constituted a threat to the integrity of the churches; one finds repeated editorial references to an "overemphasis" on social problems that was said to characterize the thinking of certain churchmen.

It is reasonable to suppose that the FCC's adoption of a preaching-mission emphasis in the late 1930s and early '40s, coupled with the related tendency to avoid stands that could prove controversial, was a necessary prerequisite to creating an atmosphere of trust between it and other interdenominational agencies, more pietistic and conservative in social outlook. Judging by accounts written by high-level council officials and by outside observers, the period from 1935 to 1949 was one of consolidation, involving reemphasis on the mission of an inter-church coordinating body and stress on evangelism. Social issues were not entirely neglected—even the Preaching Mission dealt with social questions to some degree—but they were no longer given primacy. It is indicative of growing acceptance among moderates and conservatives that when in 1949 a widely read right-wing polemic attacked the council for its alleged "apostasy" and "Communist thinking," the organization had little difficulty in lining up a committee of sober-minded business, industrial, and professional figures, headed by no less a conservative than John Foster Dulles, to issue a rebuttal. The Dulles committee recorded its "full confidence that the Federal Council functions with complete fidelity to Christian ideals." [2]

The point here is not just that the council was viewed in less controversial terms in 1949 than in, say, 1932, although this is no doubt true. It is also important that the preaching-mission emphasis resulted in a functional redefinition of the council's role in Protestantism. Whereas in the past it had stressed social reform, leaving more prosaic goals to other interdenominational bodies, by the late 1930s it had begun to deemphasize reform in favor of other matters. With the Preaching Mission it had reasserted its status as an evangelistic body, a role implicit in its 1908 mandate but heretofore largely played down. How much of this change in approach is attributable to conscious intent and how much to changing external circumstances is not entirely clear. External developments were evidently *one* factor, since a number of the issues that had marked the FCC as controversial in the 1920s and early '30s had by now been embodied in national legislation or were no longer intensely controversial. The same point can be made about Prohibition, which the council had defended in the 1920s (though not always with the fervor desired by some "drys"), but which had become a "nonissue" after the passage of the repeal amendment. Similarly, its staunch advocacy of disarmament, which had earned it the enmity of the military establishment in the years prior to 1936, had given way to an acceptance of the need for military preparedness in the face of the Nazi and Japanese threats.

For a variety of reasons, then, the council did not seem as controversial in the 1940s as it had in the 1930s; its policies and programs, once quite distinctive and unique, now could be viewed as consistent with the more evangelical emphasis favored by the other interdenominational Protestant agencies. The old justifications for maintaining a separation between these several bodies began to weaken. Joint planning and administration of programs became more common, moreover, and a whole series of inter-agency coordinating committees were created in an effort to minimize overlapping and duplication. Twenty-four of these had come into existence by the mid-1940s, but it was apparent to all that they offered no long-term solution.

FORMAL MERGER

The merger movement now gathered momentum. In 1940 a meeting was arranged between FCC representatives and those of the seven other interdenominational bodies, followed by a meeting of the eight agencies in Cleveland in December 1941. Four other agencies, founded subsequent to this meeting, would later join the merger movement. The Cleveland Study Conference surveyed the situation and came up with three different possibilities of how further progress might be made, one of which, the idea of merger, subsequently gained the widest support. On 25 April 1944 a specially constituted committee submitted a proposed constitution to a convention composed of the eight agencies, with the recommendation that it be approved. The convention acted favorably on the proposal and this action was conveyed back to the various constituencies. Ratification required action by a host of bodies, since the FCC and one or two others were themselves federations, all of which had to pass judgment. It is not surprising that the ratification process took six years.

By the end of 1949 all but one of the agencies had voted in favor of the plan, and the one holdout (The Foreign Missions Conference) was persuaded in April 1950 to reconsider and vote to join. The Constituting Convention of the National Council of Churches of Christ in the United States of America was held in Cleveland in late November 1950, and the new body was voted into existence by the 600 official delegates in attendance.

The constitution embodied assurances to the various interests represented that the goals of the old organization would not be lost sight of by the new. One-half of each denomination's representatives in the National Council would be selected by denominational program boards and agencies functioning as part of the NCC structure. It was felt that the viewpoints of these boards would continue to embody the spirit of the former interdenominational agencies to which they had been closely tied, and that their representatives would therefore protect the old agencies' programs in the merged body. To the same end it was agreed informally that each organization would be allowed (initially at least) to retain a measure of its former autonomy within the larger structure of the NCC in terms of staffing, office location, and relations with constituents. The result was a very complicated and cumbersome organization (figure 1) and a staff many of whom bore only nominal fealty to the council's executive secretary. But the decisions on organizational structure reached in the 1948 to 1950 period were sufficiently open-ended that a streamlining would be possible at a later time if so desired.

The fact that the agencies involved had felt compelled to cooperate with one another over the previous ten years suggests that the boundaries separating them were not imperme-

Figure 1 Organizational Chart of the NCC, 1951.

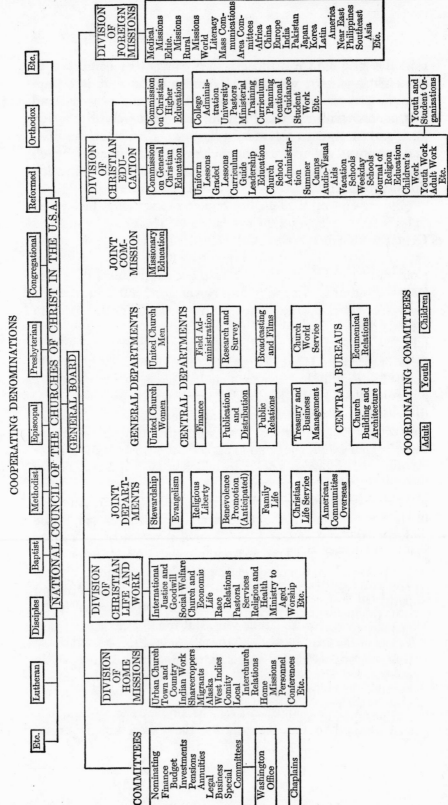

able and that the goal of one could be made to dovetail with those of the others. Also indicative of a new mood is the fact that the process of approval, though prolonged, went forward with so few interruptions. None of the organizations initially projected for the merger failed to approve it, and in all but one case approval was given the first time it was formally voted upon. Obviously, an atmosphere of trust already existed, which the merger itself both reflected and helped advance.

LARGER SIGNIFICANCE OF THE MERGER

The 1950 decision may usefully be interpreted as the transformation of twelve essentially single-purpose bodies into one enlarged organization having a diversity of goals. Those familiar with the history of the Federal Council of Churches may find this statement, at first glance, oversimplified. Admittedly, in its 42 years of existence the council had endeavored to fulfill a variety of objectives, including the promotion of interdenominational cooperation, world peace and disarmament, Jewish-Christian understanding, and increased racial harmony. In a larger sense, though, the council was single-purposed, like the other merging bodies, in that its activities had centered around one overriding objective, namely that of combatting the disruptive effects of industrialization and intergroup tension through a program of social service, social education, and disinterested research. The FCC had striven to embody at the national level Social Gospel aims, aptly summarized by the historian Charles H. Hopkins:

> The social situation produced by the industrial revolution in post-Civil War America was characterized by the rise of large scale production units that drew together vast proletarian populations in hastily built, overcrowded cities. As clergymen looked at the consequent social maladjustment, their predominant concern was with the problem of industry, a question given added concern by the strictures of socialism. . . . It may be said, therefore, that the social gospel was the reaction of Protestantism—markedly stimulated by socialism—to the ethics and practices of capitalism as brought to a point in the industrial situation.[3]

Though an important force in late nineteenth- and early twentieth-century Protestantism, the Social Gospel movement never succeeded in gaining the status of a majority or dominant viewpoint; and the Federal Council was thus viewed by some churchmen as having a narrow and sectarian outlook. Other interdenominational bodies shared their suspicion of FCC goals and sought to contain them by delimiting the domain in which the FCC could rightly function. A number of those bodies that confederated with the FCC to form the NCC had been founded at about the same time as the FCC; some important ones had even been constituted before it, a factor that had frequently been mentioned whenever the council's concerns threatened to overlap theirs. In some instances council leaders had been forced to specialize artificially in ignoring the interrelatedness of various human and spiritual needs because other agencies arbitrarily monopolized them. This is to say that prior to the merger there had been a certain division of labor among the FCC and the other merging agencies (founding dates noted):

The Inter-Seminary Committee (1880)
The Foreign Missions Conference of North America (1893)
The Missionary Education Movement of the United States and
    Canada (1902)
The Home Missions Council of North America (1908)
The National Protestant Council on Higher Education (1911)
The United Stewardship Council (1920)
The International Council of Religious Education (1922)
The United Council of Church Women (1940)
Church World Service (1946)
The Protestant Film Commission (1947)
The Protestant Radio Commission (1947)

In formal terms, then, it may be suggested that the 1950 merger of interdenominational bodies under the hegemony of the FCC (it alone, for example, had its roots in the Protestant denominations as corporate bodies, and its executive secretary was to become the general secretary of the NCC) is an important instance of what sociologists have termed "goal multiplication." In order to grasp the full meaning and significance of such a change, it is worthwhile to turn to the writings of sociologist Amitai Etzioni. In his *Modern Organizations* (1964),

Etzioni advanced a hypothesis regarding the likely consequences of goal multiplication, which has never been thoroughly
tested empirically. He suggested that organizations with multiple goals typically achieve greater efficiency than structures
having a single purpose. In multipurpose organizations, he argued, expertise developed in one area tends to expand into
other areas, resulting in a healthy cross-fertilization of thinking
in the several areas that enhances the capacity and forcefulness
of all operating units.[4] Etzioni is not suggesting that multigoal
organizations necessarily are more liberal than single-purpose
ones, the hypothesis being in no way concerned with the content or political coloration of policy. But his argument does lead
to the prediction that when an existing organization with reformist goals elects to enlarge its range of concerns through
merger with other agencies, its reformism is likely to assume a
more forceful and multidimensional character. Since the hypothesis would seem to have a bearing on the council's case, it
will be used as a point of departure in examining the council's
post-1950 development.

BUREAUCRATIC DEVELOPMENTS

Rather than analyze the impact of merger on all units, the
following discussion selects for attention two of the larger and
older departments: the Division of Home Missions (successor
to the Home Missions Council of North America) and the Division of Christian Life and Work (successor to most divisions
of the Federal Council of Churches). Although the process of
bureaucratic integration went further in these two cases than
in most (they were in fact merged to form one unit in 1965),
this does not render them atypical; and for the purposes of this
study it is important to focus on two such socially and politically
responsible units.

Increased Forcefulness in the Area of Home Missions. For
13 years after the 1950 merger, the council's Division on Home
Missions carried forward the work of the old Home Missions
Council of North America. In the early years after the merger,
the division's program and personnel changed little from those
of the 1940s, as is suggested by a 1954 *Christian Century* article:

the task of converting and churching America is too big to be accomplished by a divided Protestantism. The agency through which cooperation is being carried out is the Division of Home Missions of the NCC. It succeeds the Home Missions Council of North America. . . . a major concern of cooperative church-men of the home missions field is to evangelize the fearful or small minded and preach in season and out the principle and practice of cooperation. It is particularly in the field of home missions that the National Council is demonstrating the ca-pacity of its member churches to rise above sectarianism and achieve wholeness. . . . Toward the winning of America a beginning has been made.[5]

The "converting and churching" emphasis is apparent in the division's two leading publications of the period: the *City Church*, published from 1950 to 1964 by the division's Depart-ment of the Urban Church; and *Town and Country Church*, published by its Department of Town and Country. Though the former publication was conscious of major social issues such as crime, poverty, and racial discrimination in the 1950s, it dealt with them as essentially peripheral matters. Judging from the annual indexes of *City Church*, for example, there was not a single article dealing with race relations in the period 1950 to 1956. While black faces did appear from time to time in photo-graphs and the problem of ministering to minority groups and disadvantaged people was occasionally raised, the primary focus was not on social issues but on how to meet the churches' insti-tutional needs. *Town and Country Church* was even less con-cerned at the time with controversial matters. Photographs and printed matter conveyed an impression of rural innocence and simplicity; the spiritual, economic, and social needs of the fam-ily farmer and (white) small town resident were the center of attention. A statement setting forth the "Purposes of this Journal" was printed in each issue until it was dropped in May 1960; it stressed three goals: to encourage cooperation among rural churches, to improve administration of the local church, and to stimulate the development of a Christian philosophy of rural life. That the work of the Home Missions division should proceed along the same general lines as those laid down by its predecessor prior to merger is in no way surprising, especially since its autonomy was enhanced at the time by having division headquarters located in a building separate from that of the National Council's general secretary. In the period 1950 to 1958 the division was administered jointly by two executive secretaries: Miss Edith Lowry (b. 1897), a graduate of Wellesley College who had been serving as executive secretary of the Home Missions Council from 1940, and the Reverend I. George Nace (b. 1892), a graduate of Franklin and Marshall College and a long-time missionary to China, who had come to the Home Missions Council in 1949 after serving for three years as director of the home missions board of his denomination. Judging by their backgrounds, both were steeped in the Protestant missionary tradition.

In the late 1950s, Nace and Lowry reached the age of retirement; and instead of two successors Reverend Jon Regier was chosen to replace both of them. At 35 he was remarkably young for a division head. In addition to an A.B., he had an A.M. in social work from the University of Michigan and was thus more technically specialized than either of his predecessors, neither of whom held graduate degrees. Following ordination to the Presbyterian ministry in 1947, he had served as the director of two neighborhood houses in central Chicago, then as director of the Chicago Youth Committee and a lecturer at Chicago's McCormack Theological Seminary. Before his appointment as executive secretary in the National Council he had not been identified with the missions field as such, which may partially explain his ability to chart a new course for the division without the encumbrance of prior professional commitments.

Early in 1957, just before Regier's appointment, the Home Missions Division obtained a grant of $112,000 from the Schwartzhaupt Foundation for a three-year citizenship education project among migrant agricultural workers. The migrant ministry was not new; it had functioned in the Home Missions Council since 1920. What was new was the emphasis on helping migrants develop their own indigenous leadership and become more skillful in exercising political rights such as the right to organize and petition. In 1959, with Regier in charge, the NCC was prepared to identify itself institutionally with the legislative demands of migrant labor. While his role in this change was evidently a significant one, the decision to select Regier in the first place suggests that council leaders had felt a need for changes in the division even before his appointment, the timing of which, only a few months prior to the division's move into the Inter-Church Center, worked to his advantage as a leader because it helped break up old bureaucratic patterns of behavior. A few months after his appointment, Regier issued a statement expressing his view that in order to present a relevant Christian gospel, an integrated social, economic, and political strategy was needed:

> What is taking place in our office is an effort to understand what is taking place in America. For a century, home missions have developed and nurtured many projects geared to specific situations: to the inner city, to sparsely populated rural areas; to special groups like agricultural migrants, Spanish Americans, Indians. Each of the problems to which we have directed specific attention is worthy; each demands more positive results than we have achieved. But, too often each project has been isolated from the rest. As a result, we have developed separate *missions* at the expense of our vision of a comprehensive *mission* to the whole nation. . . .

Regier went on to propose that the piecemeal approach be replaced by one that aimed at comprehensive solutions:

> Take the problems faced by the agricultural migrant. He needs a ministry in terms of better housing and working conditions, a minimum wage, educational opportunity, health and welfare services, training for citizenship; yet similar needs apply to other Americans. The curative we have been seeking for the migrant must become one element in a broad program of diagnosis and treatment for the spiritual and socio-economic needs of all Americans.[6]

The immediate organizational implications Regier drew from this were the needs (1) to reduce the number of home missions committees from eight to two (each of the eight had been concerned with a separate program); (2) to establish overall priorities for the division through centralized planning; and (3) to restructure the training program for field-staff personnel so that they would be qualified to serve in all aspects of the division's program.

The new program assumed that home missions could no longer be viewed as an autonomous aspect of the council's work; the opportunity was opened up for closer ties with other departments and agencies whose work impinged on persons in "mission" areas, both urban and rural. For the migrant ministry this involved closer bureaucratic ties with the Department of the Church and Economic Life of the Division of Christian Life and Work in efforts both to pressure Congress to extend the coverage of the minimum-wage law to farm laborers and to encourage migrants to adopt strategies similar to those shown to be successful by urban industrial workers. The willingness of Home Missions field-staff personnel to lend encouragement to farm-worker strikes in California and elsewhere also owes something to this growing bureaucratic tie-in with the Church and Economic Life department.

The Department of the Church and Economic Life carried forward the work of the former Federal Council commission of the same name. Since its founding in 1947 under the leadership of Cameron P. Hall and Charles P. Taft, it had been identifield with an activist approach to economic issues. Its program necessarily entailed contacts with local church people who were concerned, as it was, with farm labor, industrial labor, and business enterprise issues. Since those involved in the home missions field had also manifested a concern with the problems of farmers, urban workers, and so forth, it was expectable that these two units, once brought into close physical and organizational proximity, would begin to cross-fertilize each other; and the evidence suggests that once such cross-fertilization began, the home missions staff increasingly came to take on the liberalism of the Department of the Church and Economic Life.

Increasing relationships with other non-home-missions staffs appear to have affected the editorial content of *Town and Country Church* and the *City Church*. The tone of both changed. An altered perspective was especially apparent in *Town and Country Church*, which began to document for its readers instances of injustice and exploitation in rural America, especially as they

affected the lives of farm laborers. The change in outlook of
the *City Church* was less dramatic but noteworthy. The growing informal ties between the Divisions of Home Missions and
Christian Life and Work (leading to a merger of the two agencies in 1965) were reflected in the ever greater number of
City Church articles written by NCC staff personnel whose
backgrounds were in the area of social education and action
rather than in home missions.

Increasingly the earlier rural emphasis of the Home Missions
division was matched by intensified urban action programs,
which were begun on a pilot basis in the mid-1950s in some
midwestern cities and took on mature form in the mid-1960s.
In December 1964 the division held a three-day consultation in
Philadelphia's Marriott Hotel on the role of the churches in
urban organization and development. Among the 75 persons
attending were Regier and other NCC staff personnel; lay and
clerical leaders in various urban ministries; such outside experts
as Michael Harrington, a leading member (and later party
chairman) of the Socialist Party of America and author of the
widely read *The Other America,* and Dr. Dan Dodson, director
of the Center for Human Relations and Community Studies at
New York University. A key issue at the meeting was how far
national church leaders could move in aggressively challenging
exploitative social institutions while at the same time avoiding
class-conscious factionalism among the churches. The session
was closed to the press, but a *Newsweek* reporter managed to
slip in and listen to some of the discussion until her presence
was noticed and she was asked to leave. The *Newsweek* account
inferred that

> the major Protestant denominations are preparing to bring the
> techniques of mass community organization—bloc power poli-
> tics, class conflict, and naked appeals to self-interest—into
> the churches' heretofore more reticent urban ministry pro-
> grams.[7]

While this may be overdrawn (the urban ministry had not become so hardened and militant as this suggested), the general
thrust of the observation is probably valid. The following Feb-

ruary (1965) the NCC General Board voted to approve a pilot citizenship education project in Cleveland aimed at helping blacks gain political power.

Regier emerges as the central actor in this drama of organizational transformation, his social activism finding its outlet in the major policy reorientation occurring in the division. Yet the more compelling observation to be made is that Regier's relative success did not occur in a vacuum, but rather coincided with an increasing interpenetration of one formerly autonomous NCC fiefdom by another. His essential skill lay in giving scope and direction to the expanding organizational energies and in recruiting talented individuals who would work effectively in such an environment. The findings, in short, are strongly in support of Etzioni's hypothesis.

Increased Forcefulness in the Areas of Social Education and Action. Throughout the 1950s the major programs of the Division of Christian Life and Work retained a strong emphasis on the priorities of the Social Gospel from the old FCC days. The consensus on goals was matched by one on strategy, namely a commitment to the educational approach to social problems. The prevailing view, Reverend Dean M. Kelley told the author in an interview, was that education was a necessary precondition to action, that only through heavy doses of the one could the other be achieved.[8] Characteristic of the stress on education as a means of achieving goals were the various NCC-sponsored study conferences, which were viewed as a way of educating the constituency and raising important social problems for discussion while at the same time avoiding official involvement in controversial issues, which might prove internally disruptive. Delegates to the conferences could legitimately pass resolutions; and generally these were given attention in both the church press and mass media, as in the case of a 1958 study conference that advocated Red China's admission to the UN.

In the wake of such resolutions, it was common for council leaders to stress their "advisory" and "nonofficial" character, a distinction press dispatches did not always make clear. Kelley summarized the purpose of the study conferences in these terms:

The study conferences were a way of going through the motions of confronting problems without in fact doing so. They were not intended to have any impact on the world, or the NCC for that matter. The conviction was that you couldn't do much in the short run to effect substantial change. I ran one of the study conferences myself, but I was new to the Council at the time and never was fully indoctrinated in the older tradition.[9]

Though hallowed by tradition, the attitude described above did not long survive the division's move in the late 1950s to the Inter-Church Center, where contacts with other bodies involved in the merger became more common. Growing discontent with the education emphasis found a focus in 1961, when the council had occasion to print up two statements. One of these, the "Comprehensive Program on Education for Social Action," embodied the old, deliberate, step-by-step approach to social change and had no particular topical relevance. A second publication dealt with a current and highly controversial matter, the film *Operation Abolition,* which purported to show that protest demonstrations in San Francisco were Communist-inspired and led. A critical analysis of this film by the NCC proved highly popular; it sold out its first printing of 25,000 copies in two months, and required a second and third printing to satisfy the demand.

As subsequent chapters will develop in greater detail, the division increasingly in the early 1960s came to redefine its mandate; for example, it helped to spawn the aggressively activist NCC Commission on Religion and Race, served as a focal point for Protestant pressure to effect changes in national education policy, generated church interest in the deprivations of migrant labor, and pressed for changes in national policy on this issue. The division's change in fundamental outlook, which facilitated its 1965 merger with the Home Missions division to form the Division of Christian Life and Mission (see figure 2), was not accomplished without serious organizational stresses; a significant number of the unit's executives chose to resign from the council or accept reassignment as this important strategic redefinition made headway.

While there was nothing inevitable or foreordained about

Figure 2 Administrative Organization of the NCC, Jan. 1965.

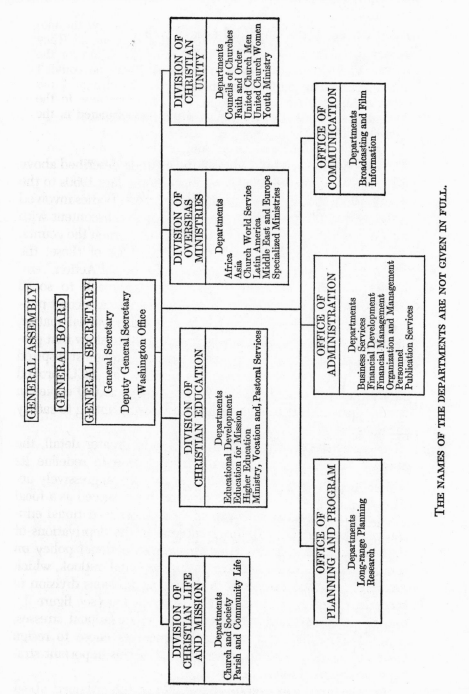

GENERAL ASSEMBLY

GENERAL BOARD

GENERAL SECRETARY
General Secretary
Deputy General Secretary
Washington Office

DIVISION OF CHRISTIAN LIFE AND MISSION
Departments
Church and Society
Parish and Community Life

DIVISION OF CHRISTIAN EDUCATION
Departments
Educational Development
Education for Mission
Higher Education
Ministry, Vocation and, Pastoral Services

DIVISION OF OVERSEAS MINISTRIES
Departments
Africa
Asia
Church World Service
Latin America
Middle East and Europe
Specialized Ministries

DIVISION OF CHRISTIAN UNITY
Departments
Councils of Churches
Faith and Order
United Church Men
United Church Women
Youth Ministry

OFFICE OF PLANNING AND PROGRAM
Departments
Long-range Planning
Research

OFFICE OF ADMINISTRATION
Departments
Business Services
Financial Development
Financial Management
Organization and Management
Personnel
Publication Services

OFFICE OF COMMUNICATION
Departments
Broadcasting and Film
Information

THE NAMES OF THE DEPARTMENTS ARE NOT GIVEN IN FULL.

what occurred, the change did accord well with the new environmental circumstances the council confronted in the 1960s, changes that one well-placed informant, the Reverend Jon Regier, summed up in these terms:

> It had become increasingly apparent that urbanization, secularization and technology had far-reaching significance for the Council's work. There were no longer the easy distinctions that had served to justify highly autonomous operating units.[10]

A more focused and integrated approach to social issues was called for; and the division, along with other units in the council, moved to meet the challenge in ways Etzioni's hypothesis leads one to expect it could, given the character of previous internal changes.

CONCLUSIONS

The merger of 1950 was an event of fundamental significance for interdenominational Protestantism, the importance of which is in no way diminished by its long gestation period or the equally protracted period thereafter, during which the long-term consequences gradually became manifest. Prior to 1950 the council was obliged to accommodate the claims of other broadly inclusive national agencies. After 1950 this was no longer the case. More positively, its headquarters staff enjoyed the benefit of increased cross-fertilization of thinking, personnel of more broadly varied talents, and an enhanced ability to mobilize resources.

The data presented can serve as a reminder that the reorganization of bureaucracies is not an entirely rational and self-conscious process and that the full implications of structural revamping are seldom fully apparent to the reorganizers. The literature on organizations sometimes conveys the impression that organizations are rational structures, that, like children's building blocks, they can be rearranged in various ways—removing a block or two here and replacing them there—without basically changing their overall constitution. The blocks (units of the organization) are assumed to be stable and nonresistant, capable of being repositioned at will without secondary consequences. The council's recent history, on the other hand, suggests that while the immediate advantages expected to accrue from the reorganization of 1950 (economies in the use of scarce resources, the elimination of duplication and overlapping, and so on) did in fact occur, the reorganizers could not in all likelihood have foreseen the degree to which the decision would facilitate comprehensive approaches to social problems and increase the general forcefulness of programming. The reorganizers would not have found the latter changes inconsistent with their goals, but at the same time they probably did not wholly anticipate them.

3. The "Active Minority" among Member Churches

Studies of the internal life of large voluntary organizations have consistently found a paradox. On the one hand their constitutions invariably provide for democratic procedures, both in elections and policy formulation. The formal rules call for the election of officers and the subordination of the board of directors to the constituent assembly and of salaried officers to the board. It is not unusual for the rules to make provision for initiative, referendum, and recall. The near-universality of such provisions testifies to the hold democratic assumptions have on American consciousness. On the other hand, it has also been shown that most mature organizations are in practice run by a few individuals whose long tenure, expertise, and command over the channels of communication afford them disproportionate power. This leadership elite is usually self-perpetuating, even though those who comprise it will see to it that the formal requirements for democracy are met. The individuals in this top stratum have been aptly labeled the "active minority." [1]

While the term is generally used in the literature on organizations to refer to a cluster of individuals, there is no reason why "active minority" may not also connote a pattern of alliances among factions. Such a definition would be appropriate in characterizing the elite not of a unitary organization but of a federation, whose "members" are by definition themselves or-

ganizational entities. The present chapter therefore undertakes
to identify an active minority of member denominations in the
council. In focusing attention on differing degrees of involvement among participating churches, it is not suggested that the
motivation, commitment, and expertise of individuals are unimportant in determining which persons wield organizational
power. Individual factors, however, may come into play only
after the number of contestants for top leadership posts has
been narrowed down on the basis of denominational identifica-
tions. The result is a disproportionate representation of the
leaders of the more active and committed churches in the federation's higher stratum and a policy bias that reflects the
stances of these few churches. In regard to the NCC, we shall
first attempt to find such an "active minority," then (in a subsequent chapter) we shall analyze its composition in an effort
to explain the council's overall liberal disposition.

PARTICIPATION IN THE COUNCIL:
THE PROBLEM OF MEASUREMENT

In an organization as complex as the National Council of
Churches, any attempt to measure the impact of a member
church on the formulation of policy is confronted with problems. One might want to quantify or rank the relative influence
of individual delegates or denominational delegations, but mea-
suring influence is difficult. Although meetings of the council's
General Board are open to the public, the behavior of delegates
in these meetings may not be a true indicator of relative influence: delegates from churches with the least influence may
do the most talking; and formal votes on important questions,
sometimes a valuable source of data, are in the General Board's
case usually near-unanimous, thus, not very revealing. It is
reasonable, then, to set aside the nebulous question of delegates' relative individual impact on policy, adopting instead as
an index of influence member-body participation, gauged by
relatively objective measures (contributions to budget, denominational affiliation of key personnel, and rates of attendance of denominational delegates at key council meetings).

LOW LEVEL OF MEMBER-BODY COMMITMENT
IN THE EARLY YEARS

From the time of its inception in 1908, the council fulfilled two related, though not altogether harmonious, functions: social service as defined by the Social Gospel movement and the co-ordination of the activities of members in an effort to avoid wasteful competition. For the first three decades of the council's existence, the social service motive was dominant, while the goal of achieving greater coordination (except in the social service area) was only minimally satisfied. Top officials of the constituent churches took little interest, for the most part, in council affairs, and the persons chosen to represent member churches in the council were in many cases predisposed toward its Social Gospel outlook by virtue of their identification with their denomination's social action or social service board.

On the one hand, this unusual relationship to constituent bodies gave the council's leaders a degree of freedom from the constraints that are typical of most federations. But on the other hand, it weakened the leaders' capacity to speak for the churches, produced an unhealthy financial dependency on *individual* donors, and raised questions about the legitimacy of board meetings, often only poorly attended by the delegated representatives of the denominations. Church historian John A. Hutchinson observes in *We Are Not Divided* that the council borrowed prestige and status from its members, but managed to maintain sufficient autonomy from the several denominational hierarchies to avoid their characteristic conservatism.[2] Much of its work was carried on through semiautonomous agencies known as "commissions," whose relationship to the constituent churches was often tenuous. Denominational involvement was mostly limited to the protection of vested interests, as is suggested in the following *Christian Century* editorial from the early 1930s:

> It is difficult for any but the initiated to realize how tenuous a connection this body [FCC] has with its constituent denominations, how little authority is committed to it, and how jealously the denominations guard their own prerogatives

against any encroachment or usurpation by the Council which is their creature.[3]

Furthermore, the Federal Council during most of its years (1908–1950) was chiefly dependent on income derived from individuals and other non-member-body sources. That member-body contributions as a percentage of total income ranged from a high of 38 percent in 1913 to a low of 23 percent in 1933 suggests a lack of sustained denominational concern. Another indicator of member-body apathy is the wide disparity between assigned delegate strength in the Executive Committee (the top policy-making board in these years) and actual delegate attendance at meetings (table 1).

Table 1 ATTENDANCE OF OFFICIAL DENOMINAL REPRESENTATIVES AT ANNUAL MEETINGS OF THE FCC EXECUTIVE COMMITTEE BY YEAR AND DENOMINATION*

Denomination†	Year			
	1913	1923	1933	1943
Baptist Church North	5/4‡	5/1	4/4	17/3
Congregational Church	3/1	4/4	3/1	15/5
Disciples of Christ	5/5	4/2	4/3	29/6
Methodist Church	9/6	7/3	10/3	103/13
Methodist Church South	4/2	6/2	6/2	**
Presbyterian Church in the U.S.	2/2	2/1	§	8/1
Presbyterian Church in the U.S.A.	7/3	5/1	5/2	22/4
Reformed churches	4/4	5/5	4/3	5/3
All black bodies††	4/0	8/2	8/1	64/10
Smaller white denominations§§	42/20	43/20	29/8	43/12
Total	85/47	89/41	73/27	306/57

* Source: FCC, Annual Reports.

† The Episcopal Church, although represented in the FCC by its Commission on Christian Unity and Social Service, did not elect to affiliate formally with the council until 1940 and is thus excluded. In 1943 its assigned delegates numbered 25, 5 of whom attended the annual Executive Committee Meeting.

‡ The first figure is the number of delegates assigned the denomination; the second figure is the denomination's average attendance at meetings.

§ Temporarily withdrew from the council.

** Merged with the Methodist Episcopal Church.

†† Includes African Methodist Episcopal Church, African Methodist Episcopal Church Zion, Colored Methodist Episcopal Churches, and Negro Baptists.

§§ Includes all white member bodies with fewer than 5 officially assigned representatives (principals) on the Executive Committee. In 1913 these numbered 21; in 1923, 20; in 1933, 13; and in 1943, 9.

INCREASED MEMBER-BODY INVOLVEMENT
IN RECENT YEARS

Beginning slowly in the 1930s and moving with increasing momentum in the 1940s, the attitudes of the various Protestant bodies toward the council began to undergo significant change. On the one hand, the Social Gospel movement, as a semiautonomous force in Protestantism, was faltering. The reasons for this decline have been explored in other works (see the notes, annotations for chapter 3), and we may simply note here that it appears to have been caused by a loss of relevance when the old "progressive" answers were no longer suitable to emergent social issues. The implications of this for the Federal Council were only too clear: it could no longer rely upon the movement to arouse the support necessary for its survival; new ways of defining and appealing to its constituency would have to be found. In addition, basic sociological changes were occurring in American Protestantism, reducing the social distance between denominations and causing Protestant churches to desire increased cooperation, something they had previously resisted. In the late 1930s and early '40s, the churches came to recognize that they had a genuine stake in the survival of ecumenical bodies like the council. Church bodies that had heretofore remained outside of it now manifested an interest in joining; the number of member churches increased from a low of 21 in 1939 to 29 by 1951. Existing members tended to become more actively involved, as is suggested by a comparison of the data in tables 1 to 3. Table 2 points to a shift in the proportion of income derived from official denominational sources. The change is paralleled by increased attendance at board meetings, as revealed by the relatively high rate of attendance in the 1960s (table 3) as compared to earlier years (table 1). As the comparison indicates, the rate of participation on the part of the larger, doctrinally conservative, main line denominations now clustered around 75 percent, whereas in the Federal Council years it had usually been below 50 percent.

Thus, the present distribution of power in the NCC is probably more typical of that prevailing in other large federations, whereas in an earlier period the degree of actual involvement

Table 2 INCOME OF THE FCC OR NCC BY SOURCE AND BY YEAR
(IN DOLLARS)*

	Year		
Source of Income	1943	1953	1963
Individuals, foundations, and other nonchurch sources	$251,126	$2,818,082‡	$ 4,503,475‡
Member-church bodies	177,473	3,055,762‡	7,119,137
Self-generated income†	76,987	1,336,884	3,190,537
Total	$505,586	$7,210,729	$14,813,149

* Sources: FCC, *Annual Reports*; NCC, *Triennial Reports*.
† Includes income from sales, subscriptions, royalties, and investments.
‡ The increase over the ten-year period largely reflects the council's participation in the U.S. government's "food for peace" program (P. L. 480), not an increase in donations from individuals.

on the part of member bodies was limited. With the decline of the Social Gospel movement as a self-conscious force and the simultaneous increasing emphasis on Protestant ecumenism, the federation's role in Protestantism shifted fundamentally. Member churches became more aware of the need for genuine cooperation; beginning in the 1940s, they manifested increased willingness to accept responsibility for the council's maintenance and leadership. Though once governed by a group of activists the majority of whom were closely identified with the Social Gospel movement, a minor force in Protestantism even at the peak of its influence, the federation's governing elite now was largely made up of denominational officialdom, especially the officials of the larger, doctrinally traditional churches.

DIFFERENCES IN MEMBER-BODY
PARTICIPATION RATES

The preceding discussion has hinted at, without fully documenting, the possibility that participation varies significantly among the member bodies of the council. Since degree of participation is important to the thesis of the present chapter, it is worthwhile inquiring into it at some depth.

Delegate Attendance at Top Levels. A church-by-church comparison of the ratio of appointed delegates to delegates actually in attendance reveals the existence of gross differences.

Table 3   Attendance of Denominational Delegates at Regular Meetings of the NCC General Board by Year and Denomination*

Denomination	Year						
	1960	1961	1962	1963	1964	1965	1966
American Baptist Convention	8/3†	8/4.5	8/3	10/5	10/9.3	10/7	12/7.6
United Church of Christ	8/5.5	8/5	8/8	12/7.6	12/7.6	12/9	13/9.6
Disciples of Christ	10/4.5	10/6.5	10/7.3	12/5.3	12/8.3	12/10.3	11/9.6
Methodist Church	40/16.5	40/18	40/23.7	44/17.3	44/24.7	44/20	44/24
Evangelical United Brethren Church	4/2.5	4/1.5	4/1	3/1	3/2.3	3/2.3	6/3
Lutheran Church in America	7/6	7/5	7/5.3	12/4	12/6.6	12/7.6	11/9
Episcopal Church	10/5	10/4.5	10/9.3	12/6.3	12/8.6	12/10	12/10
Presbyterian Church in the U.S.	6/4.5	6/2	6/4	8/3	8/5	8/5	6/4.3
Presbyterian Church in the U.S.A.	14/9.5	14/9.5	14/11.3	16/10.3	16/12.3	16/12.6	19/14.6
Aver. of all Protestant main line churches	11.8/6.3	11.8/6.3	11.8/8.2	14.3/6.6	14.3/9.4	14.3/9.3	14.9/10.2
Aver. of all black bodies	41/7	41/9	41/9.6	56/9.3	56/13	56/8.6	56/11.3
Aver. of all Orthodox bodies	20/3	20/3	20/4	26/3.6	26/3.3	26/3.6	33/6
Aver. of other churches	(no data)/8	(no data)/6	(no data)/5.3	32/6	32/12	32/11	36/11

* Source: Minutes of the NCC General Board (selected years).
† The first figure is the number of delegates assigned the denomination; the second figure is the denomination's average attendance at meetings.

The main line Protestant bodies (the first nine churches listed in table 3) taken together average well over 50 percent delegate attendance at General Board meetings (table 3), with only the American Baptist Convention and the Methodist Church dropping below this percentage with any degree of frequency. On the other hand, attendance by blacks, Eastern Orthodox, and several small, white Protestant bodies is without exception well under 50 percent.

Fiscal Involvement. An analysis of member-church contributions in 1963 and 1966 reveals that over 90 percent of donations to the NCC came from just seven bodies, each of which gave over $300,000 annually. In order of decreasing average amounts these were the United Presbyterian Church in the U.S.A., Methodist Church, United Church of Christ, Lutheran Church in America, Disciples of Christ, Episcopal Church, and Presbyterian Church in the U.S. (Southern Presbyterian). Four other bodies contributed between $25,000 and $300,000: the American Baptist Convention, Evangelical United Brethren Church, Reformed Church in America, and Church of the Brethren. The combined contributions of the remaining 21 member churches in both years was under 1 percent of total denominational support.

The above figures might be criticized on the ground that they consider only absolute dollar figures and fail to take into account differences in *ability* to contribute. A modest contribution from a small or less prosperous church may represent a greater commitment of its available resources than a large contribution from a more affluent denomination. In order to control for this factor, it is useful to consider denominational records concerning meeting assigned quotas. The NCC Department of Financial Development sets quotas based on a denomination's resources, determined more by total income than by number of members. A church having a large percentage of lower-income members (the National Baptist Convention, for example) should not be expected to contribute to a church of equal size whose average income is substantially higher (Episcopalians or Presbyterians, for example), and the quota system takes this factor into account.

When member churches are ranked in terms of donations

as a percent of assigned quotas (again, for 1963 and 1966), some interesting shifts occur in the rank order of particular bodies, but the basic picture of strongest support coming from churches in the main line Protestant group remains unchanged. In the category of highest contributors (over 80 percent of quota) were the Church of the Brethren, Religious Society of Friends (Quakers), United Presbyterian, United Church of Christ, and Lutheran Church in America (which, incidentally, overfulfilled its quota in both 1963 and 1966). Churches donating between 60 and 80 percent of quota were the Disciples of Christ, Methodist, Evangelical United Brethren and Episcopal. Those churches averaging between 50 and 60 percent for the two years included the Presbyterian Church in the U.S., Reformed Church in America, and five churches characterized by their very small membership—the Armenian Church, Hungarian Reformed, Polish National Catholic, Seventh Day Baptist General Conference, and Church of the New Jerusalem. Thirteen churches have the poorest record of meeting denominational quotas: the five black churches, Eastern Orthodoxy (seven churches), and the American Baptist Convention.

A still more discriminating index of financial commitment, which again highlights the greater involvement of main line churches in the NCC, is amount of contribution to the budgets of special council programs that are in some degree controversial. (One would not wish to suggest that the reluctance of denominations to make specific provision for these budgets springs in every case from a concern over the controversial character of the programs.) The three budgets chosen for analysis are "Religion and Race," "Priority Program for Peace," and "The Delta Ministry." A tabulation reveals for 1963 and 1966 that eight denominations provided over 95 percent of the donations to these special budgets, and the eight constitute a by now familiar list (in alphabetical order): Disciples of Christ, Episcopal, Evangelical United Brethren, Lutheran Church in America, Methodist, Reformed Church in America, United Church of Christ, and United Presbyterian. (The inclusion of the Reformed Church in this list is noteworthy, since it did not rank among the top donors in the previous tabulations.) It should be noted that the absence here of small, relatively low-budget denominations like the Church of the Brethren and Quakers is not to be construed as evidence of lack of concern for these particular issues. The absence of other churches, however, is obviously significant.

Participation in Leadership. The third and final area in which member-body participation in the council may be studied is denominational affiliation of top officials. As may be expected, those churches that assume the greatest financial obligation and have the best attendance record at board meetings are also the best represented among the top elective and appointive leaders. But the degree to which certain churches are over- or underrepresented is unexpected.

Background information was collected on the 31 executive staff personnel who in 1967 occupied key policy-making posts:

United Presbyterian	9
Methodist	6
Episcopal	5
United Church of Christ	3
American Baptist Convention	2
Evangelical United Brethren	2
Lutheran	2
Black churches	1
Not ascertained	1

An interesting parallel is revealed when the above data on top staff personnel are compared with the affiliations of non-salaried officers during the period 1950 to 1968, given in table 4. The table makes the distinction between members of the board with some executive responsibilities (totals given in parentheses) and those whom the council designates vice-presidents-at-large. Although the boundary between these two groups is not an exact one, persons in the former category (president, treasurer, recording secretary, and vice-president for a division) carry a more immediate responsibility than those classified in the latter category.

Table 4 reveals that the vice-presidents-at-large were recruited in the 1950s and '60s with a view toward achieving a cross-sectional representation of member churches, while in

Table 4   Nonsalaried Officers of the NCC by Term and Denomination*

Denomination	Term							Total
	1950–52	1952–54	1954–57	1957–60	1960–63	1963–66	1966–68	
American Baptist Convention	1†	—	1	1 (1)	1	—	2	6 (1)
United Church of Christ	1	1 (1)	2 (1)	1	2	—	3 (2)	10 (4)
Disciples of Christ	1	—	1	2 (2)	1 (1)	2	1	8 (3)
Methodist Church	1	4 (3)	2 (1)	2 (1)	2	2 (1)	3 (2)	16 (8)
Evangelical United Brethren Church	1 (1)	1 (1)	1	1	1 (1)	1 (1)	—	6 (4)§
Lutheran Church in America	—	—	1	—	2 (2)	1	1	5 (2)
Episcopal Church	1 (1)	1	1	2	—	1	1	7 (1)
Presbyterian Church in the U.S.	—	—	1	—	1	1	—	3
Presbyterian Church in the U.S.A.	3	3 (1)	5 (3)	3	3 (2)	2 (2)	4 (1)	23 (9)
All black bodies	—	1	1	1	—	1	3	7
All Orthodox bodies	—	—	2	1	1	1	1	6
Church of the Brethren	—	—	—	1 (1)	1 (1)	1 (1)	—	3 (3)
Other‡	1	1	1	—	2 (1)	3	1	9 (1)
Total ascertained	10 (2)	12 (6)	19 (5)	15 (5)	17 (8)	16 (5)	20 (5)	109 (36)
Not ascertained	1	1	1	1	1	3	0	8

* Sources: *Yearbook of American Churches* (annually, 1951–67); *Handbook of the National Council of Churches of Christ U.S.A., 1967–69*; *Who's Who in America* (selected years).

† Numbers in parentheses refer to individuals explicitly having executive responsibilities: president, treasurer, associate treasurer, recording secretary, vice-presidents of divisions. The number not in parentheses includes these and all individuals having the title vice-president-at-large.

‡ Includes the Moravian Church, the Reformed Church in America, the Quakers, and United Church Women. (Although United Church Women is not a denomination, it is here treated as such for representational purposes.)

selecting those to occupy executive positions on the board, representation was clustering by denominations. The United Presbyterians, Methodists, and United Church of Christ captured a disproportionately high number of officers. Although these churches presently comprise 36.5 percent of the council's 43 million individual members, they collectively held 45.4 percent of all general officer positions in the period 1951 to 1969 and 61.8 percent of the executive positions on the board.

The question arises of whether the larger-than-average numbers from these denominations might have been the result of carrying over individual board members from one term to the next. The office of treasurer has been carried over, for example: only two individuals have served as NCC treasurer; and, since both were United Presbyterians, the figure for that church may be slightly inflated. Aside from the treasurer, the only individual to have served for an extended period among the general officers was the Reverend Reuben Mueller (Evangelical United Brethren), who was a divisional vice-president for several terms before being elected president of the council in 1963. No person has ever served more than a single term as NCC president; and among divisional vice-presidents, vice-presidents-at-large, and recording secretaries, there is typically complete turnover from one triennium to another. Thus, the tendency for certain denominations to monopolize top positions (especially executive ones) suggests that identification with one of the more active churches in the council is an advantage for those seeking high office. It also may be the case that persons so identified have greater incentive to become actively involved in the first place. This is suggested by the fact that, with minor variations, the same churches predominating among the top staff also tend to predominate among the nonsalaried executive officers.

The pattern of selective denominational representation in leadership is also apparent in the affiliations of those elected to the post of NCC president. Since the formation of the NCC in 1950, eight persons, drawn from just six member denominations, have held this office: two Episcopalians (Henry Knox Sherrill and Cynthia O. Wedel), one United Presbyterian (Eugene Carson Blake), one Evangelical United Brethren

(Reuben Mueller), one Disciple of Christ (J. Irwin Miller), two Methodists (William T. Martin and Arthur Flemming), and one American Baptist (Edwin T. Dahlberg). Of the eight, all but two (Miller and Dahlberg) are identified with churches labeled above as "most committed," while only one (Dahlberg) is a member of a church having a low level of council involvement. This is to say that twenty-eight of the council's 1967 constituent churches, having a combined membership of 21.4 million (just over half the total inclusive membership of 42.5 million), have never once been accorded the important symbolic reward the presidency represents.

THE FORMAL DECISION-MAKING PROCESS AS A FACTOR SUSTAINING EXISTING PREDISPOSITIONS

As noted previously the council resembles other large voluntary organizations in its adherence to democratic procedures for selecting officers and deciding policy. In view of the formal procedures prescribed by the Constitution and by-laws, a highly motivated body of churchmen, assuming they had the necessary votes, could in short order wrest control of the organization from established leaders and reverse or drastically modify existing priorities. The organization is above all an "open" system, and its policies must find acceptance among constituents if it is to survive for any period of time. Yet, as has already been intimated, its policies have not in fact undergone any such drastic short-run changes. This is in part because of a rather stable denominational alliance pattern in which certain member communions, more so than would be anticipated on a chance basis, predominate among those attending meetings of policy-making boards, among the elective officers, and among the executive staff. This pattern has been the subject of analysis of this chapter.

Before leaving the topic of NCC elites, it is important to take note of an additional factor tending to sustain long-standing NCC commitments in the face of momentary fluctuations in constituency backing. The factor in question is the NCC's formal decision-making process.

By its very nature a federated structure departs from the

model of direct democracy. In a federation individuals are only indirectly represented, basic voting rights being granted to the member bodies as a group. Insurgents who might wish to alter the basic thrust of policy face a more prolonged and difficult task than would be the case in an otherwise similar but "unitary" body. The preceding point is rather obvious and requires little elaboration. Not so obvious is the fact that in the case of the National Council the top leadership elites are, if anything, somewhat more removed from grass roots pressures than the federated structure alone suggests. Some attention to the 1950 Constitution can help to show why this is the case, even though this document has subsequently been modified in certain details.

Under the Constitution policy-making authority is vested in two bodies: a General Assembly, the official "governing body," which in recent years has met every three years but which in the 1950s met biennially; and a General Board, a much smaller unit, which is granted "the full powers of the Council ad interim, except the power to determine the membership of the Council and the power to revise the Constitution and by-laws." Members of the General Board are in all cases drawn from the larger General Assembly membership.

The basis on which these two bodies are constituted is interesting in several respects. First, no attempt was made by the framers to separate sharply the policy-making and policy-execution functions. Paralleling the practice of many other private organizations, but unlike the separation of powers provided for in the U.S. Constitution (article 1, section 6), executive officers of the council were not prohibited from sitting on either of the above-mentioned assemblies. As a matter of fact, article 9, section 3, of the 1950 document specifically mandated that a number of executive officers—namely, the general officers of the council (four); the chairmen of the general departments, joint departments, and joint commissions (in 1950, two, seven, and one, respectively); the chairmen of three designated central departments; and the immediate past president of the organization—all should sit on the board and assembly.

Second, the 1950 Constitution provided that the assembly and board should contain several other groups of persons not formally representative of any member communion. Among them were state and local councils of churches, represented in the General Assembly by one delegate each from cooperating state councils of churches and ten additional ones chosen from local councils and on the General Board by one-seventh of this total (but not less than five persons). Provision was also made for the selection of a number of laymen-at-large: up to one-third of the total denominational delegates eligible for General Assembly membership and up to twelve (three each from the four NCC divisions) eligible for General Board membership.

Still further qualifying the NCC as a democratic federation of denominational assemblies were certain stipulations affecting the selection of denominational delegates. The basic formula for setting voting strength was contained in article 4, section 1, paragraphs (a) and (b), which specified that each member communion was entitled to five representatives on the assembly, an additional delegate for each 100,000 communicants or major fraction thereof, and an undesignated number of lay delegates, the number of which was not to exceed one-third of the regular delegate total. But paragraph (d) of the same section made it clear that denominational assemblies were to have complete discretion only in the selection of part of their respective delegations: ". . . of the total number of [denominational] representatives at least one half shall be nominated by the boards and agencies of that communion cooperating in the work of the Divisions of the Council. . . ." The distinction between freely chosen denominational delegates and ones elected but not nominated by them might seem unimportant in view of the fact that all denominational boards are ultimately answerable to denominational assemblies and presiding officers and have no basis of authority other than this. Nevertheless, in the short run, such bodies of delegates often enjoy substantial de facto autonomy, including the capacity to "ride out" momentary upsurges of adverse sentiment as reflected in the votes of their parent bodies. The framers of the NCC Constitution evidently aimed to regularize the internal life of the federation and to insure the survival of programs that long predated the council's own inception. But an important indirect consequence of this objective was to insulate the NCC General Assembly from con-

stituent denominational opinion, especially when it was oppo-
sitional. In the same way the stipulation in article 4, section 1,
paragraph (c), that denominations might elect additional lay
representatives, but only from among those nominated by the
NCC General Board, presumably had an important stabilizing
effect.

A further stabilizing factor has been the fact that the Constitution did not rule out the possibility of salaried NCC staff
personnel serving on NCC policy-making boards as denominational delegates, local council delegates, and so forth. Since
interdenominational bureaucrats have a special incentive to attend board and assembly meetings and to do what they can
there to influence policy, they are likely to be influential out
of proportion to their number, which is small compared to the
total number of delegates. Such individuals constitute still another reinforcement of the policy status quo.

This is not to suggest that NCC policy has been static.
Indeed, one of the major purposes of this study is to show that
important changes in policy content have occurred in recent
years. The point is rather that any prevailing tenor of policy
always enjoys powerful support, which makes it difficult in the
extreme for dissidents to successfully challenge the basic thrust
of NCC policy, even if their grass roots support is momentarily
substantial. Only in the unlikely event that their backing were
to be both widespread and sustained would they be in a position to interfere with the continued implementation of policies
preferred among the long-time NCC activists.

It is possible to classify the 31 member bodies that participated in the council at the time of this survey (1967) in terms
of their relative commitment, though it should be kept in mind
that any such ranking is to some extent arbitrary. The denominations that could be characterized as "very committed" are the
United Presbyterian Church in the U.S.A. (Northern Presbyterian), United Church of Christ (successor to the old Congregational and Evangelical and Reformed Churches), Episcopal,
Lutheran Church in America, and the Quakers (two member
bodies). The United Methodist Church, which combines the
former Methodist and Evangelical United Brethren Churches,
can also be placed in this category, bearing in mind its excep-

tional size and the fact that not all of its factions are in warm support of the council. In the "moderately committed" group could be placed the Reformed Church in America, Disciples of Christ, Moravian, Church of the Brethren, and Presbyterian Church in the U.S. The "least committed" churches would then include the black churches (three Methodist and three Baptist), the seven Eastern Orthodox churches, the American Baptist Convention (though it has contributed to the council more than most others in this category), and the five small denominations previously identified.

It should be stressed that member-body involvement in support and leadership of the council has increased from what it was in its first quarter-century (1908 to 1933). However, the increase in involvement has been principally with the main line Protestant bodies; it has not been so apparent in the other membership categories, where the involvement has remained low.

CONCLUSIONS

Variations in the extent and intensity of member-church commitment are associated with a disproportionate tendency for individuals with certain denominational backgrounds to move into leadership positions. In the case of the executive staff and nonsalaried officers, the data indicate a decided preference for the selection of persons from certain denominations, especially for the more sensitive and vital posts. It is not implied, of course, that the council self-consciously favors some denominations over others or that a deeply concerned individual identified with one of the less committed denominations would not stand a chance of elevation to high office. What has been shown is a subtle process of shared expectations in which certain member bodies see fit to make a substantial contribution and are rewarded with prestige offices out of proportion to their numerical strength.

4. Liberalism versus Conservatism

*H*aving identified in the preceding chapter three clusters of churches that vary in degree of council involvement, it remains to consider the twin questions of whether the churches comprising the active minority (including all of those in the "very committed" category and some in the "moderately committed" group) share a roughly comparable outlook on social issues distinguishing them from the less involved members and whether, assuming this to be the case, there is a pronounced correlation between the policies of the active churches and those of the council.

Both primary and secondary sources were searched for data relevant to this question. For some of the council's members, especially the main line Protestant churches, information was found in abundance; in the cases of the black and Eastern Orthodox bodies, materials were more limited, though still reasonably adequate. For the five bodies labeled "smaller white Protestant churches" above, published information was almost totally lacking, so this cluster of churches will not be included in the following discussion. This omission raises no serious problem for the argument, however, since the combined membership of the five bodies (511,800) is only slightly over 1 percent of the council's total inclusive membership.

POLITICAL PREDISPOSITIONS OF THE MOST ACTIVE
AND MODERATELY ACTIVE MEMBER BODIES

In probing for possible parallels in the social attitudes of
those churches found to be the most committed to the NCC, one
must examine them over a period of decades in order to correct
for possible idiosyncrasies of behavior related to a particular
issue and time. (In a later section a similar investigation for
the less involved members will be undertaken.) For the sake of
convenience, the social outlook of these churches will be considered at three crucial stages: the late nineteenth and early
twentieth centuries (era of the original Social Gospel), the
early 1930s (depression era), and the 1940s, '50s and early '60s
(era in which race emerged as an overriding national concern).

Era of the Social Gospel. The leading authorities on the
Social Gospel era in American Protestantism support the view
that the movement made its greatest impression on those
churches in the main line, rather than more fundamentalist,
category.[1] All the main line churches, with the exception of the
Lutheran, responded to the Social Gospel to some degree, so
that by the outbreak of World War I

> the Social Gospel forces had gained enough influence to compel
> the churches to recognize the movement officially. . . . The
> large denominations, except only the Lutheran, had appointed
> social service boards or commissions.[2]

The churches made room for the movement in part out of their
anxiety over loss of support among working class migrants to
the cities, a situation that Social Christianity seemed capable
of alleviating, and in part out of genuine concern over the material, social, and spiritual deprivation of the urban masses.

But not all churches took this step at the same time. One
cluster, more liberal in outlook, established social service boards
around the time of the founding of the Federal Council, while
another did not see fit to do this until the 1920s or '30s. In the
former group were the Protestant Episcopal, Northern Presbyterian Church, Methodist, and Congregational churches. The
less socially involved cluster included the Evangelical and Re-

formed, Southern Presbyterian, Southern Methodist, Disciples of Christ, Lutheran, and Northern Baptist churches.

In comparing these findings to the ranking of relative church commitment to the church offered in chapter 3, one finds that the bodies listed as having established social service boards early all are in the "very committed" category, while those that created such boards only later are ranked, with only one exception, as "moderately committed" to the council. (The exception, the Northern Baptists, since renamed the American Baptists, is categorized as "least committed.") Information on how several churches (for example, the Church of the Brethren and the Moravian Church) handled the social service board question is unfortunately lacking, so a cross-tabulation of them is not possible. The comparison is nevertheless suggestive.

Depression Era. A roughly parallel line of demarcation between liberal and moderate churches was apparent in Protestantism's response to the Great Depression and the New Deal of the 1930s. Even the more liberal churches avoided outright support of the Democratic platform, partly because of Franklin D. Roosevelt's unacceptable advocacy of repealing Prohibition and partly because of their traditional policy of nonpartisanship. But the more liberal churches did sharply question the existing capitalist order and responded to the same economic conditions that had paved the way for the New Deal. As early as 1930 the Methodist bishops resolved that "there is something fundamentally wrong with a system that in the midst of plenteous abundance dooms untold numbers of our people to unbearable poverty." In 1933 the same assemblage resolved that "merely to 'restore the system to its normal functioning' as we have been advised to do is to trifle with a terrible catastrophe and assure its return." The counterpart body in the Protestant Episcopal Church, the House of Bishops, resolved in 1933 that "No mere re-establishment of the social order will suffice. Christ demands a new order which will substitute the motive of service for the motive of gain." The Presbyterian Church in the U.S.A. (a precursor to the United Presbyterian Church in the U.S.A.) announced that "if the right to live interferes with profits, profits must necessarily give way." By far the most radical departure from the apolitical, gradualist bias of the original Social Gospel was that embodied in positions adopted by the General Council of the Congregational Church in 1934. Speaking as the highest representative assembly of that denomination, the General Council called for "abolition of the system responsible for these destructive elements in our common life by eliminating the [capitalist] system's incentives and habits, the legal forms which sustain it, and the moral ideals which justify it" and went on to propose "the abolition of our present competitive profit-seeking economy." [3]

Without implying that stands adopted by the less liberal churches were necessarily contradictory to those mentioned above, it can be said that their statements were less inclined to question the basic premises of capitalism or to suggest that the present emergency required radically new approaches. The Presbyterian Church in the U.S. was unprepared to go beyond voicing "concern over unemployment." The Evangelical and Reformed Church, while affirming in a 1932 resolution that the present order was "built upon greed and selfishness," saw no need to propose an alternative order. For the United Lutheran Church (a precursor of the present Lutheran Church in America) the 1930s was a period of transition, during which the denomination clung to its traditional reluctance to question the social order but increasingly came to doubt the justifiability of this policy as a matter of general principles, especially at its 1936 national convention.[4] Summarizing the attitude of the Northern Baptist Convention of the U.S. in a study originally appearing in 1950, Robert G. Torbet remarked that

> with respect to economic reform, one may generalize quite safely by saying that their strong emphasis upon individualism has caused Baptists to shy away from radical theories; at the same time it has made them willing to support the capitalistic system of individual enterprise.[5]

In summary, incomplete information makes it difficult to assess the behavior of all FCC member churches in the depression era; but it is reasonably clear that the most radical statements of the period arose from bodies long identified with, and deeply involved in, the council, while more cautious statements emanated from churches in the "moderately" or "least committed" categories.

Era of Racial Involvement. By the mid-1940s national Protestantism's concern with social questions was increasingly finding its expression in action on the civil rights front, though its earlier interest in economic issues was still prevalent. Admittedly, the race issue taps a somewhat different vein than the issues heretofore dealt with in this section; it is scarcely surprising, therefore, that at least some bodies identified as liberal (or progressive) on economic issues would behave conservatively on race issues, and vice versa. For example, there was support from economically conservative churches for the FCC's 1946 resolution calling upon member churches to "renounce the pattern of segregation" and "work for a nonsegregated church in a nonsegregated society," a decidedly liberal statement vis-à-vis the race issue for the time. Though the FCC statement was officially endorsed by such denominations as the Presbyterian Church in the U.S.A. and the Congregational Church, as might have been expected, it was also subscribed to by the Northern Baptist Convention (1948) and the United Lutheran Church (1952), neither of which had been previously regarded as being especially liberal on social issues.[6]

Notwithstanding the willingness of many churches to support the principle of racial justice and nondiscrimination, there is evidence that in the late 1950s and early '60s the traditionally liberal churches were more prepared than the other council members to commit money and staff to the civil rights cause. The United Presbyterian Church first authorized establishment of a Presbyterian Interracial Council and later an even more activist Presbyterian Commission on Religion and Race. The Methodist Church sponsored conferences on human relations, the resolutions of which addressed themselves strongly to civil rights matters. The United Church of Christ voted sanctions against member churches and church-related institutions guilty of racial bias and authorized establishment of a Commission on Racial Justice. Though for tactical reasons the Episcopal Society for Cultural and Racial Unity did not request official endorsement from the Episcopal Church, it exerted significant influence on that body. (Indeed, as the first of the racial action bodies in a major Protestant body, ESCRU occupies a place of special importance in the history of these years.)

Among the moderate churches, on the other hand, there was a tendency to deal with the race issue in more modest terms. A convention sponsored by the Disciples of Christ in October 1963 devoted major attention to the need for relocating men who had lost pulpits because of their integration stands. About the same time the Southern Presbyterians voted to ban discrimination from church-related institutions but chose not to go so far as to establish an official racial action body such as the one voted into existence by their brethren in the United Presbyterian Church. These and other "moderate" NCC supporters endorsed the civil rights work of the NCC but stopped short at creating their own official race action arms.

It is important not to make value judgments prematurely in regard to these findings. To conclude that a given denomination manifests a preference for confronting social issues in an activist manner is not equivalent to suggesting that it is therefore necessarily more compassionate or humanitarian, any more than a more pietistic emphasis that views activism with misgivings is to be considered evidence of indifference to injustice and evil. Whatever the professed reasons for approaching issues in a certain manner, one must also keep in mind that all churches have a prudent regard for their own survival, this motive being as much apparent in the more activist bodies (concerned with the need not to appear irrelevant to important moral issues confronting the nation) as it is in the others (concerned with maintaining rapport with well-to-do supporters inclined toward conservative social views). This is not to suggest that social involvement may be accounted for purely in terms of self-interest, but it is to suggest that this consideration is never wholly absent.

POLITICAL PREDISPOSITIONS OF THE LEAST ACTIVE MEMBER BODIES

The following churches or clusters of churches have previously been identified as ranking relatively low in their commitment to the NCC: the Eastern Orthodox bodies (seven), several white Protestant bodies distinguished by their small membership (five), the American Baptist Convention, and the black denominations (six). Taken collectively these churches have a membership of 15.7 million, approximately 37 percent of the council's total. With the exception of the second of these clusters, consideration of which must be omitted for reasons noted above, these churches will be investigated to determine whether they deviate significantly from the tendencies marking the more committed churches. Our hypothesis is that there is a correlation between conservatism and lack of involvement with the NCC. To test it, it is not necessary to demonstrate that all "least committed" denominations are equally conservative. Indeed, in the case of the American Baptist Convention, for example, or the African Methodist Episcopal Zion Church, a strong argument could be made that they have been more supportive of social action than has been true of some "moderately committed" bodies. It will be enough to show that the general tone of policy in these denominations is markedly more conservative than that of the NCC itself, in contradistinction to those churches most actively involved.

Eastern Orthodoxy. Two factors have historically conditioned the Eastern Orthodox attitude toward politics and society. First, these churches have organized themselves along nationality (autocephalous) lines. Although the titular leader of all Orthodoxy is the patriarch of Constantinople (Istanbul), the real power lies in separate churches, each administered by an archbishop with a constituency consisting predominantly of a single ethnic group. Second, prior to their coming to the United States, Eastern Orthodox churchmen lived in the Balkans, Russia, and Asia Minor, areas marked for centuries by economic and political instability. Taken in combination these two factors have caused the Orthodox churches to stress those portions of scripture emphasizing obedience to secular authority and to play down those passages that might justify church involvement in social protest. For related reasons, Orthodox Christians have favored a fusion of sacred and temporal authority, church and state, so as to better insure social order and promote adherence to the "true Faith." While their experiences with anarchy and disorder in the Balkans did not necessarily *insure* their continued adherence to conservative views following immigration to the United States, these experiences did perhaps reinforce their conservatism. In contrast, the emphasis in American Protestantism on separation of church and state, though not necessarily leading to a *liberal* political attitude, does imply a high degree of autonomy for the church and the option to criticize government in the name of social justice when church leaders deem it appropriate.

Protestant-Orthodox differences on church-state matters more than once have contributed to sharp differences within the NCC. At a meeting of the General Board in June 1963, for example, Archbishop Iakovos of the Greek Orthodox Church voiced strenuous objection to a draft proposal for a pronouncement dealing with "The Churches and the Public Schools," which endorsed the 1962 Supreme Court decision in the Regents' Prayer case, *Engle* v. *Vitale*. Though the Protestants on the board found the statement unobjectionable, Iakovos insisted that it capitulated to secularist sentiment and that it posited an unrealistic dichotomy between church and state. "If this statement goes out with NCC endorsement," Iakovos warned, "it may be necessary for the Orthodox to repudiate membership in the Council." [7] The General Board nevertheless voted approval of the pronouncement.

Such an incident reveals not a mere disagreement over policy, which might occur even among groups of closely similar outlook, but the conflicting predispositions and often inarticulate major premises of Orthodoxy and non-Orthodox Protestantism. Protestant annoyance at Orthodoxy's seeming arrogance in repeatedly insisting that it is "the one true way" is matched by Orthodoxy's anxiety that liberal Protestants are only interested in secular matters. Thus, for example, the *Christian Century*, the leading organ of interdenominational Protestantism, once expressed editorially the view that

> Never a large ecumenical meeting is held that a representative of the Orthodox wing of the World Council of Churches does not rise before final adjournment to explain that, while Orthodox Christianity is glad to have been involved in the discussion, it must clearly disassociate itself from the conclusions. . . . [These statements] are galling to the Protestant Christian,

who can hardly be expected to rejoice in this regular rejection.[8]

The annoyance is reciprocated. Orthodox intellectual John Meyendorff, for example, has worried over the possibility of "the Protestant majority in the Council leading the organization more and more in a direction incompatible with Orthodox principles."[9] Both the *Christian Century* and Meyendorff had the World Council of Churches specifically in mind, but the same basic problem is present in the NCC.

By the late 1960s, Orthodox dissatisfaction with liberal NCC stands on such issues as abortion, race, and family planning had crystallized. A group of leading Orthodox theologians at St. Vladimir's Orthodox Theological Seminary in Tuckahoe, New York, drew up a scathing memorandum calling for a reevaluation of Orthodoxy's relationship with the NCC, including the possibility of dropping out. The memorandum charged that the NCC had encouraged "hasty mergers and the dilution of Christianity in secularism" and contended that the NCC "almost totally ignores the most terrible moral degradation of our world." Singled out for particular criticism was the NCC's friendliness with black militants and its advocacy of peaceful coexistence with Communism. In a subsequent interview with a *Newsweek* reporter, the principal author of the memorandum, Father Alexander Schmemann, alluded to the fact that the Orthodox churches were unhappy not only over the substance of NCC statements but the style of its official behavior: "The whole style of the NCC's operation is completely alien to the Orthodox churches."[10]

In light of all this, the question quite naturally arises as to why the Orthodox churches remain in the council. It is possible that in the future one or two of the Orthodox bodies in the NCC (especially the Russian Orthodox Church of North and South America, of which Schmemann himself is a member) will secede, their affiliation being tenuous at best. Yet the more impressive fact is that despite persistent and highly vocal Orthodox criticism of the council and despite repeated threats to withdraw, all nine churches have thus far stopped short at secession. In response to the statement at St. Vladimir's, for example, Archbishop Iakovos told a *Newsweek* reporter that "Withdrawal is out of the question." [11]

It is not difficult to see why withdrawal has been avoided. The Orthodox churches are too few in number and not well enough placed in terms of access to key centers of decision-making in the United States for a "go it alone" strategy to appear attractive. While an Orthodox alliance with Roman Catholocism appears feasible on doctrinal grounds, collaboration with the Catholic hierarchy is precluded by rival claims to primacy in the family of churches. Protestants are more flexible in this respect and less inclined to raise troublesome theological problems. Also there is the long-standing quarrel between Rome and Constantinople going back more than a thousand years. Given its relatively small constituency in the United States and its marginal social and political status, to ally with neither Catholicism nor Protestantism would involve real risks for Eastern Orthodoxy. Its need for church allies is illustrated by an incident in 1966, when Turkish authorities adopted policies that would have adversely affected the freedom and deference accorded the Greek Orthodox patriarch of Constantinople. These were protested by the Greek Orthodox Church of North and South America through United States diplomatic channels, but the protest was all the more effective because the NCC was willing to use its influence in behalf of the Orthodox position and to issue a public statement on the matter.[12]

The essential point, then, is that Eastern Orthodoxy continues to participate in the NCC not because of but despite the NCC's pronounced liberal outlook. Weighing the relative advantages and drawbacks, Orthodox leaders have apparently concluded that their status in American life is not yet sufficiently secure to justify the severing of formal ties with their more numerous and more socially prestigious Protestant brethren. Events could occur to make Orthodoxy reassess its social outlook and embrace liberal assumptions, much as a generation ago the denominations that now comprise the Lutheran Church in America reassessed the traditional Lutheran view on church involvement in social issues. Perhaps like the Lutheran Church in America, a stalwart supporter of the NCC, Orthodoxy may one day adopt an equally sympathetic view. On the other hand, it is equally possible that as Orthodoxy's prestige rises (as a result of the acculturation of its constituency and its consequent upward social mobility) it may decide that its basic conservative outlook rules out any need for continued affiliation with Protestant liberalism. In that event, some or all of the Orthodox bodies might elect to withdraw from the council.

Fundamentalist Impact on the American Baptist Convention. Although differing from them in most other respects, the American Baptist Convention (ABC) resembles the Eastern Orthodox churches in one important way: the strong emphasis on the Baptists' unique creed and social outlook. This creedal emphasis makes the Baptists distinctive, giving them a competitive edge over many churches that look doctrinally alike to the casual observer and thus have difficulty attracting and holding members. Yet this very emphasis on distinctive points of theology and structure tends to frustrate cooperation with other churches, even when cooperation is deemed desirable by Baptist leaders.

The American Baptist Convention is more modernized than the Eastern Orthodox churches and is more inclined to temper a basically conservative outlook with liberal views on certain issues. Formerly the Northern Baptist Convention, it was among the original members of the FCC; and unlike some churches that withdrew from membership in the FCC or NCC for varying periods of time (such as the Southern Presbyterians and United Lutherans), it has remained in the council continuously since the FCC's founding in 1908. Given the council's progressive bias, this fact is itself evidence of liberal inclinations. Also, the American Baptists, with a large black minority in its membership, were among the first denominations to lend their prestige to a call for stronger stands against racial segregation in the churches and in society. The ABC has a highly decentralized structure, and certain local Baptist congregations have involved themselves actively in social service and protest movements.

Nevertheless, during the past generation a marked conservative tendency has dominated the ABC. As Paul M. Harrison has shown, the decentralized structure and emphasis on direct, plebiscitary democracy has made it difficult for the

American Baptists to press for social change with any degree
of consistency, especially in view of the unusual ethnic and
social class cleavages among its constituents and its highly
competitive relationship to the Southern Baptist Convention in
border states and in California. Since the Southern Baptist
orientation is distinctly conservative, the ABC dare not become
too liberal for fear of antagonizing potential supporters.[13]

The contest between fundamentalists and liberals has been
evident within the convention, with the liberals generally having the worst of it. The priorities established through the
budgetary process, specifically the Committees on Budget Research and on Finance, have tended to discriminate sharply
against social action efforts. The convention's Council for Christian Social Progress (CCSP), a liberal, action-oriented body,
has had to struggle simply to survive. In the 1950s, "after many
years of dedicated effort," the CCSP's annual appropriation
reached a mere $37,549 or 0.0043 percent of the convention's
total budget. The "reserve" (or miscellaneous) item in the
budget was about the same size.[14] Other less controversial agencies were fully funded and were in a position to make long-
range plans with the assurance that funds would be available
when needed. The CCSP's lack of support at the grass roots
level, given the Baptist commitment to local autonomy, greatly
intensifies its survival problem. Harrison quotes one official as
remarking:

> Other denominations have their Fundamentalist problem,
> especially in rural areas, but not like the Baptists have it. If
> we started an open discussion of theological issues we'd blow
> the lid off a boiling pot. I know—we fear this more than any-
> thing else and it conditions everything we do and say.[15]

Generally speaking, convention officials have sought to con-
ciliate the fundamentalists, whereas their gestures toward the
liberal faction have been far less forceful. The result is that
while the convention avoids becoming quite as conservative as
the fundamentalist faction would prefer, it falls substantially
short of meeting the liberals' demands for stronger commitments in behalf of social justice and reform efforts.

Nevertheless, the settlements of issues preferred by the top elective and appointive officials have not always proved acceptable to the convention delegates. A main focus of controversy has been the ABC's involvement in the National Council of Churches, a body the fundamentalist faction views with deep distrust but one the liberals would like to see the convention more committed to. At the 1946 annual meeting in Grand Rapids, the fundamentalists, having grown considerably in the years just previous, launched a vociferous campaign aimed at reversing, or at least substantially altering, the generally liberal line adopted by the denomination in the late 1930s and early '40s. The campaign was two-pronged, having both a theological and an immediate practical dimension. On the theological front a prominent Baptist layman, a certain Judge Fickett, urged that the convention go on record as requiring all staff executives employed by the convention to give assent to a statement embodying a literalist interpretation of the Bible. Among other arguments the judge insisted that this would help defend the convention from the inroads being made by the Southern Baptist Convention, "whose representatives tell people that 'the National Baptists do not believe in the Bible.'" [16] When after considerable controversy the motion was voted down, the fundamentalist faction launched an attack on the convention's $4.4 million "general benevolence" budget and in particular on funds earmarked to support special programs sponsored by the FCC and the World Council of Churches (WCC).

Two years later the fundamentalists returned to the fray in larger numbers. A group calling themselves "Conservative Baptists" held a meeting attended by 500 people immediately in advance of the convention's own annual meeting. The seriousness of their threat was later acknowledged by the convention president, the Reverend Dr. Edwin T. Dahlberg, who reported that between 25 and 45 local Baptist churches had informed him of their intention to withdraw unless substantial concessions to fundamentalist views were forthcoming. The issue had resolved itself into a dispute over the convention's right to authorize, by majority vote, the spending of denominational funds in support of the FCC and WCC. The more conservative faction maintained that any effort to settle the matter by majority vote would infringe upon the sovereignty of those local churches not in the majority, thus violating the sacred Baptist principle of local autonomy. The result of behind-the-scenes negotiations on the matter was a compromise giving something to both sides but leaning toward the fundamentalist view: distribution of money to the Federal Council's general operating budget would be ended, except in the case of funds specifically designated for that purpose by donating local churches, which were likely to be only few. The liberals, on the other hand, took satisfaction from the fact that this would not in actuality diminish greatly the *overall* convention support of the council, since the 1948 resolution was officially interpreted as not applying to convention funds going from its own societies, boards, and councils to the parallel activities of the National Council of Churches. Thus, whereas in 1966 the total American Baptist official assignation to the NCC was a minuscule $22,109, the total of all remittances to NCC divisions and departments was a more substantial $311,159.[17]

The fundamentalists' long-term goal remained complete withdrawal from the council as a token of the ABC's return to biblical absolutes. By the late 1950s it was becoming more difficult for top convention officials to paper over the theological-political dispute and to placate wealthy churchmen concerned about the direction of the denomination's social thinking. A report issued in 1957 indicating that the American Baptist Convention was losing an average of 10,400 members a year presumably helped to sharpen the bite of fundamentalist invective.

At the convention's 1960 meeting the seething dispute once again erupted on the floor of the convention, with American Baptist participation in the National Council of Churches again the key issue. Delegates from the First Baptist Church of Wichita, Kansas, arranged for publication of a searing indictment of the council entitled *Why One Church's Conscience Spoke Out Against the National Council of Churches*, copies of which were made available to delegates as they entered the meeting hall. As the debate opened, Preston Huston, spokesman for the Wichita group, spelled out the case against the NCC, calling it a "mish-mash of watered down Christianity and its leaders supporters of Communist causes." "We feel we should be preaching the true Gospel," he continued, "instead of trying to find ways of cooperating with infidels." [18] Another Wichita delegate introduced a resolution castigating the NCC and calling for the ABC to end any official contributions to its budget.

In the face of this barrage, the moderates did the best they could to mount a defense of present ecumenical commitments. The fact that the Reverend Dr. Edwin T. Dahlberg, a prominent churchman and a leading moderate in the 1948 struggle, was then completing his three-year term as NCC president was perhaps a factor in the fundamentalists' timing. In any case, he was obliged to rise in defense of the National Council. The moderates sought to counter the fundamentalists' attack by introducing a counterresolution acknowledging the diversity of views among local churches but reaffirming the convention's membership in the NCC and avoiding any direct criticisms of it. It went on to provide, however, that local Baptist churches that could not in good conscience support or affiliate with the NCC should be allowed to so list themselves in special sections of the convention's annual yearbook. The resolution was adopted.[19]

The continued strength of the right-wing faction in the early 1960s was attested by the fact that the Conservative Baptist Association of America, founded in 1947 for the purpose of opposing "modernism, all forms of inclusivism and ecumenicalism," had by 1961 grown in membership to 1,300 churches and was in a position to support four theological institutions, three colleges, two Bible institutes, a foreign missions society, and a home missions society with combined staffs numbering in the hundreds.[20]

Thus, over a 15-year period the fundamentalist faction in the American Baptist Convention had met defeat on a number of specific issues, in particular the proposal to withdraw from the NCC, but had nevertheless managed to secure considerable influence in the convention. The view that the ABC should withdraw from the NCC was at least regarded as respectable, even if it was not persuasive to most convention delegates. Although the 1948 resolution regarding the allocation of funds to the NCC did not prevent some ABC money from going to the council (especially for programs that were of direct tangible benefit to the convention), these allocations were substantially less than what might have been expected of a denomination of 1.5 million members.

Conservative Bias of the National Black Churches. There are six almost exclusively black denominations in the National Council of Churches: the African Methodist Episcopal Church, the African Methodist Episcopal Zion Church, the Christian Methodist Episcopal Church, the Progressive Baptist Convention of America, the National Baptist Convention of the U.S.A., and the National Baptist Convention of America. The combined membership of these six churches is approximately 12 million, which is roughly 29 percent of the council's total membership. There are no national black churches of any appreciable size that are not members of the NCC. In view of their great diversity, it is difficult to generalize about black churches: they are so varied that a simple liberal-conservative dichotomy may obscure their richness and variety. Nevertheless, much of the behavior of black denominational assemblies becomes clear when this dichotomy is used as an analytical framework.

Though the dominant tendency in black ecclesiastical life appears conservative, it would be misleading not to take account of evidence indicating the opposite tendency. Black clergymen in both northern and southern communities have played prominent roles in challenging racial discrimination and economic exploitation of black people. Indeed, given his role as "race man" in the black community, a pastor cannot afford to openly disavow the black protest movement, although many presumably have their reservations about the strategies of race protest groups.

While the black church may thus under certain circumstances play an important role in racial struggles, this seems to be atypical. Despite forays by certain individuals into the arena of politics, there is reason to believe that the black clergyman has not taken on the role of black civic leadership commensurate with his prestige in the black community. It is even arguable that the churches have more often served to dampen and deflect the consciousness of social injustice than to articulate social grievances. Indeed, there is considerable evidence that the basic function of the black church is escapist and compensatory. The church has been found to provide a place for the fulfillment of personality needs inadequately met by a white-dominated caste society. In sociologist E. Franklin Frazier's words, "the Negro church has provided an arena for the political struggles of a people shut out from the political life of the American community." [21]

As long as black people resided mainly in southern rural and small-town communities, the black church remained a relatively autonomous institution and enjoyed mass support among its constituents. The leadership the church had earned in the South carried over into the early years of the black migration north, so that as late as the 1930s an informed observer of a city like Detroit could state that the leadership of the black people was in the hands of their clergymen. Yet this same observer was conscious that even then the autonomy of the black church was jeopardized by a growing dependency on white business, political, and industrial interests, which created doubts among constituents about the church's motives. In many northern areas the church was coming to be looked on by black people as a racket—more an exploitative and parasitical force than an indigenous aspect of black urban culture. No doubt there were many individual churches that were not viewed in this light, but the tendency existed nevertheless. Frazier, in a controversial interpretation, went so far as to suggest that the black masses had come to regard the black church as "an instrument for the advancement of the black bourgeoisie" and as a "force divorced from any real religious sentiment." [22]

There is no question, certainly, that from 1930 to 1960 black churches were experiencing a decline in prestige due to the failure of black clergymen to keep pace with the rising educational levels among elite groups in the black community. Despite some recent increases in the number of black clergymen with seminary backgrounds, a 1963 study found that only about one black preacher in ten had attended seminary.[23] Largely because of the educational lag, the prestige of the black ministry, formerly *the* profession open to young black men, had declined rapidly and recruitment into the black clergy had become a major problem. Moreover, a low level of educational attainment presumably reinforced the characteristically conservative character of the black clergy, since higher education, particularly in liberal arts and humanistically oriented colleges and seminaries, is known to contribute to more liberal social and political views among the clergy. Among blacks in northern and western cities, according to James Q. Wilson, the role of civic leadership gradually passed from the hands of the clergy to "race relations professionals," who from time to time called upon the clergy for support, resources, and publicity.[24]

It is true that the black churches' tendency to escapism is in part a function of social class, not race per se. At the time of their study of black life in Chicago, St. Clair Drake and Horace Cayton found that roughly three-fourths of the black churches were of the "store front" variety (that is, lacking a permanent edifice of their own). In terms of membership, the lower class churches comprised roughly 65 percent of church membership (much higher than among white churches). While the lower class pastor typically remains almost exclusively within the boundaries of his racial subculture and has a narrow, pietistic conception of his role, the pastor serving a middle to upper class black congregation is more likely to join a plethora of organizations, even interdenominational ones, such as the local church federation, in which whites may be in the majority. Nevertheless, among black pastors at all levels of the social scale researchers have found a common reluctance to act in civic leadership roles or to support protest organizations like the NAACP. More than one observer has concluded that black churches, regardless of class composition, on the whole exert a conservative influence in black communities.[25]

Conceivably, local findings do not provide a valid indication of the social and political predispositions prevailing among national officials of black denominations; delegates to a national assembly may reveal liberal tendencies for which the local church provides little avenue of expression. To explore this possibility it is worthwhile to study one black denomination, the African Methodist Episcopal Church (AME), in its national dimension. There is no reason to believe the AME to be atypical, and in terms of total membership it stands somewhere between the largest black body in the National Baptist Convention (NBC) and the smallest (Christian Methodist Episcopal Church). Selection of the AME was also based in part on the relative availability of published materials on this body over a period of years.

The African Methodist Episcopal Church was one of the founding members of the Federal Council of Churches in 1908. It is therefore of some interest that the official record of its Twenty-third General Conference in Norfolk, Virginia, in May of that year makes no reference to the then-upcoming FCC constituting convention—this, despite the fact that the convention was already being widely discussed in church circles and despite the intention of AME leaders to attend. Furthermore, a careful examination of the official minutes of subsequent AME General Conferences through 1922 failed to uncover a single mention of the council, either of a general nature or with specific reference to the AME role in the FCC. Also revealing is the fact that these minutes contain references to the most minute aspects of internal denominational affairs in the 1908 to 1922 period but do not once broach what might be termed a broad social issue. A partial exception is the matter of lynching, touched on more than once in the minutes; but issues affecting the lives of black people in equally serious, if less sinister, ways are absent.

Moreover, not until 1948 was the matter of establishment of an official social service department given serious consideration, even though, as Bishop Richard R. Wright observed in his Episcopal Address of that year, the FCC had maintained such a department for many years and most other national churches had long since established parallel agencies. As of this writing no social service board has been established.

Even in the era of civil rights militancy beginning early in the 1960s, available materials suggest that the AME was reluctant to become officially involved. An examination of two official AME publications over the past several years (*AME Review* and *Christian Recorder*) provides little evidence of interest in political, economic, social, or even racial issues of broad national importance. With an upsurge in militancy and emphasis on group pride among blacks, a number of younger black clergymen have begun to reassess the potential of churches for political action. But while this has resulted in the organizing of black caucuses within predominantly white Protestant denominations, caucus leaders doubt their ability to "radicalize" black communions. The racial activists' attitude toward the black denominations is summed up by one of them: "There are no militant associations in the [all black] churches because [their] posture has been one of accommodation to the white middle class ethos." [26] Even Joseph R. Washington, an informed black observer who is generally optimistic about the capacity of black churches to assume a political leadership role in the black community, is critical of the conservative bias still prevailing among the leaders of black denominations.[27]

CONCLUSIONS

There is evidently a significant association between the NCC's pronounced policy preferences and the basic predispositions of certain of its member churches; its liberalism derives more from the outlooks of its most committed members than from a consensus among all its participants. Moreover, its own tradition of liberalism is self-perpetuating, since it makes it all the more difficult for denominational leaders who are not committed liberals to have much impact on the organization. Thus, neither the criticism from the chief prelate of the Greek Orthodox Church nor that implicit in conservative stands adopted by the American Baptist Convention is influential in altering the prevailing NCC ideology.

It would be misleading to suggest, however, that the greater deference accorded the more liberal churches derives simply from their greater relative commitment. Another significant factor, implied by the data of the preceding discussion, is that liberal Protestants enjoy greater cohesion on social issues than do their conservative brethren. Though occasional issues have threatened the consensus (Episcopalians and Lutherans, for example, were by no means entirely supportive of the "Protestant crusade" to enact Prohibition), on a great many issues (for example, social service, child labor, industrial democracy, national economic planning, and racial justice) liberal Protestantism has found itself united in agreement. On the other hand, conservative churchmen have had divergent rather than parallel attitudes toward several of these issues. The relative degree of racial and ethnic diversity among the more conservative churches is one factor involved in their greater diversity of opinion. Many of them have a distinct ethnic character in contrast to the heterogeneity that characterizes each main line church. Struggles over policy issues that go on *within* the more liberal, pluralistic bodies tend to divide one conservative church from another. Theological differences, on which conservatives place a good deal of emphasis, also have a divisive effect much greater than among liberals.

These considerations probably help to account for the fact that the more conservative churches have not banded together to form a distinct bloc in the council. The absence of such a bloc has made it easier for liberal churchmen to have their way on major social questions.

5. The National Lay
Committee Controversy

*I*n the ordinary course of things, the Federal Council's social activism, espoused from the outset and reaffirmed in later decades, could have been expected to persist in the enlarged body established in 1950. The personnel, the traditions, the mystique of the old FCC remained intact. As it developed, however, this expectation did not go unchallenged in the NCC's early years.

The present chapter focuses attention on an effort by a group of conservative business and professional church people to rearrange the council's priorities so as to minimize its programs aimed at social and economic justice and to emphasize, instead, the importance of traditional moral and spiritual values. Known as the National Lay Committee, this group was called into existence around the time of the Federal Council's 1950 merger because of a concern over opening up new revenue sources and securing greater lay involvement in leadership. The Lay Committee was denied formal constitutional status, and its position vis-à-vis the General Board remained ambiguous. But this did not prevent it from wielding significant influence over the general content of policy, an influence that persisted for some time, even after the committee itself was formally abolished. This group's history thus merits detailed attention both for insights into the organization's outlook in the "pre-civil rights" era and for a fresh perspective on the liberal-conservative tension in American Protestantism, which from the beginning has conditioned council behavior.

FORMATION OF THE LAY COMMITTEE

The founders of the National Council of Churches intended to maintain the activist orientation identified with the FCC. This was not their only intention, however; they also wanted the merger to facilitate an expansion of operations well beyond the total programs of the parties to it. Since those in a position to donate the necessary large sums of money were inclined to be conservative, it was not clear whether such an expansion could actually be carried out. The funds required were significantly larger than those that had been raised in total by the confederating groups. As of 1950, the last full year of FCC operations, the merging bodies had a combined income of approximately $2,435,000, the FCC's share of this being $695,000. The total budget projected for the new organization's first year was $4,435,000, almost double the previous figure. By 1953 the council's *actual* budget totaled $7,210,000; and while it may not have been foreseen in 1950 that the budget would grow at quite this pace, it seems reasonable to suppose that the NCC organizers had projected plans beyond the first year of operations and that the $7 million budget was therefore not unexpected.

Much of the new money was to be raised among the participating Protestant and Orthodox denominations, whose contributions to the FCC had been less than what many believed they could have afforded. In its last year of existence, the FCC had received only about $300,000 from its member churches. Additional sums may have been donated by the churches to the other interdenominational bodies involved in the merger, but in any case the total had been small. As a result of assiduous cultivation of this source of income, the NCC leaders succeeded in raising additional funds from the denominations, which by 1953 totaled $3.1 million.

The projected expenditure plans still exceeded even the most optimistic estimates of what might be forthcoming from member churches, and substantial additional funds had thus to be sought outside "regular" membership channels. It was believed that pledges from individual lay people and from other "nonchurch" sources such as business firms and foundations, could be solicited. Some lay people had felt that the FCC was too progressive for them, since it had been labeled Communist and socialist in several widely read books. Although they had doubtless discounted the more hysterical accusations, the fact that the charges had been repeatedly made had helped reinforce their anxieties. Others had charged that the FCC was run in the interests of ordained clergymen, who dominated all the major committees. It is easy to see how such an impression originated, since of the five men elected president of the Federal Council during its last decade, only one, Charles P. Taft, was a layman. Figures on the lay-clergy ratio of the FCC Executive Committee are not available, but the situation probably resembled that of the NCC's early years; in 1952, for example, 84.7 percent of the General Board (similar to the old Executive Committee as the highest policy-making body) were clergymen. To demonstrate the sincerity of their stated desire for greater lay participation (hoping thus to receive more lay financial support), those who had arranged the merger had to go to the lay people with a new plan.

GENESIS OF THE NATIONAL LAY COMMITTEE

The problem of how to increase lay participation was a major concern for the Planning Committee for the Proposed National Council of Churches, created in 1948. On 16 June 1950 the members drew up a "Memorandum of Conclusions," which provided for the establishment within the NCC structure of the National Lay Committee to advise on the best method of securing the "vital participation" of lay members in the council's work. The Lay Committee was to have more than "advisory functions," the planning committee being of the opinion that men of stature in the business and financial community would not serve unless they were given their say on substantive issues in the life of the NCC.

Obviously, the selection of a man to serve as chairman was a matter of considerable importance, since the NCC's initial progress would depend upon generating a sense of involvement among lay people able to donate generously. A man only moderately wealthy or only moderately well placed in the corporate business community would not be in the best position to attract the sums of money expansion plans required. NCC leaders were doubtless pleased, then, when, on 6 July 1950, Mr. J. Howard Pew made known his willingness to accept the position of Lay Committee chairman offered him. In the first place, Pew was a man of substantial means, having a personal fortune estimated in 1957 as being at between $75 and $100 million.[1] His full financial resources may have been even greater, since the extended Pew family, of which J. Howard was the senior member, is believed to own over half the common stock of the Sun Oil Company. If true, the Pews are, after the Rockefellers, du Ponts, Mellons, and Fords, the fifth richest family in the nation. Secondly, Mr. Pew's position at that time as chairman of the board of Sun Oil Company gave him access to other corporation officials, upon whom he could call without embarrassment for donations to the NCC. Finally, Mr. Pew was an active Presbyterian layman in good standing with his church and was respected even by critics of his ultraconservative economic and political views.

In accepting the Lay Committee chairmanship, Pew was given a free hand in selecting the other members. By the time of the NCC Constituting Convention in late November 1950, a total of 86 men and women had agreed to serve. "Though active in their local churches, most of the members of this National Layman's Committee had not previously had any close identification with denominational affairs at the national level."[2] The members' lack of pronounced denominational involvement reduced to a minimum whatever uneasiness they might have felt about taking issue with official denominational stands on social issues. Though all of the major Protestant denominations appear to have been nominally represented on the committee, Pew made no particular effort to balance the membership in proportion to the varying sizes of NCC member churches, as was the case for the NCC General Board. The committee was made up predominantly of persons affiliated with just two churches, the Episcopal and United Presbyterian, a point later raised against it by spokesmen for other denominations, especially ones not in the same socially elite category.

In recruiting members for the new committee, Pew stressed their opportunity to redirect the council's energies away from "social and political matters" and toward true religion and evangelism. In view of the exuberant self-confidence with which the Lay Committee set about challenging the council's friendship with organized labor and its receptiveness to state planning embodied in the 1932 "Revised Social Creed," it would appear that the motivation of members owed something to what John Kenneth Galbraith refers to as the "revival of the Market" and the "rediscovery of the Benthamite world of the nineteenth century," which characterized the late 1940s and early '50s.[3] The "revival of the Market" had its origins in the academic community, especially in F. A. von Hayek's *The Road to Serfdom* (1944) and among his followers at the University of Chicago, but was soon taken up by *Fortune,* the *Wall Street Journal,* and other business journals. New Deal-Fair Deal liberals found themselves on the defensive in economic matters during these years.

EARLY STRUGGLES OVER THE LAY COMMITTEE'S ROLE

Resistance to the Lay Committee's special status in the council soon became apparent. Though Pew accepted his post in July 1950, it was not until the NCC Constituting Convention that November, after the entire committee membership had been selected, that most Protestant leaders even so much as knew of its existence. It had not, for example, been mentioned in the proposed constitution for the NCC. The *Christian Century* reported that many delegates, presumably the more liberal ones, were amazed and perplexed when J. Howard Pew, already well known for his ultraconservative views, was introduced as someone who would play a prominent role in the newly formed council. Their amazement increased when they heard Pew announce,

The Planning Committee has expressed its willingness to recommend to the General Board the adoption of a procedure whereby the National Lay Committee will be given an opportunity to collaborate . . . with other units of the Council as they formulate pronouncements and strategy and statements of policy in areas in which the lay groups have special competence and interest, and in which collaboration may be mutually advantageous in strengthening the Council's program.[4]

Doubts about Pew's role had only begun to crystallize when the NCC's newly elected General Board gathered for its initial meeting on 2 December 1950, immediately following the Constituting Convention's close. Dr. Samuel McCrea Cavert, general secretary of the newly formed body and a man of considerable stature in the Protestant ecumenical movement, introduced the Lay Committee concept. He spoke of the committee as "overarching" the whole structure of the council, yet without final authority, as having sweeping powers of participation and review. Bishop G. Bromley Oxnam (Methodist) was the first to speak out in opposition, replying to Cavert that the very use of the word *overarching* disturbed him and insisting that there be no arrangement for censorship of the NCC's pronouncements. The upshot of the discussion was that whereas the General Board quickly ratified the other major recommendations submitted to it by the Planning Committee, it balked at the Lay Committee idea. Yet there seemed reason to hope that an acceptable compromise would be achieved, since even critics of the proposed committee agreed that greater lay participation in the council was desirable. Given the growing internal opposition to Pew's committee, however, an acceptable compromise was not achieved until 28 March 1951, when a plan was approved whereby it would be established as an "advisory" and not a regular standing committee of the board.[5]

As an important concession the General Board voted that five laymen and five laywomen should be designated to sit on the board as "consultants," enjoying all member privileges except the right to vote. In spelling out the Lay Committee's mandate, the federation officers stressed the need "to make the most effective use of the experience of laypeople . . . and provide a partnership between them and ministers in all areas of the Council," and also "to assist in obtaining needed financial support." Though the resolution did affirm the Lay Committee's status as an affiliated body in the NCC, Pew was distressed over its failure to affirm the committee's right to be consulted on major policy issues coming before the board for action. He regarded this as a departure from the "partnership relationship" he had had in mind in accepting the chairmanship, and he strove, although unsuccessfully, for a definite commitment on this crucial point. Despite the chairman's anxieties, the Lay Committee agreed to a formal request that it help raise a minimum of $600,000 by the end of 1951 to finance operations already undertaken by the NCC.

THE LAY COMMITTEE REACHES THE PEAK
OF ITS INFLUENCE

The president of the council during the first two years was the Right Reverend Henry Knox Sherrill, presiding bishop of the Protestant Episcopal Church and a man of immense prestige among Protestant churchmen. Judging by the written record, Sherrill made an effort to placate Pew by making concessions on a number of relatively minor matters, while avoiding any compromise on the crucial issue of allowing the Lay Committee to review NCC policy statements. He thus sent a warmly worded telegram to the group's first annual meeting in April 1951, in which he underscored the need for "an increased partnership between ministers and laymen" and the "vital role" the Lay Committee had in this endeavor.

At a General Board meeting on 28 November 1951, a resolution was proposed by the Department of the Church and Economic Life that would have the NCC speak out strongly on certain "ethical issues" raised by inflation in the national economy. Pew objected, and Bishop Sherrill indicated his own uneasiness about the resolution, raising "a question of whether the General Board can or ought to take action on a variety of complicated questions." He suggested that pronouncements be kept to a minimum on these subjects "on which no general agreement can be reached readily." It was Sherrill's opinion that the larger issue of the circumstances under which the council ought to issue pronouncements should be considered in more detail, and he appointed a committee of five to study the matter and report back to the next meeting. The committee came back with a recommendation that J. Howard Pew was later to quote with warm approval:

> We have come to the clear conclusion that it would be wise, as a matter of policy, for the Board to limit the number of occasions on which it makes a pronouncement in the name of the churches and to confine those pronouncements to those matters in connection with which there is an unmistakable ethical or religious concern and which seem to require an utterance by the church.[6]

The committee also recommended that NCC departments be permitted to prepare and circulate objective studies of ethical import (something they had long been accustomed to doing). As a concession to Pew it was made clear that the studies did not represent the official thinking of the organization; and in order to insure compliance with General Board policy, it was proposed that a subcommittee of that body, the Committee of Reference, be created to review "the manuscripts of all studies undertaken and to determine whether it was of such a character that it may properly be issued by the authority of the division concerned."[7] The board agreed to this suggestion, and a reference committee was constituted. The decision meant that the various divisions of the council, especially those carrying on the work of the old Federal Council in the social action area, were henceforth to be deprived of a certain measure of their former autonomy. Studies relevant to social policy questions might still be prepared, but their printing and distribution would depend upon approval by a committee composed of General Board members. There was no guarantee that such approval would be routinely forthcoming.

Though this represented a significant victory, the Lay Committee soon came to the conclusion that loopholes remained, which the liberal activists might exploit. Pew became alarmed when he learned that the newly established Committee of Reference had met and authorized printing and distribution of two controversial studies recently completed by the Church and Economic Life department, one concerning U.S. agricultural policy and another the matter of how to deal with the inflation problem. He particularly objected to the fact that the reports as approved contained no statement of the "minority viewpoint" (i.e., that of the business community). While not so powerful that he could dictate terms, Pew was in a position to insist that he be given serious attention by the council's highest officials. A meeting between a Lay Committee delegation and top NCC officials was held June 20; it ended inconclusively because the participants were unable to agree on how to interpret certain ambiguous sections of the NCC Constitution.

Although not successful in curbing "political" statements as fully as it desired, the Lay Committee's influence in the council continued to wax in the latter half of 1952 and throughout 1953. The General Assembly, meeting in December 1952, renewed the committee for another year and related it more closely to the board by naming four *voting* members to replace the ten "consultants without vote" previously provided for. An additional eight laymen were to be named by other agencies in the council. Three members of the Lay Committee were elected to the post of vice-president-at-large, one of them being Mrs. Norman Vincent Peale, wife of the nationally prominent conservative author and preacher. The officials of the federation also approved a resolution that "noted with concern" the continued lack of adequate lay participation in the council and asked the Lay Committee to redouble its efforts in this direction.

Encouraged by what it took to be warm approval of its efforts, the Lay Committee held its third annual meeting at a retreat in Hershey, Pennsylvania, and rededicated itself to the propagation of conservative economic and social views. Admiral Edward B. Harp, chief of chaplains, U.S. Navy, addressed the body concerning the need to safeguard the moral welfare of members of the armed forces, both in military installations and in adjacent communities. Walter H. Judd, the ultraconservative congressman from Minnesota, delivered a plea in favor of Bible reading in the nation's public schools. His resolution to this effect was passed. Howard E. Kerschner, editor of *Christian Economics,* delivered an address entitled "God, Gold and

Government," in which he argued that "our freedom is rooted in Christian faith. . . . But faith must be supplemented by knowledge, 'know how', in the form of a sound currency, i.e. the Gold Standard," which, abandoned by the nation in an ill-advised moment in 1933, must be restored. He contended that no civilization has survived for more than 42 years without "trusted money." [8]

During the final session of the meeting, the members turned their attention to a statement recently prepared by the council's Department of Church and Economic Life now being circulated prior to its presentation for formal action at the General Board's next meeting. The Report, "Basic Christian Principles and Assumptions for Economic Life," read like a liberal manifesto. Its basic premises were related to those of the Social Gospel, which the old Federal Council of Churches had long sought to embody. It asserted that excessive economic power, even when held by those of benevolent intentions, can lead to irresponsible actions and has a strong tendency to corrupt its wielder, just as political power has a tendency to corrupt public officials. The report noted caustically,

The existence of such benevolent intentions has been used with sincerity to justify slavery, to give a religious sanction to white supremacy and the continuance of imperialism, to prevent the poor from having education or suffrage, to discourage land reform or the organization of the poor.

Having thus cleared up some "misconceptions," the report went on to set forth a "more adequate" series of objectives and norms:

there is no 'Christian economic system' that is suitable for all situations; an economic system that permits large scale unemployment or long continued unemployment for a few is gravely defective. . . . The church should keep under strongest criticism those economic institutions which increase the self-interest of men and which develop a moral climate within which money is regarded as the chief good and in which success in acquiring it is most highly honored. . . . It is essential to preserve the role of government and the activity of private business, free labor unions, and many types of voluntary organizations.[9]

The report challenged the rhetoric of free enterprise and insisted upon the need to foster social balances as a way of protecting the interests of society at large.

According to Pew's account of the meeting, the response of Lay Committee members to the report was one of strenuous criticism and denunciation. He observed that every single member rose to speak against the proposal, with "one speaker after another contending that every paragraph justified the most severe criticism." The castigations continued for four hours; then the Lay Committee voted its disapproval, 47 to 0. The accompanying resolution labeled the report "totally unsound" and "basically defective" and went on to suggest "a completely new approach and a completely revised statement" that would "take cognizance of the contribution which the American [free enterprise] system has made to human welfare, to the establishment of freedom, justice and order and in the implementation of Christian principles." [10]

The Lay Committee's objections were subsequently presented to the General Board at its meeting of 20 May 1953. After discussion the board voted to return the proposed statement of principles concerning economic life to the department that had originated it.

At the same meeting J. Howard Pew and the two other Lay Committee members also voiced objection to a statement originating in the Department of International Justice and Goodwill that condemned the Bricker Amendment, then pending before the U.S. Senate. The board sustained the objection and voted to return the proposal to the department for further study.

Either one or both of the proposals might come up again before the board, but the Lay Committee delegates were clearly influential enough to delay their enactment. There is evidence that its opposition was unflagging. As early as January 1952 it was reported in a leading interdenominational journal that NCC staff personnel were becoming discouraged by the repeated rebuffs of their policy proposals: "members of one department [unnamed, but presumably Church and Economic Life] are tempted to think that the kind of cooperative work in which they are engaged is fruitless." [11] Morale among liberal activists was being lowered.

Had the Lay Committee been content simply to exert influence within the board and not attempt to oversee the various divisions by means of its "unofficial" capacities, it is conceivable that it would have found a permanent place for itself in the council's life and structure. It was unwilling to limit itself in this manner, however.

CLIMAX OF THE STRUGGLE

J. Howard Pew and the other Lay Committee members continued to be disturbed by the fact that the General Board rules failed to prevent either resolutions (passed by delegates to NCC-sponsored meetings) or studies (made by NCC departments and agencies) from endorsing positions the board had not approved. Pew's *procedural* objections were closely related to his disagreement with the *substance* of policies recommended. Yet if the subordinate units of the council were to be disciplined, it would first be necessary to tighten still further the procedures in the board governing the way in which resolutions could properly be brought up for discussion and vote. Though the Lay Committee had succeeded in getting the members to tone down resolutions and delay action in some cases, it was still disturbed by the board's tendency to overstep the "proper" boundary between religion and politics. This tendency would have to be corrected before actions of subordinate NCC agencies could be challenged.

At its meeting on 17 March 1954, the board, having voted to extend the Lay Committee's life for another year, authorized the Informal Conference of Council and Lay Leaders for the purpose of considering Pew's objections. The meeting, held on May 1, brought Pew and other Lay Committee leaders together with the council's president (Bishop William Martin, a Methodist), the chairmen of the three key policy subcommittees of the board, and top staff executives. From Pew's standpoint, the results of this meeting were "greatly encouraging," since the participants agreed to propose a new set of procedures for board actions. Major policy statements and pronouncements to which any substantial minority on the board objected would now be subjected to an elaborate process of review. The new rules, to which the council president and the other top elective officers present nominally committed themselves, would require an 80 percent affirmative vote of board members present before controversial resolutions could properly be taken up for action. Since the suggested changes would require board approval, the matter would be presented to the board at its next meeting, scheduled for September 14 to 15 later that year.

But the Lay Committee had in mind more than mere procedural changes. It also stood in opposition to the Social Gospel tradition. It challenged the notion that the churches had a responsibility to involve themselves in social issues or attempt to reshape the "Divinely ordained" social order. At its fourth annual meeting on 7 to 9 May 1954, the Lay Committee adopted a resolution known as the "Lay Affirmation," which offered a theoretical rationale for defining the "proper" sphere of religious activity and applied this in a manner highly critical of recent council pronouncements. While *economic* activity has as its proper sphere "the market place," the resolution affirmed, and *politics* the sphere of "representative government," "*Christian* activity" is solely concerned with "the furtherance of the coming of the Kingdom of God . . . through worship and evangelism." Judged against this standard, recent NCC behavior appeared seriously reprehensible:

> Our committee believes that the National Council of Churches has impaired its ability to meet its prime responsibility when, sitting in judgement on current secular affairs, it becomes involved in economics or political controversy having no moral or ethical content, promoting division where unity of purpose should obtain, nor do we believe that the National Council has a mandate to engage in such activities.[12]

The Lay Committee decided to submit the resolution for action at the next NCC board meeting, the meeting of 14 to 15 September.

A third major item for the September board agenda grew out of a proposal introduced in May by B. E. Hutchinson, vice-president of the Lay Committee and one of its four representatives on the board. Hutchinson wanted curbs put on the public statements of the Department of the Church and Economic

Life. The board gave Hutchinson's resolution to a subcommittee, with instructions to report back to the September meeting.

The "Lay Affirmation" and the Hutchinson resolution were evidently intended to counter the growing support for the statement of "Basic Christian Principles and Assumptions for Economic Life," which the board had referred back to the Church and Economic Life department and which was now scheduled to come up in revised form as a fourth major item on the September agenda. Among the several individuals who had participated in drafting the statement were three prominent laymen, Charles P. Taft (a lawyer and brother of Senator Robert A. Taft), Kenneth E. Boulding (an economist), and J. Irwin Miller (an industrialist). The stature of the laymen made it difficult for the Lay Committee to claim this was merely a struggle between laymen on the one hand and clergymen on the other.

Evidently opposition to the Lay Committee was growing in the council, not only among the activist liberals, but more especially among the moderate conservatives, who at this time occupied the top-level posts. Opposition to the Lay Committee had been held in check in its early years by its usefulness in alleviating severe financial stringencies, but these were becoming less a problem. Furthermore, whereas in the 1952 to 1953 period council leaders had been concerned over statements made by Senator Joseph McCarthy, the House Un-American Activities Committee, and J. B. Matthews (an ex-Communist now speaking in behalf of the anti-Communist cause) alleging that the Protestant churches were riddled with Communists and with Red sympathizers, by mid-1954 the McCarthyism hysteria had begun to wane and church leaders were no longer on the defensive. While opposition to the Lay Committee had presumably been latent for some time, the top leaders appear to have been optimistic as late as the 1 May "Informal Conference," as it was called, about chances of coming to terms with Pew. Opposition began to crystallize a week later with the adoption of the "Lay Affirmation," which, if accepted, would undercut the whole basis of delegated responsibility in the council and probably provoke a major crisis among the member churches in the federation. Pew was entitled to his interpretation of Scripture, the top leaders apparently felt; but he was not to impose it at the expense of the integrity of the organization.

The September 1954 board meeting thus represented the climax of the struggle. It was now evident that compromises and delays were no longer possible and that major decisions had to be made. Pew had already begun to cut back on his personal financial contributions to the council, and a rebuff at this stage would doubtless contribute to still further cutbacks in budget. It was feared that acceding to the "Lay Affirmation" while refusing to adopt the statement of "Basic Christian Principles and Assumptions for Economic Life" would endanger the survival of the organization, on the one hand, by subverting the authority of delegated representatives of member bodies and, on the other, by provoking a crisis of confidence among staff and appointive personnel.

Faced with this choice, the General Board acted decisively. First, the report of the Conference of Council and Lay Committee Leaders (the recommendations flowing out of the 1 May meeting) was referred to the Committee on Policy and Strategy, which amounted to burying it. Second, the board voted merely to "receive" the "Lay Affirmation," expressing its "gratitude" and assurance that "Lay Committee Communications will always be given the most thoughtful consideration." On the other hand, the board voted to adopt the statement of "Basic Christian Principles and Assumptions for Economic Life." Third, it agreed to lay aside the original Hutchinson resolution concerning the Department of the Church and Economic Life and adopt a drastically amended version offered by Bishop Sherrill without the concurrence of Hutchinson. This retained some of the original language but stripped away all references to the department, while reaffirming the authority of the National Council to issue pronouncements arrived at after deliberation among denominational delegates acting "under the guidance of the Holy Spirit." Pew later maintained (doubtlessly correctly) that Sherrill's version "produced the opposite meaning" of the original.[13]

Since the decisions the board reached placed the status of the Lay Committee in doubt, the committee resolved to have a meeting between five of its leading members and five board representatives appointed by the president to discuss the "Lay Affirmation" with the "hope that this may lead to further understanding." As if it wanted to underscore its determination to continue speaking out on public matters, the board closed its meeting by passing two "political" resolutions, one endorsing self-determination for the Island of Cyprus and another authorizing a letter to the U.S. delegation at the UN setting forth the council's position on such matters as collective security, the need for assistance to underdeveloped countries, and the international refugee problem. Pew's objections were brushed aside.

DECLINE AND FINAL DEMISE

The conference between the Lay Committee and council officials provided for in the board resolution represented the last hope of achieving compromise so the committee might continue to function. Committee leaders had decided in advance to request reconsideration of the "Lay Affirmation," extension of its own official mandate beyond the 30 June 1955 expiration date, and increased representation for itself on the General Board. Selected to represent the NCC leadership at the conference were President William Martin (Methodist); the past president, Henry Knox Sherrill (Protestant Episcopal); and the man whose name was soon to be officially recommended by the Nominating Committee for the three-year presidential term beginning December 1954, Eugene Carson Blake (Presbyterian). In addition, the NCC chose the top elected officials of the American Baptist Convention and the Lutheran Church in America, Reuben E. Nelson and Franklin Clark Fry, respectively. Also in attendance were the council's top staff personnel, General Secretary Roy G. Ross and Associate General Secretary Roswell P. Barnes. The five-member Lay Committee delegation was led by its vice-chairman, B. E. Hutchinson (Pew himself had decided not to attend), and it was Hutchinson who officially presided. The meeting was held 29 October and lasted several hours.

Hutchinson opened the meeting with a statement indicating the urgency of reaching some kind of understanding. The anxiety among NCC members that the Lay Committee was endangering the representative character of the council is reflected in the following interchange, which occurred before Hutchinson had completed his preliminary remarks:

> Hutchinson: I want to be in a position where out of ten [laypeople on the Board] I can count on having two or three people of my persuasion who will stand up and be counted and feel their backing. You were all most generous to me, most courteous. I have no complaints whatever, but I felt awful lonesome at [the last General Board meeting]. That is what we have in mind in suggesting that we would like to be able to designate ten people from the Lay Committee [to serve on the Board].

> Bishop Sherrill: How many votes has the Lay Committee on the General Board? Of a body of roughly 200 people you would have more representation than the Protestant Episcopal Church with two and a half million members has on the General Board.

> Hutchinson: If I may rule you out of order. It is the first time I have ever had an opportunity. The discussion has not started and I want to lay my whole report before the Committee before we proceed with discussion of it.
>   The next point, and the final point, is this: That we would like to ask that, on the initiative of someone other than ourselves, a motion to reconsider the Lay Affirmation be made at the next meeting and that it be brought up and that it be published, not as a pronouncement—not only published, but publicized. I think it was Dr. Blake who said it was full of heresy.

> Blake: I am afraid it was.

> Hutchinson: Someone else said that it was illegitimate. It was with difficulty I restrained myself under the circumstances from saying that in formal debate I have been called everything, but that this was the first time anybody found a way to call me a bastard! . . .[14]

At a later point in the discussion, the NCC delegates began to hint that if the National Lay Committee could not find a way of "meshing gears" with the duly elected officials of and delegates to the council, some other way might be found of representing lay opinion. Again, it was Blake who took the lead:

4 6 6 1 3

Blake: . . . I think that one of the difficulties comes in your [Hutchinson's] use of the word "hierarchy" [in his preliminary remarks] to describe the National Council.

Hutchinson: For the record, in using the word "hierarchy" I asked whether it was objectionable.

Blake: It was objectionable in one sense, I want to get at something it interprets. The word "hierarchy" I think does reflect a distrust, not on your part, a distrust of the kind of organization that the National Council is, and the kind of organization any of our denominations are. . . . We have a representative form of government which surely is led by leaders, it is ultimately responsible to the setup of our church. . . . Hierarchy to my mind at least takes the connotation of not representative government, but a class of offiers who are not responsible to the whole.

Hutchinson: In my use of the word "hierarchy" I had no such implication. I was simply referring to the central authority that exists.

Blake: There has been expressed to me by various individuals that the real representatives of lay opinion in our churches is the National Lay Committee and that the lay opinion of the Presbyterian Church is better represented by that than by official representation. There is a question that is important, and what one does in terms of his organization is that say, that if you believe in representative government as I do, that, it [ought to] be utterly representative. . . . I would say basically we have been struggling for four years with a problem of distrust. I think it is mutual. . . .[15]

Whereas Hutchinson charged that the NCC inadequately reflected lay thinking on major issues, one of the NCC spokesmen questioned whether the Lay Committee was any better qualified to do this, or indeed as well qualified:

Nelson: . . . I might mention very briefly that the demoninations are not equally represented on the National Lay Committee. An analysis of the membership, I think you will find, shows an overwhelming membership of Presbyterians and Episcopalians. . . . If you are going to have any kind of representation it will have to be a representation that is somehow related to the balance within the group itself, and are all the consequences taken into the picture as you think about it? I could not help being impressed by the fact that implicit in this whole matter there was an equal criticism of denominations as well as the Council.

Back of this whole thing, however, there is another viewpoint that has not been expressed. I know there is a danger in even expressing it, and I would not want to inject anything that would cause hard feelings in any way. What I have to say I say out of kindness. I am always fearful when any group within the Christian church consists entirely of people within a certain [income] bracket.

Hutchinson: That does not obtain in the Lay Committee.

Nelson: My analysis would indicate that it is largely true. This is a group of people upon whom the stamp of success has been laid. Is it right within the Christian church to give preference to any group upon which there is written the label of success over against any other?

.   .   .   .

Hutchinson: You talk about success. I do not know what you mean by success. . . . If you want to accomplish things in this world and have outreaching influence in the community, I think you have to turn to people who have demonstrated capacity for leadership. . . .[16]

The meeting ended on an inconclusive note, with the various participants doing the best they could to appear hopeful that a compromise settlement was still feasible. It was evident on reflection, however, that the differences were now revealed as irreconcilable.

On 19 January 1955, a month after his election as president of the council, Eugene Carson Blake wrote to J. Howard Pew (coincidently a fellow member of the Presbyterian Church), informing him that the 29 October meeting "had developed no new factors with respect to termination of the Committee on June 30, 1955," and that the Committee on Policy and Strategy of the General Board had thus recommended discontinuance of the committee as of June 30. Though he did not explicitly say so in this letter, Blake himself had made the final decision to disband the Lay Committee.[17]

Despairing of the National Council of Churches, J. Howard Pew soon found other outlets for his conservative religious, economic, and political views. He was instrumental in the founding of *Christianity Today*, which began publication in 1957 and now has the largest circulation of any Protestant publication in the country. *Christianity Today* has become one of the NCC's severest critics.

CONCLUSIONS

The deathblow to the Lay Committee was struck by a group of men (Blake, Sherrill, and others) who might best be described as nonideological or perhaps as moderately conservative. Deeply committed to the church as an ecclesiastical structure, these men were concerned, not that the Lay Committee was inhibiting the council's move toward the political left, but that, in its insistence on having a major voice on policy independent of the member churches, it was endangering the internal stability of the NCC. Though a loss of income was to be expected (the NCC indeed suffered a loss of funds when the Lay Committee disbanded), this was more than offset by the NCC's having averted the debilitating factional strife the Lay Committee's existence threatened to initiate. The "Lay Affirmation" presented such a threat, and on this point the moderate conservatives in top leadership posts would not compromise. Even Eugene Carson Blake was probably looking at the Lay Committee from the standpoint of internal cohesion rather than as a progressive. While he would later gain a reputation as a crusading liberal on the civil rights issue, at this time he was dissociated from that camp, having disavowed it in a 1952 article.[18]

The demise of the Lay Committee in 1955 did not lead to immediate changes in the council's cautious social policy. For several years the NCC remained reluctant to become involved in controversial issues. J. Irwin Miller, the NCC's first layman president, for example, began his tenure with sentiments J. Howard Pew could not have found objectionable. Shortly after his 1960 inauguration, Miller charmed a group of Chicago businessmen, who were not easily impressed by anyone speaking for the NCC, by affirming that "our society has intrusted business with the present opportunity to lead America." In October 1961 he said that although the NCC favored "promo-

tion of Christian *study* of social problems," in the future it
would make fewer actual *pronouncements* on "hot subjects."
He urged that the NCC was more moderate than its constituent
denominations, implying that moderation was the ideal toward
which council leaders strove.[19]

Nevertheless, if the demise of the National Lay Committee
was not to the immediate advantage of activist liberals, they
were the chief long-term beneficiaries. With the removal of
this ultraconservative faction, liberals were now contending
primarily with moderates. In the same way as the victory of
General Dwight D. Eisenhower over Robert A. Taft for the
1952 Republican nomination settled the issue of whether the
New Deal would be repealed should the Republicans be
elected (it would not), so Eugene Carson Blake's election in
1954 as NCC president put an end to the question of whether
the Protestant churches and the interdenominational agencies
would repudiate the Social Gospel. Policy debates could now
go on within a broad "Social Gospel consensus"; while this by
no means guaranteed success to the more activist churchmen,
it did obviate the necessity to carry all questions back to first
principles.

A moderate like J. Irwin Miller may have superficially resembled J. Howard Pew (both were prominent industrialists
and took active interest in their Ivy League alma maters), but
at a more basic level they had significant differences. Miller
was identified with the view that the churches should concern themselves with social questions, while Pew was an
economic fundamentalist whose views paralleled those of Herbert Spencer. It was thus possible for Miller to preside over the
council without discomfort during a period when it was becoming identified with reform causes (1960 to 1963). Within
limits he lent his prestige to this liberalization. The influence of
Miller and the decline of Pew's marked the fundamental change
in the balance of forces between the 1950s and 1960s.

part 2

RESOURCES

It is clear from research done on large organizations that bureaucrats have their own policy preferences and that, short of outright defiance of the formal policy-makers, appointive executives have a significant degree of discretion in interpreting the mandates given them. Thus, policy decisions with which appointive executives disagree may be resisted indirectly through procrastination and minimal compliance; those with which they agree in principle but to which they attach low priority may be implemented in ways that fall short of initial expectations. Characteristically, it is only those decisions the appointive officials like that are enthusiastically carried out. The issue of compliance typically arises with special urgency during times of rapid change, when executives recruited in an earlier period are expected to implement decisions for which their prior experience has not fully prepared them.

In the NCC, top-level staff executives attend meetings of the main policy-making bodies, the General Board and the General Assembly, where they can influence decisions, and it is thus unlikely that those vested with formal voting power would adopt policies to which the executive staff in general is adamantly opposed. The possibility of a diversity of views nevertheless is present, especially since policy decisions are typically phrased in broad language and thus admit of conflicting interpretations between board and staff.

The problem raised in part 2 is how best to account for the willingness of executives serving in high-level NCC posts and in its member churches to go along with the redefinition of goals and strategies already under way, as the previous part has noted, in the first dozen years or so after the 1950 merger. Does the staff routinely carry out policies laid down by the official bodies? Or is it better to conceive of their role in this instance as being more dynamic, involving a maximum fulfillment and even an apparent liberal interpretation of received mandates?

A complete answer to this will be developed in part 3, where the question of the council's response to the Birmingham crisis is analyzed. Yet the broad outlines of an answer will emerge in the chapters immediately to follow. The concern here is the nature of staff policy predispositions—whether these are essentially liberal-activist or cautious and expressive of a self-defensive regard for bureaucratic status.

A major premise underlying the following three chapters is that not all of the executives who are responsive to changes in strategic thinking are necessarily employed on the NCC's own staff. The council's influence is presumed to extend beyond those over whom it exercises formal authority and to include personnel serving such autonomous agencies as state and local councils of churches and editorial staffs of liberal Protestant publications. Though some might choose to dispute this premise, it appears to be a reasonable one, given the frequent references in conversations and published accounts to such concepts as "interdenominational Protestantism" and the "Protestant conciliar movement." To narrow the definition of "bureaucratic resources" in such a way as to include only persons on the NCC payroll seems unduly restrictive.

6. Liberal Trends in the Council's Staff

The recruitment of a large cadre of full-time staff professionals has been an important development over the past quarter-century of the council's life. Contrary to what might have been expected, this bureaucratization of the organization does not appear to have fostered a more conservative, status-preserving atmosphere at the top level. On the contrary, it has if anything encouraged an activist stance with respect to social issues and a more vigorous pursuit of the council's original goal of finding solutions to social problems. The reason for this unusual effect of bureaucratization is found in the tendency for full-time salaried staff to be recruited from sources identified with more progressive views.

CHURCH BUREAUCRACIES

The council's operating budget grew substantially between the mid-1920s and the mid-1950s. Between 1923 and 1943 the annual income had nearly doubled ($269,000 to $505,000); and a decade later, by 1953, it had increased fourteenfold to $7,210,-000. The need for a larger bureaucracy was related to new program responsibilities assumed as part of the 1950 merger. But even the older programs, such as social service and social action, grew in scope and complexity. By 1967 the council thus found it necessary to employ an executive staff of over 200 persons and an additional 500 in other employee categories. Under the impact of these changes, the organization's internal affairs became more formal and routinized, and the staff came to play a more significant part in policy deliberations.

Given this change, how might one expect the council's policy to have been affected? In the literature on organizations, bureaucratization has been viewed as tending to distract attention from original goals in favor of the goals and requirements of the organization itself. Referring to one large ecumenical body, J. Milton Yinger has remarked, ". . . it is one thing to be dedicated to ecumenical work, it is another thing to be dedicated to the World Council of Churches,"[1] intimating that bureaucratic survival increasingly becomes the dominant purpose of complex organizations. In the same vein other observers have documented how church bureaucracies foster a preoccupation with precedent, rules, procedures, and tradition so as to preclude serious discussion of radical alternatives. Paul M. Harrison has found marked conservative tendencies associated with the emergence of bureaucracy in the American Baptist Convention, one of the NCC's constituent bodies.[2] Since the NCC resembles the WCC and ABC in many ways, one might expect its bureaucratization to have had the same effect.

Yet it was just when a large, highly specialized bureaucracy had begun to make its weight felt that the council shifted toward the more venturesome and explicitly political stance discussed in part 2. Furthermore, there is evidence in at least one published account to suggest that the bureaucracy may have helped *cause* the leftist shift in NCC policy views. The editor of *Christianity Today,* a widely read publication not noted for its support of the ecumenical movement, made the following observation in an article published in the mid-1960s:

Espy [R. H. Edwin Espy, NCC general secretary] gets more severe pressure from bureaucratic radicals [than from President Arthur Flemming, himself a liberal] who have little respect for the consensus of the NCC's vast constituency. Some are on the NCC payroll, constantly thinking up new programs and position papers. Other radicals are denominational employees who have won themselves seats on the Board and have ample time to attend the meetings. They often seize the added leverage provided by the absence of busier or less interested lay members and clergymen who give priority to pastoral responsibilities. Espy [felt obliged to say] publicly last month that the charge could be refuted that the National Council is "tightly run by a small clique of bureaucrats." [3]

While the remarks were intended as a mild rebuke to the council, persons more closely identified with it have made similar observations. Thus, Harvey G. Cox has pointed out that the bureaucratization of

religious organizations is [one of two factors] contributing to the entrance of church groups into the political arena as forces to be considered. Although this may sound unlikely to some church members, there can be little real doubt that it is true.[4]

Cox went on to offer an explanation as to why bureaucratization has tended to liberalize the policy views of the Protestant churches. In the first place, the church bureaucrats, by virtue of their greater technical competence and command of information, tend to see social problems in a larger perspective than do the people "whom they are supposed to represent." They are more conscious of the interconnectedness of issues and thus more inclined to favor comprehensive solutions. In the second place, the "managerial revolution" (Cox's term) in the churches has intensified the tendency toward social activity by providing a pool of men who are free of the constraints imposed on the local pastor. Thus, whereas

activist ministers must frequently contend with the socially conservative laymen who sit on the boards and committees that rule the churches, . . . ministers who do not serve a local parish and hence are more insulated from direct lay control are much more likely to [become involved in protest demonstrations] . . .[5]

The bureaucrats' relative lack of subservience to laymen stems in part from the fact that they are physically removed from and therefore not subject to immediate lay observation in their work, in part because their salaries, though dependent on continued lay generosity, are derived partially from denominational investment portfolios, which cannot be cut off, in the way pledges can, on short notice and without explanation.

It is important to caution at this point that Cox was not intimating that the process of bureaucratization is itself an explanation for increased liberal activism. The case of the American Baptist Convention has already been mentioned as one in which bureaucracy is associated with a generally conservative predisposition on social issues. The most that is implied is that the process described provides organizational elites with an increased degree of insulation from grass roots opinion. When for any reason elite opinion tends toward liberalism and grass roots opinion toward conservatism, bureaucratization may enhance the former's ability to implement its preferences. The question then becomes whether there is anything in the background of top-level NCC executives that would predispose them toward liberal policy views. An answer to this question

Table 5.1 EDUCATIONAL BACKGROUNDS OF 31 NCC TOP STAFF PERSONNEL, 1967:* TYPE OF INSTITUTION ATTENDED†

Type of Institution	Number of Persons‡
College or university	
Private, nonsectarian	9
Church-related	11
Public	8
No college or university	1
Not ascertained	2
Total	31
Seminary§	
Interdenominational only	14
Denominational only	5
Interdenominational and denominational	6
No seminary	6
Total	31

* Includes all executive staff attached to the Office of the General Secretary, all division heads, and all department heads (with the exception of the Office of Administration).

† Source: Personnel Department, Office of Administration, NCC.

‡ Graduate degrees earned by the 31 executives were: Ph.D., 5; Th.D., 1; and terminal A.M., 5. There was one candidate for the Ph.D. who did not finish the doctoral degree.

§ Multiple counting for individuals with more than one seminary degree. Of the 25 seminary graduates, 21 subsequently became ordained clergymen.

will require delving into the social backgrounds of key persons on the NCC staff.

With this problem in mind, the author analyzed the higher-educational backgrounds of 31 top staff personnel serving in the NCC in 1967 (tables 5.1 and 5.2). These persons occupied the major "policy-relevant" posts, specifically those executives attached to the Office of the General Secretary, the heads of the four divisions in the council (all with the rank of associate general secretary), and the 22 heads of departments, with the exception of those in the Office of Administration, whose functions are presumed to be more related to internal management than to broad policy. As table 5.2 shows, certain seminaries

Table 5.2 EDUCATIONAL BACKGROUNDS OF 31 NCC TOP STAFF PERSONNEL, 1967: SEMINARIES ATTENDED*

Location	Number of Persons†	Institutions	Number of Persons‡
Northeast	17	Union Theological Seminary	9
Midwest	3	Yale Divinity School	4
West	2	Harvard Divinity School	1
Border	1	Pacific School of Religion	2
Foreign	2	Ten denominational seminaries	12
No seminary	6	No seminary	6
Total	31	Total	34

* Source: Personnel Department, Office of Administration, NCC.
† Individuals who received a bachelor degree from more than one seminary are classified by the institution attended last.
‡ Numbers include some individuals who attended more than one seminary.

stand out as contributing a disproportionate share (roughly 60 percent) of all Bachelor of Divinity degrees earned by these NCC staff members. Since most individuals earned more than one degree at the bachelor's level and at different institutions, and others studied theology at more than one institution, only a rather small proportion of council staff executives have had an education that is wholly within their own particular denomination. The predominance of interdenominational and nondenominational seminaries (Union, Yale, Harvard, and Pacific School of Religion, especially) is perhaps not wholly unexpected in view of the NCC's own interdenominational character; but this does not deprive the finding of interest and significance. Equally interesting is the breakdown of seminaries by region, with the Northeast (usually considered the most liberal region) far ahead of all others combined. Again, the fact that the NCC itself has its headquarters in a major eastern metropolis and is immediately adjacent to its largest single sources of staff, Union Theological Seminary, obviously influences the pattern.

Four institutions, Yale, Union, Harvard, and Pacific School of Religion, have granted over half the Bachelor of Divinity degrees conferred upon the 31 individuals in our sample. The heavy preponderance of these four seminaries is by no means what one would expect on a chance basis. According to the *Statistical Abstract of the United States,* there were 50,000 persons enrolled in 1965 in "independently organized professional schools of religion and theology." The *Abstract* offers no breakdown on the relative proportion of students attending institutions in various categories; but additional useful information is obtainable from figures put out by the American Association of Theological Schools, whose membership comprises the older and more firmly established seminaries in the country. As indicated by table 6, 11,837 or about half of AATS student en-

Table 6 ENROLLMENT IN INSTITUTIONS AFFILIATED WITH AATS, 1965 *

Type of Institution	Number of Institutions	Enrollment
NCC-related denominational	16	11,837
NCC-nonrelated denominational	95	6,986
Nondenominational or interdenominational	16	3,156
Total	127	21,529

* Source: *Yearbook of American Churches* (New York: NCC, 1967), pp. 222–24.

rollment in 1965 was in institutions identified with one of the NCC-related denominations. This total contrasts sharply with the combined enrollment of the four seminaries mentioned above, which in 1965 was only 1,049. Though in theory one would expect that the products of seminaries attached to NCC-related churches would be at least as eager as the products of other seminaries to seek NCC employment, this is not the case; nondenominational or interdenominational seminaries of a certain type, such as Yale, Union, Harvard, and Pacific School of Religion, are the ones that contribute most heavily to NCC top elective staff.* The question therefore arises, What, if anything, do these four institutions have in common that might account for their graduates seeking employment in a liberal body like the NCC?

Striking resemblances exist among the four interdenominational seminaries most prevalent in the backgrounds of the 31 persons. One is their location in large urban centers (Union in New York, Yale in New Haven, Harvard in Cambridge/Boston, and Pacific School of Religion in Berkeley/San Francisco). Another is their status either as an organic part of or as a co-operating institution with an adjacent university (Columbia, Yale, Harvard, and the University of California at Berkeley, respectively). By virtue of their location and institutional affiliation, the four schools not only reflect the intellectual and liberal ethos of a great university, but are more likely to be affected by the urban social problems of their immediate environment. Union's commitment to the East Harlem Protestant Parish is perhaps the best-known example of how urban seminaries have sought to relate to such issues. Most Protestant seminaries, however, are isolated from the realities that give rise to these issues. Many were deliberately located in areas away from city life and universities. As Franklin H. Littell has put it:

> A long line of denominational seminaries followed [the split of Andover Theological School away from Harvard in 1808], many of them deliberately set out in the countryside to spare the young men the perils of encounters with "pagan learning" in the liberal university and temptations in the city. With the

* This is probably true of NCC executives in general. On the basis of conversations with a number of NCC executives, the author is under the impression that the proportion of interdenominational seminary degrees awarded them was substantially higher than would have been anticipated assuming random recruitment from among the three types of seminaries covered in table 6. Even when seminaries affiliated with denominations not in the NCC are excluded from consideration, seminaries of the interdenominational type are still disproportionately represented among the executives whom the author encountered during his extensive interviewing at the NCC.

highest proportion of Protestant clergy coming from village and farm, the dislocation of many seminaries simply served to blind seminarians further to the main direction of American thought and social direction.[6]

These four seminaries also resemble one another in terms of the degree to which they have been receptive to radical views on society. Though this progressivism is presumably in part an outgrowth of the above-mentioned affiliation with another university and major metropolitan location, it also inheres in a particular biblical perspective that places emphasis on social justice as espoused by the Old Testament prophets and exemplified in the life of Jesus. This biblically grounded radicalism was pronounced in the decade of the Great Depression.

Union Theological Seminary, the largest single source of current NCC executives, "led in the production of young radicals in the early 'thirties."[7] A 1937 examination of the professional backgrounds of the twelve persons described by one writer as "America's foremost religious radicals" reveals that eight were either then teaching or had recently taught on the faculties of three leading urban interdenominational seminaries: Union Theological Seminary (Reinhold Niebuhr, Halford Luccock, Harry Ward, and George A. Coe), Yale Divinity School (Jerome Davis, Kirby Page, and Francis J. McConnel), and University of Chicago Divinity School (Charles Clayton Morrison).[8] The membership of the influential "Theological Discussion Group," which in the early '30s did much to recast the Social Gospel movement along more radical and politically self-conscious lines, largely consisted of seminary professors from urban interdenominational institutions.[9] Thus, it would seem that in precisely those years, the 1930s, when many NCC executives of the 1960s were enrolled as seminary students, the faculties of the institutions they attended were marked by an openness to radical views on social issues.

CHANGES IN POSTSEMINARY CAREER PATTERNS

Though illuminating in one sense, the preceding discussion falls short of an adequate explanation as to the increasing progressivism of council executives over the 60-year life of the organization. Seminary backgrounds cannot account for this change, since council executives from the beginning have come predominantly from the same kinds of academic institutions. Therefore, comparison of postseminary experiences may provide clues to the reasons for the change in social views. One hypothesis is that top staff personnel in earlier years typically served for a long period of time prior to NCC employment in an environment marked by conservative assumptions about society and politics, while top staff personnel in more recent years have been employed in a more markedly liberal setting. This possibility will be investigated in the following discussion.

The overwhelming majority of Protestant clergymen are employed in the local church pastorate. Only a small fraction are in one of the various nonparochial ministries, such as hospital and prison chaplaincies and seminary teaching. Of the latter group a small percentage, indeed only a minute percentage, of the total ordained are employed as staff officers in denominational (judicatory) offices or interdenominational agencies such as councils of churches at the national, state, or local levels. A recent study dealing with how ordained clergymen in the Episcopal Church are deployed found that more than three-fourths are in the parish ministry and less than one-fourth in such diverse fields as missions, administration, and chaplaincies.[10] The same situation probably prevails in other main line denominations.

Prior to the 1940s career backgrounds of staff personnel in the council mirrored this heavy preference for the parish ministry. Those recruited tended to enter staff posts at a high level laterally, after having served for some time in a local church. There were exceptions to this, but the tendency was quite pronounced. In 1931, a typical year of the decade for the council, only three out of nine staff executives were without parish experience; six had parish experience, averaging an extensive 18.5 years.[11]

An analysis of the career patterns of the 31 "policy-relevant" executives serving the council in 1967 reveals a sharply contrasting pattern. The council's Office of Personnel made available to the author dossier summaries containing background information on all 31 persons. The summaries indicate that only three of this group had parish experience of any note. The relative proportion of persons with parish experience was thus roughly the reverse of what it was in the 1930s: in 1967 parish background was the exception, not the rule.

Supportive evidence for the decline in participation of pastors in the council's affairs can be drawn from an analysis of the occupational characteristics of delegates to the constituent assembly, the General Assembly. Unfortunately, available records do not permit a year-by-year breakdown of the occupational composition of this body. The council only began gathering systematic data on this point in 1957, which is too recent to use as a base line. A search of existing records revealed one earlier occupational listing, for the founding convention of the Federal Council of Churches in 1908. Data exist, then, for three recent assemblies (1957, 1963, 1966) and for the very first, but for none of those in between. This permits identification of some gross changes across a very long span of time (half a century) but precludes charting a more precise trend. Despite this difficulty, the findings in table 7 are revealing. It appears that the

Table 7   Vocations of Delegates and Alternates Attending FCC or NCC Constituent Assembly Meetings, Number and Percent by Year*

	Year			
	1908		1966	
Vocation	N	Percent	N	Percent
Pastors and other local church staff	137	41.1%	40	17.9%
National church executives and church publication editors	65	19.7	93	41.7
Regional church executives	29	8.8	21	9.4
Interdenominational agency executives	7	2.1	6	2.7
Laymen and others not otherwise identified	93	28.1	63	28.2
Total	331	99.8%†	223	99.9%†

* Sources: (For 1908) Report of the *First Meeting of the Federal Council of Churches* (New York: FCC, 1909), pp. 554–69 (available in the Research Library of the NCC); (for 1966) "Survey of National Council of Churches Triennial Assembly, 1966" (New York: Office of Planning and Program, Department of Research, NCC, 1967) (details of the breakdown were supplied by the Planning and Program office).
† Does not total 100.0% because of rounding.

relative positions of pastors and national church executives in
the constituent assembly is now strikingly different from what
it was at the beginning. Whereas in 1908 over two out of every
five delegates and alternates were identified with local churches,
the proportion in the 1966 General Assembly (the composition
of which was comparable to the 1957 and 1963 assemblies, according to informants in the NCC Office of Planning and Program) was only about one out of every six delegates.

What significance may be attached to this difference over
time in the backgrounds of council staff and official member-
church delegates? There is considerable evidence, some of it
summarized in the introductory chapter to the present work,
that the typical white Protestant congregation in this country
disproportionately represents the Republican party (generally
regarded as the more conservative nationally) and is less supportive than most other social groups of governmental intervention in behalf of deprived minorities. This situation was recognized as a problem by Christian socialists and other religious radicals as early as the 1930s. Reinhold Niebuhr, for
example, in a 1936 article struggled with the problem presented
by the middle class church and pondered how new congregations prepared in their own self-interest to engage in progressive politics might be organized.[12] Similarly, Gerhard Lenski,
using survey data assembled in the late 1950s, concluded that
"with class controlled, white Protestants proved to be the most
opposed to any expansion in the powers of government [in
eight of ten income brackets] and in the other two ranked second in the degree of opposition." [13] In addition to matters concerning the welfare state, Lenski found white Protestants to be
the group most likely to adopt a conservative stance on the
issue of racial integration, although when those born in the
South were excluded from the analysis, Protestants ranked
slightly below white nonsouthern Catholics in segregationist
attitudes.[14] Moreover, comparing white Protestants deeply involved in churches with ones only marginally involved, Lenski
found the former group generally to have more conservative
leanings: more were Republican in their political preferences,
and they were less favorably disposed as a group toward increased governmental intervention for the sake of promoting

social welfare ends.[15] He also concluded that the middle class ethos of the typical white Protestant parish served to reinforce the middle class political leanings of clergymen. When asked their views, for example, on the important issue of possible nationalization of basic industries, a proposal long identified with socialism, the clergy were even more united in their opposition than were their white Protestant parishioners.[16]

It is a reasonable inference that among the NCC elite the decline in number of local pastors and laymen identified solely with a local congregation has been a factor in the waning conservatism of top NCC leaders and in their growing acceptance of the premise that solutions to the problems of deprived groups may necessitate more active governmental intervention. As the NCC and its associated state and local councils have increasingly come to offer careers to men recently graduated from seminary, the impact of local parish conservatism has appeared to have diminished. Of course, the council has never actually been dominated by parish opinion; in all periods it has found it possible to adopt reformist policies. But the increasing extent to which the national headquarters staff has been prepared not only to go along with but to support aggressively and implement progressive stands seems attributable partly to the NCC's greater insulation from local congregational opinion. This insulation has exacted a price in terms of diminished internal cohesion. In chapter 12 this loss of cohesion will be dealt with in some detail. For the moment it is enough to reiterate that grass roots restiveness has not thus far been sufficient to undercut the liberal NCC consensus.

CONCLUSIONS

The present data reveal suggestive patterns in the route by which a number of high-ranking NCC executives have reached their present posts; from these patterns inferences may be drawn in order to better account for top-level executive behavior in recent years. The fact that the officials in many cases received seminary training at institutions of a particular type and did so at a time when these institutions were more than usually receptive to radical social thought evidently has a bearing on their long-term social policy views. Moreover, the declining tendency for officials to be recruited from among those with backgrounds in the parish ministry and their increasing tendency instead to be career-church bureaucrats offer a reason for the officials' growing ability to identify positively with the progressivism of the organization.

Unfortunately, the findings provide no entirely satisfactory answer to the important question of why career church bureaucrats, not ex-parish clergymen, now predominate among top-level NCC executives. Could it be that their social policy views, more liberal on the whole than those of otherwise similar local pastors, are considered more acceptable? Or is it because such career bureaucrats, though not regarded as necessarily more competent or more ideologically congenial, are more inclined to seek council employment and, once employed, to remain in the organization until such time as their seniority makes them candidates for the top posts? In the recent period they would have an especial competitive advantage, since lateral entry into the NCC from different fields of endeavor is now more difficult than in the past.

The data provide us with no clear answers to these questions. But while *causation* remains obscure, the *effect* of increasing numbers of career church bureaucrats is reasonably clear: activist liberal tendencies have become institutionalized in the council's headquarters. While this staff liberalism is not the only component in the mix out of which policy emerges, it does have an influence.

7. Local Councils of Churches

A group that wishes to wield influence in the name of goals as broadly comprehensive as "social justice" and "moral progress" cannot in the mid-twentieth century rely on a highly trained staff and the prestige attaching to organized religion solely to achieve its legislative ends. Before the day of instant mass communication, interest groups often depended on direct lobbying techniques—buttonholing, "social lobbying," promises to give and threats to withhold money and other tangible material rewards—which were largely conducted at state and national capitals. While these approaches are not now obsolete for organizations whose interest in public policy is defensive and narrowly circumscribed, they are no longer adequate for those like the National Council of Churches that want to promote reforms affecting broad sectors of the American population. For groups of this type, direct lobbying carried on in Washington, D.C., or in state houses or city halls, may prove relatively ineffective unless it is backed up by indirect lobbying aimed at arousing legislators' constituents in the home districts. Such "lobbying at the grass roots" is a direct function of the communications revolution and has become increasingly common. The present chapter thus takes up the matter of how the NCC has generated grass roots backup for its stands, bearing in mind the fact (as noted in the introduction to this work) that Protestant church people at the local level are by no means united in their support of the liberal sentiments embodied in official pronouncements of interdenominational bodies or even of ones adopted by the national assembly of their own denominations.

To the casual observer it might appear that the council is ideally suited to mobilize constituents for objectives approved of by its member communions. It has an inclusive membership of extraordinary size (roughly 43 million), which is broadly dispersed throughout the country, not, as is the case with Roman Catholicism and Judaism, concentrated in a few heavily populated urban centers. Furthermore, one might think that the presence of so many Protestant church members in Congress, especially in the key committee chairmanships, would insure the Protestant churches unusually good access to the centers of decision-making in Washington.

In fact, the organization is not especially well adapted, by virtue of its formal structure, to wield influence in Congress and the executive branch. In part its disability stems from a factor that impinges on all religious organizations in this country, the doctrine of separation of church and state, which, though it does not legally preclude church action on controversial questions affecting the larger community, does inhibit it, except in the special case where the churches can show that their institutional stakes are clearly in jeopardy (taxation of church assets, for example). On matters that they do not choose to define as falling within the proper sphere of religious concern, many members of Congress allege that church activism violates the established "rules of the game."

A second factor, the social composition of the organizational constituency, constrains Protestant political behavior more so than it does with many other religious groups. In its role as spokesman for the majority religion in this country and for a group of churches whose status in society is that of a "quasi-establishment," the council finds it difficult to mobilize its grass roots constituents in the name of social change, change that will necessarily require many Protestants, themselves generally inclined in favor of the status quo, to give more than they receive in a tangible or political sense. Lacking a minority-group consciousness to appeal to, the NCC frequently finds it difficult to arouse vocal grass roots support, even on issues in which the churches' interest is well recognized and considered a legitimate basis for political action.

In 1961, for example, executives in the Washington Office were embarrassed by their inability to generate grass roots support for the National Council's announced position on the Kennedy administration school bill. It was noted with dismay that the Roman Catholic position was backed by an "avalanche" of mail. "The lack of follow up machinery to demonstrate popular support," an NCC executive was later to write, "seriously weakens presentations arranged for by the NCC's Washington Office."[1] Only on matters involving a threat to Protestantism's privileged status in American society (for example, President Truman's 1950 proposal to appoint an American ambassador to the Vatican) is the council likely to enjoy a mass upsurge of grass roots support.

A third factor arises out of the council's federal structure. *Individuals* cannot join it, only *denominational bodies* (or communions). In many cases the 33 bodies that comprise the NCC are themselves highly decentralized, perhaps best thought of as de facto federations. The chief locus of authority in Protestantism is in local units of church government: the presbytery, the diocese, the conference, and, in the case of some denominations, the local congregation. The council is almost devoid of sanctions with which to discipline nonconforming member bodies and must carefully avoid the implication that it "speaks for" the great number of church people comprised in its member bodies. There are also such factors as the cleavage within Protestantism along racial lines and sharp ideological differences between liberals and conservatives, which limit grass roots support.

Though the difficulties outlined above must be accepted as givens by council officials, there are certain strategies that can be pursued to reduce the severity of their impact. The thesis of the present chapter is that the council has succeeded in partially offsetting its relative lack of a fully articulated structure, with branches reaching down to the local level, by helping to promote a body of people, scattered in communities throughout the country, who are supportive of its liberal social views and who, though officially autonomous of the parent organization, can normally be counted on to provide it with backup support. More particularly, it will be argued that this body of people consists largely of full- and part-time executives ("secretaries") serving state and local councils of churches, who tend to be the embodiment of their respective councils. This is not to suggest that the NCC, in fostering the growth of councils of churches, has had explicitly political motives or that its officials have been consciously endeavoring to create a network of grass roots "contact men" through which indirect lobbying can be carried on. What is suggested is that the same functional requirements that brought the council into existence in 1908 (the need to organize for social service, desire to promote denominational cooperation, etc.) are felt among churchmen in local communities, and that the national organization has assisted in meeting these needs by maintaining an Office for Councils of Churches and otherwise by providing assistance to these councils. The fact that the local councils so created do agree in large part with the parent body's social views is an unintended, but significant, by-product.

Before presenting data bearing directly on the above thesis, it may be helpful to trace the emergence of the "Protestant conciliar movement." This collectivity began to take on concrete organizational form around 1890 in the northeastern part of the country, when the old Evangelical Alliance (U.S. branch formed in 1867), having concluded that church unity would greatly contribute to fostering the social application of religion (a goal central to its thinking), helped organize federations of churches in several of the larger cities and more urbanized states of that region. These in turn laid the basis upon which the first federation of national scope, the Federal Council of Churches of Christ in America, was to be established early in the twentieth century.

The Federal Council accepted as one of its primary tasks the promotion of the conciliar movement in localities not already organized. Acting through its Office for Councils of Churches and several regional offices, it helped increase the number of state and local councils having full-time staff from 50 in 1930 to 147 in 1945. By 1960 the number with full-time staff approached 300, which represented a sixfold increase in 30 years. In the meantime, existing councils had become larger and more specialized (the Council of Churches of New York City, for example, set up in its present form in 1943, had grown by 1965 to a budget well in excess of one million dollars). This flourishing of bureaucratic structure reflected the increasing urbanization of American Protestants and a heightened awareness that denominational competition tended to undermine Protestant influence at a time when Protestantism no longer enjoyed undisputed ascendancy.*

With the purposes of the present study in mind, the author took a survey of all full-time state and local church-council secretaries in the country, using a list of 279 addresses made available by the Office for Councils of Churches of the NCC. First, a pretest questionnaire was distributed to a representative sample. The responses to the pretest helped guide the preparation of a revised schedule, mailed out in the summer of 1965 to all names on the list. After repeated follow-up postcards, a total of 161 schedules were returned, of which 145 (52 percent of the total list) contained fairly complete responses and the remaining 16 (6 percent) had at least some usable information.

Perhaps the most striking initial impression from the completed questionnaire is its evidence of widespread support for the NCC among the respondents and their heavy involvement in the conciliar movement. Only a small minority (table 8) failed to report approval of NCC stands and willingness to support NCC programs relevant to their concerns.

The same basic pattern emerges when one examines questions dealing with the secretaries' reading habits. Responses indictated that official NCC publications were received and actually *read* by a solid majority. Moreover, the secretaries showed a marked tendency to subscribe to and read general circulation journals noted for support of interdenominational Protestant cooperation while avoiding publications unfriendly

---

* It may be noted that roughly comparable developments occurred about this time among farmers, businessmen, and professionals as they likewise sought to cope with disruptions in preexisting relationships associated with rapid urbanization and industrialization. See: Truman, *Governmental Process*, pp. 26–33, 106–8.

Table 8 Local Councils' Secretaries' Attitudes toward the NCC by
Response to Questionnaire, 1965 (in Percent)

(1) "How do you feel about the general tenor of the NCC's pronouncements?"

"Highly favorable" or "generally favorable"	Reaction mixed or "generally unfavorable"	No answer
92.2	7.2	0.6

(2) "How do you respond to specific NCC pronouncements?" (composite score based on 15 selected official statements).

"Highly favorable"	"Less than highly favorable"	No answer
77.1	12.1	10.8

(3) "Do you regard your council of churches as part of the Protestant conciliar movement in which local, state, national, and the World Council of Churches are *partners?*"

Yes	No	No answer
88.5	11.5	0.0

(4) "Have you ever cooperated in the distribution of official NCC literature?"

Yes	No	No answer
76.4	18.5	5.1

to the NCC and inclined to be skeptical regarding such co-operation. Thus 67.6 percent of respondents reported reading the *Christian Century* regularly, while only 18.5 percent indicated regular reading of even one of the widely circulated journals *National Review, Christian Beacon,* and *Christianity Today,* which are antagonistic to the NCC.

This predisposition toward the NCC was reflected in the secretaries' actual behavior. The survey results showed that well over two-thirds of the respondents attempt in various ways (attendance at meetings, correspondence with NCC head-quarters, maintenance of personal friendships with other secretaries) to manifest commitment to the conciliar movement.

It is an interesting question whether this involvement in the movement affects the way in which the secretaries define the nature of their jobs. The data provide some fragmentary and admittedly inconclusive evidence on this point. As the organizational focus of the movement, the NCC has long been identified with a point of view on social problems that stresses the weaknesses in American social structures as an underlying cause of immoral action and that tends to reject the traditional pietistic notion that social problems result from the personal myopia and moral incapacity of "fallen" individuals. It is note-worthy, for example, that whereas NCC pronouncements from 1950 to 1965 dealt on only one occasion each with the consumption of alcoholic beverages and gambling (both somewhat pietistic issues in character) and with pornography never, racial discrimination was the subject of three and "human rights" of six formal statements. It appears more than coincidental, therefore, that when asked about their interest in gambling, obscene literature, and liquor, a majority of respondents indicated "no interest" whereas in response to a question about their concern with racial injustice, a substantial majority indicated "very active interest," the greatest concern that could be registered on the four-point scale used. Differences did exist, however, in the degree of local council involvement in traditional, pietistic concerns; but, as will be documented later, the more favorable a secretary's opinion of the NCC, the less his interest in issues of this type.

Since the proportion of responses favorable to the NCC was so large, it became clear that an analysis of responses using a simple "friendly"-"unfriendly" (to NCC) dichotomy was not likely to prove adequate; with only a mere handful of secretaries classified in the "unfriendly" category, the seeming resemblances among them might well have appeared simply on a chance basis and might be thus of little analytical value. In order to increase somewhat the number of less-than-completely-supportive cases, therefore, it was decided to classify all respondents either as "consistent supporters" or as "ambivalent supporters," the latter category including any who failed to approve as many as four of the fifteen NCC policy statements respondents were asked to evaluate, the former including all the rest. Perhaps this classification understates support for the NCC, since lack of unqualified assent to only a handful of statements could cause an individual to be classed as "ambivalent" when he might have classified himself in the "consistent" category. But an examination of the findings showed that the results would not have been significantly changed if another arbitrary cut-off point had been used. Making use of this dichotomous attitude scale, the author then proceeded to find out whether degree of friendliness toward the NCC was systematically related to several important structural variables.

One structural factor the author predicted would be significantly associated with varying attitudes toward the NCC was the degree to which the local secretary served an urbanized constituency. Since the conciliar movement originated in response to specifically urban problems, it is significant, though not surprising, that local secretaries serving in the more highly urbanized areas turned out to be a good deal more warmly disposed toward the council than ones serving in less urbanized areas, the difference being on the order of 21 percent.

It was also predicted that attitudes would vary on the basis of diversity of church membership, that is, whether a given council's constituent churches were affiliated only with denominations that participated in the NCC (more friendly) or whether some conservative, non-NCC denominations were also represented (less friendly). Since a decision taken by a national denominational assembly regarding affiliation or nonaffiliation with the NCC is not binding on local churches of that denomination in regard to affiliating with a local council, it is entirely possible for the local council to include some member congregations not affiliated with the NCC. With the single exception of the Unitarian-Universalists, nonaffiliated churches are decidedly conservative in theology and social outlook; in order to avoid spurious results, this denomination was coded in the same category as NCC member bodies. (In their outlook on major issues, Unitarian-Universalists share much of the council's thinking; it was strictly on theological grounds that their 1946 bid for council membership was rejected.) Respondents were given a list of Protestant churches that have refused (or, in the case of the Unitarian-Universalists, have been denied) membership in the FCC/NCC and were asked to check the names of any represented in their local council. The results were as anticipated: the most "consistent supporters" tended to serve in councils whose denominational composition resembled the NCC's, whereas those with the most non-NCC denominations were the least supportive (table 9).* Although the distribution

* In view of the fact that certain NCC denominations have been identified previously as conservative on social issues, a surer index of local council similarity to the National Council would have been the relative proportion of liberal churches, *regardless* of whether they are affiliated with the NCC. Unfortunately, this consideration did not enter into the author's thinking in making up the questionnaire and the required structural information is thus unavail-

Table 9   LOCAL AND STATE COUNCIL SUPPORT FOR THE NCC BY NON-NCC
DENOMINATIONAL CONCILIAR REPRESENTATION, 1965
(IN PERCENT)

	Non-NCC Denominational Representation		
Support for NCC	Two or more	One	None
Consistent supporters	64%	81%	85%
Ambivalent supporters	36	19	15
Total	100%	100%	100%
N	14	26	103

in the three columns is as predicted, it is significant that the
preponderance of councils fall in the third category, an indication of the fact that a large number of them closely resemble
the NCC in denominational representation. A more basic question, for which the data provide no direct answer, is why the
conservative, non-NCC churches would join a local council.
Quite possibly, local councils are in a position to provide services
that local churches of all types find valuable, and since many
local councils are not as identified with controversial stands as
the national council, non-NCC churches would have fewer
qualms about joining the local councils.

The data also lend support to a hypothesis the author
initially formulated, that attitudes among the council secretaries would vary in terms of the basis on which member bodies
were allowed to participate in a local council of churches. When
a given council is composed in part of local parishes and congregations, one might expect its outlook on social issues to reflect their marked conservative tendencies. In contrast, a local
council composed only of local denominational assemblies
(synods, dioceses, districts, and so on) would be likely to think
more in *denominational* terms and reflect the more liberal biases
of the major denominations nationally. As shown in table 10,
the data lend support to this hypothesis.

Another hypothesis predicted that executives serving councils in areas of the country with a large number of fundamentalist churches would be less friendly to the NCC than
executives located in other regions. Unfortunately, the propor-

able. Had it been so, however, the pattern observed in table 9 would probably
have been even more marked.

Table 10 LOCAL COUNCIL SUPPORT FOR THE NCC BY CONCILIAR
MEMBERSHIP COMPOSITION, 1965 (IN PERCENT)

	Membership Composition		
Support for NCC	No local churches	Some or all local churches	Percentage Difference
Consistent supporters	87%	66%	21%
Ambivalent supporters	13	34	21
Total	100%	100%	
N	24	99	

tion of responses from the South, the area of the country having
the greatest fundamentalist strength, was low. For this reason
the findings on this point must be reported with considerable
caution. Preliminary interviews revealed that a number of
local and state councils in the South were brought into existence at the behest of the NCC acting through its regional office
in Atlanta. This was controlled for in analyzing the findings. It
appears from table 11 that support for the NCC among re-

Table 11 SUPPORT FOR THE NCC BY REGION AND BY INVOLVEMENT
OF THE NCC IN FOUNDING THE LOCAL COUNCIL, 1965 (IN PERCENT)

	NCC Initiating Role		
Regional Support	Yes	No	Percentage Difference
South			
Consistent supporters	100%	50%	50%
Ambivalent supporters	0	50	50
Total	100%	100%	
N	5	2	
Non-South			
Consistent supporters	71%	66%	5%
Ambivalent supporters	29	34	5
Total	100%	100%	
N	43	59	

spondents in the South was quite high, but it is also evident
that most of this support came from councils the NCC had a
hand in forming. Except where the NCC was directly involved
in initiating a council, southern councils of churches do appear
to be less consistent in their support. The differences, though

based on a very small sample, are as predicted, and it seems reasonable to suppose that a more adequate sample would have brought out the regional factor more sharply.

A final hypothesis predicted that secretaries serving councils actively involved in social reform movements would be more well disposed toward the NCC than secretaries in councils having a more traditional, pietistic emphasis. In the survey respondents were asked to indicate which of several social problems had actively engaged their council's attention in recent years. Some of the issues related primarily to social and political phenomena (table 12.1), while others concerned individual impropriety (table 12.2).

Table 12.1 LOCAL COUNCILS' SECRETARIES' SUPPORT FOR SOCIAL ISSUES, 1965 (IN PERCENT)

Issue Support	Percentage Interest		Percentage Difference
	Little or no interest	Active or very active interest	
Social welfare			
Consistent supporters	68%	87%	19%
Ambivalent supporters	32	13	19
Total	100%	100%	
N	41	98	
Voter registration			
Consistent supporters	64%	93%	29%
Ambivalent supporters	36	7	29
Total	100%	100%	
N	109	30	
Racial justice			
Consistent supporters	62%	72%	10%
Ambivalent supporters	39	29	10
Total	101%*	101%*	
N	13	125	

* Does not total 100% because of rounding.

With one exception the findings reported here are consistent with the hypothesis. Secretaries who had been heavily involved in social welfare, racial justice, voter registration, and problems arising out of alleged structural defects in society were more supportive of the NCC than secretaries whose councils were

Table 12.2 LOCAL COUNCILS' SECRETARIES' SUPPORT FOR PIETISTIC ISSUES, 1965 (IN PERCENT)

	Percentage Interest		
Issue Support	Little or no interest	Active or very active interest	Percentage Difference
Obscene literature			
Consistent supporters	73%	64%	9%
Ambivalent supporters	27	36	9
Total	100%	100%	
N	97	42	
Liquor			
Consistent supporters	73%	68%	5%
Ambivalent supporters	27	32	5
Total	100%	100%	
N	75	65	
Gambling			
Consistent supporters	62%	77%	15%
Ambivalent supporters	38	23	15
Total	100%	100%	
N	61	79	

more involved in matters of the "personal piety" variety. The percentage differences are not especially large, but they are as predicted. Only the councils involved in the pietistic matter of gambling ran counter to expectation, being more friendly to the NCC on the whole than those not involved in this issue. This finding may not be as anomalous as it first appears, since the secretaries were quite likely viewing this issue in essentially structural, not pietistic, terms. Reflecting the main locus of conciliar movement strength generally, the panel of respondents was heavily urban and nonsouthern. In northern metropolitan areas gambling is thought of as a social evil insofar as it is associated with menacing social institutions, such as organized crime and the Mafia, not insofar as it tempts people into sin. Rather than stemming from an essentially pietistic motive, Protestant crusades against legalized gambling are part of a larger effort to protect insecure and politically inarticulate groups, in much the same way that efforts in behalf of racial justice are geared more to changing oppressive structures, in the short run at least, than to "changing the hearts and minds" of individuals. Interviews conducted with the Council of Churches of New York City and Massachusetts councils of churches confirmed that gambling was primarily regarded in these terms by local secretaries.

Let us consider the implications for state and local councils and for the NCC. It was suggested at the outset of this chapter that the decentralized, fragmented, and pluralistic nature of American Protestantism, coupled with doubts among churchmen about the appropriateness of churches acting as pressure groups, make it understandable that the churches have found it difficult to translate their numerical strength into concrete political leverage.

Yet, assuming that the local secretary is himself a liberal, and the above discussion suggests that his generally favorable view of the NCC often inclines him toward liberalism, the secretary's council of churches may become a focal point for activating liberal sentiments among ministers and lay people in the vicinity. He thus provides a counterpoise to the conservatism typical of most white Protestant and Orthodox congregations. In seeking to arouse liberal responses, the secretary can find legitimacy not only in stands officially adopted by councils of churches (state, local, and NCC), but in the formal pronouncements of national denominational assemblies, characteristically more progressive than most rank-and-file church members.[2] Though the absolute number of persons in his constituency with pronounced liberal-activist leanings may be relatively small, it is not insignificant; and the political mobilization of such persons can make a difference on closely divided national policy struggles.

The argument that local councils generally have a liberalizing effect on local denominational policy must necessarily be advanced cautiously, given the limited percentage of response in the survey and the underrepresentation of the South. But to the extent that the respondents were representative of the total universe of church council secretaries (and we have no reason to believe the respondents atypical, notwithstanding the above mentioned problems with the sample), the inferences drawn appear to have a basis in empirical fact.

NCC leaders have generally behaved in ways consistent

with this hypothesis. Throughout the life of the organization, they have budgeted money to sustain the NCC Office for Councils of Churches. In periods of crisis it is not uncommon for NCC staff personnel to be assigned the task of contacting local councils for the purpose of generating increased grass roots supportive pressure behind NCC stands. This was the strategy employed in the 1964 civil rights struggle.[3] Local councils were also contacted for back-up support concerning the 1961 NCC General Board resolution on the Kennedy administration school-aid bill.[4]

Yet the local secretary is not as free as his NCC counterparts to identify forcefully with social changes that threaten to disrupt the status quo. Being a step closer to the grass roots, he is that much more vulnerable to the conservatism of the local congregation. The striving for a measure of institutional autonomy on the part of the local council often conflicts with the ambition of local congregations to exploit it for their own particularistic ends. Too close an identification with such a body is often viewed as inimical to the career aspirations of the local pastor and to his smooth relationship with parishioners. As William B. Cate has observed, ". . . cooperative activity in a council of churches can become a threat to a minister in his work. He faces a dilemma of loyalties."[5] Similarly, there is evidence that local denominational officials are in many cases less tolerant of any liberal-activist behavior on the part of a local council secretary than on the part of their national counterparts on the staff of the NCC. An official of the Massachusetts Baptist Convention remarked to the author, for example,

> We cooperate with the Massachusetts [state] Council because it is there. But we have to keep a pretty close rein on it. It is a service providing agency, not a church! . . . Of course cooperative church planning [which the council seeks to encourage] is a good thing. It's much better that we work together on this than compete in ignorance.

Interviews with denominational leaders in both the Boston and New York areas indicated their fear that the local council might infringe on jealously guarded "church functions"; hence, their felt need to monitor the local council's activities with a wary eye. The local council secretary with liberal-activist leanings is thus in many instances subject to serious constraints and is less in a position to devote himself to social reform with the single-minded intensity often achievable in the headquarters of national denominational or interdenominational agencies.

CONCLUSIONS

In summary, the conciliar movement fulfills a number of functions in American Protestantism, and the present evidence makes it appear highly plausible that one of these is that of mobilizing Protestant grass roots strength on national issues deemed of major importance. The data suggest that while the overwhelming majority of local secretaries who responded to the survey share the NCC's policy preferences, there exist interesting variations in the intensity of this support, with the most wholehearted support coming from secretaries whose council resembles the NCC in terms of the degree to which constituent churches are urbanized, the degree to which liberal denominations are involved, the basis on which churches are admitted to membership, and, finally, its priorities on social issues. Taking the present respondents to be typical of the conciliar movement, there is suggestive evidence that local councils are in many instances responsive to NCC suggestions on matters of broad national importance and that NCC leaders, aware of this fact, have used local councils (along with other channels) as a means of arousing the essential grass roots support.

part 3

ACTIVISM

Part 3 begins with a discussion in chapter 8 of the years prior to 1963, in which the council's response to major domestic issues was one of ambivalence revealing, on the one hand, a continued attachment to an "educational strategy" (as discussed in chapter 2) and, on the other, growing awareness of the need to respond creatively to an increasingly politicized environment. Chapter 9 describes how this dilemma was resolved, with special stress being placed on the spring 1963 Birmingham, Alabama, crisis and the embarrassment and deep concern over the matter manifested by leading churchmen. In an effort to assess the depth of organizational change associated with this event, the chapter goes on to determine whether NCC leaders, having made an initial commitment on the civil rights front, would elect to withdraw at the earliest opportune moment or, instead, would persevere even when the immediate issues raised by Birmingham were no longer current. Continuing the same general theme chapter 10 analyzes the council's response to the issues put forth in the late 1960s and early '70s by militant black churchmen, especially in connection with the "Black Manifesto."

Assuming that a major strategic redefinition in fact occurred in the early 1960s the following chapter seeks to find out how this affected other areas of council concern, specifically its behavior on national educational issues.

The section is brought to a close with a chapter dealing with *constituency responses to council activism. Particular attention is paid to the efforts of NCC leaders to steer a middle course between critics on the right, who denounced the organization for having gone too far, and those on the left, who insisted that it would never truly come to grips with the issues until it moved a good deal further left than it had.*

8. Prelude to Activism

Organizations resemble physical bodies in the sense that inertia conditions their behavior. The greater the organizational "mass" (its size and complexity), the more the inertia and the more force that consequently must be exerted to effect any predetermined change in course. Those in the organization who seek to bring about significant innovations often have little force at their disposal relative to the mass present, thus are most likely to achieve their ends, if at all, by a series of incremental changes, not by a single, dramatic change. The gradual manner in which the National Council of Churches edged away from its traditional "educational strategy" for dealing with social issues (see p. 41), climaxed by the sweeping General Board decisions of June 1963 (to be discussed in the following chapter), testifies to organizational inertia present in this large body.

The educational strategy had been adopted, it will be recalled, in a period when liberals of all types were optimistic about the chances of effecting reforms through persuasion, appeal to moral instincts, the marshaling of objective social evidence, and avoidance of coercion. So firmly had this stance become rooted in the organization that it was not to be dispensed with quickly, simply on the basis of reasoning and analysis. Indeed, the 25 year period beginning around 1935 inaugurated an era of rethinking in the council, in which a growing number of persons, though still a minority, came to accept the necessity of governmental intervention in behalf of deprived groups and the use of coercive sanctions where necessary to achieve significant reforms. In the present chapter the argument will be advanced that during these years the council was faced with a dilemma: it was uncertain whether to persist in its emphasis on identifying moral principles at stake in social situations while leaving to others the task of political implementation, or whether to commit its own prestige and resources as a direct participant in national policy struggles. In 1963 the organization would opt essentially for the latter of these alternatives (at least with respect to the issue of civil rights). Yet in order to fully grasp the significance of this move, one must first consider what preceded it, which is the concern of the present chapter.

ARGUMENTS AGAINST POLITICAL ACTIVISM

Weighty arguments can be raised by Protestant churchmen who are inclined to oppose interdenominational church involvement in political protest or reform causes. These center around four considerations:

First, in common with most interest groups in American society, the NCC does not like to admit any continuing interest in politics, as that term is conventionally used. Lobbying activity in favor of particular goals, which is what politics often involves, has a negative connotation in American life. A democratic system that extols the "rule of the majority" is inclined to condemn legislation passed at the behest of "special interests," however irrational such a view may seem to the informed person.

Second, lobbying *by churches* is doubly suspect for reasons stated by James Allen Nash:

> The institutional church is frequently expected to refrain from political involvement. According to a popular interpretation of the doctrine of church state separation, the church should remain altar-bound, adhering strictly to its spiritual function.[1]

Third, the above norms are reinforced by federal statutes, the effect of which is to complicate, even when they do not actually proscribe, church political involvement. Of primary importance are the Federal Registration of Lobbying Act, which requires organizations for which lobbying is "one of the main purposes" to formally and publicly acknowledge this fact, and the Internal Revenue Code, section 501 (c) (3), which forbids the granting of tax-exempt status to organizations that exist to "carry on propaganda or otherwise attempt to influence legislation . . . [or which] participate in . . . any political campaign or in behalf of any candidate for public office." These two statutes pose difficulties for all Protestant bodies maintaining representation in Washington, D.C., although one such body, the Quakers, has dealt with the problem by officially registering as a lobby, the Friends Committee on National Legislation. Though registering under the act has proved feasible for a highly cohesive sect like the Quakers, this option is far less attractive to the council, given its broader and more diversified constituency.

Fourth, some churchmen maintain that church political action, where called for, is best handled separately by each denomination, rather than jointly through the NCC. Though the Protestant communions usually see eye-to-eye on major policy questions, this is not always the case; and this is one important reason why most of the churches have their own autonomous Washington representatives. In the face of the well-staked-out claims of its several constituent bodies, the NCC's Washington representatives often feel constrained to play a passive role, except occasionally when issues arise on which the churches are substantially in agreement. An NCC study conference called in 1966 to consider political representation highlighted the diversity of denominational concerns. The conference minutes recorded these facts:

(1) Whereas the Methodist Board of Christian Social Concern employs a staff of eighteen people in Washington, "there is not much cooperation with other denominations."
(2) The American Baptist Joint Committee has a staff of four, but all "are concerned solely with church-state relations."
(3) The Friends Committee on National Legislation, despite a somewhat broader range of interests, "concentrates largely on issues related to peace."

(4) The Church of the Brethren, with one full-time staff member, works full time on assignments related to peace."
(5) The United Presbyterians' only staff executive concentrates on "civil rights, civil liberties, and church-state relations."
(6) The Episcopal Church and the Lutheran Church in America do not maintain full-time staff personnel in Washington.[2]

Efforts are made to achieve a measure of coordination between these various staff executives and agencies, especially through the NCC's Washington Staff Conference, but this has been only modestly successful in offsetting the centrifugal tendencies.

DEFENSIVE POLITICAL INVOLVEMENTS

These considerations are related to the fact that prior to 1963 the council saw fit to commit itself on a political matter only in those cases in which the interests of Protestantism generally, or of churches in particular, were clearly and unmistakably endangered. Four council actions may serve to illustrate this essentially defensive posture.

Navy Department Criticism. On 10 September 1935, Congressman Maury Maverick of Texas inserted into the *Congressional Record* a memorandum issued by the Department of the Navy that described the Federal Council of Churches, along with certain other organizations, as giving "aid and comfort to the Communist movement and party." The same message was repeated by the chief of naval operations, Admiral Stanley, in an address in Atlantic City on 17 September. Information coming to the attention of a Washington, D.C., Presbyterian pastor, the Reverend Joseph R. Sizoo, indicated that Navy Department officials, angered by the council's earlier work in behalf of disarmament, were releasing a barrage of attack against Protestant churches in general and the Federal Council in particular. The Federal Council of Churches was highly distressed by this intelligence. On 14 November the Administrative Committee of the FCC voted to request a meeting with President Franklin D. Roosevelt, which was arranged for 20 November. At the meeting Roosevelt expressed "solicitude and concern over what had happened" and assured the Federal Council delegation of his high regard for it and the churches, adding that he had no personal misgivings about anything the council did. He informed the delegates that he had issued orders to prevent any recurrence of the derogatory statements.[3]

Establishment of a Permanent Washington Office. On 1 October 1945 the Federal Council opened a permanent Washington office with a small staff and modest budget of $15,600 for the first year of operation. There is a good deal of evidence that the primary factor in creating the office was defensive and institutional. This seems implicit, for example, in the officially defined purposes of the Washington Office, as spelled out by the Executive Committee in 1946:

(1) to give notice regarding legislation and governmental decisions affecting the interests of the churches *with special reference to financial and administrative questions* [italics are mine]

(2) to give interpretations for interested persons of legislative and administrative acts where application was ambiguous

(3) to provide indications of proper channels for contacts in Washington[4]

It was apparently not contemplated that the office would serve as a staging area for lobbying in behalf of NCC stands on moral and social issues, judging by the absence of reference to that effect in the official statement. The specific concerns that underlay the Executive Committee's ambiguous phraseology were identified for the author in interviews with informants. A series of legislative measures in the decade prior to 1945 had raised a number of questions to which the churches desired more precise answers. Of chief importance was the 1935 Social Security Act and later amendments thereto, which made clergymen eligible to participate in social security. There was also uncertainty over recent measures providing for such things as exemption from federal taxes of income derived from church-owned property, special tax deductions for clergymen, and, finally, the Fair Labor Standards Act of 1938, setting minimum wage scales and overtime pay standards for blue collar workers, some of whom were church-employed.

The council's leadership explicitly prohibited the Washington Office from "making decisions regarding policy," an admonition that its first executive, Benson Y. Landis, was scrupulous to observe. Given its limited scope, a single executive was adequate. A number of the constituent churches maintaining Washington offices saw fit to coordinate their efforts in behalf of humanitarian and social reform legislation, acting through a loose organization known as the Joint Washington Staff of Church Legislative Representatives; but Luke E. Ebersole's enumeration of the membership of this activist body does not show any of the council's Washington Office executives among the 17 members.[5] Such involvement would have been inappropriate to the essentially defensive purpose for which the NCC Washington Office was established.

Proposed Ambassador to the Vatican. On 20 October 1951, President Harry S. Truman nominated General Mark Clark to serve as United States ambassador to the Vatican. Truman acted in the face of repeated entreaties from the council and other Protestant groups not to name an ambassador, a move they insisted would breach the separation of church and state. In 1939, President Roosevelt had sent Myron C. Taylor to Rome to serve as his "personal representative," and Taylor continued to serve in this capacity under Truman following Roosevelt's death. On two occasions (5 June 1946 and 14 November 1947) representatives of the council had called upon Truman, urging him to terminate Taylor's appointment, and had been told by him that it was temporary and would end with the establishment of full peace. When Truman "laid down the gauntlet" to Protestant forces by his 1951 action, the response was immediate and outraged. Episcopal Bishop Henry Knox Sherrill, the NCC president, called an emergency meeting of the NCC's General Board, which voted to issue a strongly worded statement and take whatever other actions might be in order. Hundreds of other statements followed daily from Protestant leaders. Under a shower of abuse, General Clark requested on 13 January that his nomination be withdrawn. Truman announced that he would secure another nominee, but he never did.

From one standpoint the NCC's action may be considered a reasoned response, based on a well-formulated theory of the proper relationship between church and state. But to consider the matter exclusively in terms of its rational elements is to miss much of the essence of the struggle. The staggering total of messages that poured into Washington in the weeks following the president's announcement (*Time* reported 21,000 letters and telegrams received at the White House in the first week alone, more than that produced by any issue of recent years except the dismissal of General MacArthur) points to the symbolic importance of the issue to many Protestants. In this sense the National Council of Churches was helping to lead a crusade in defense of Protestant status in American life, a status sharply challenged in recent years by the emergence of Roman Catholicism as a major political, economic, and social force.[6]

Air Force Training Manual. A final instance of the council's readiness to employ its resources in defense of Protestantism's good name and standing in the community is reminiscent of the 1935 controversy between the council and the navy. A training manual employed by the air force was discovered to contain allegations to the effect that the council was a Communist agency and that Protestant clergymen in large numbers had subversive connections. Among the "evidence" cited to support this charge was the claim that 35 of the 95 ministers involved in preparing the Revised Standard Version of the Bible (prepared and published under NCC auspices) were subversive or had Communist leanings. It developed that much of the material in the manual came from the pen of the far right evangelist Reverend Billy James Hargis, particularly from his pamphlets *The National Council of Churches Indicts Itself on Fifty Counts of Treason Against God and Country* and *Is the National Council of Churches Subversive?*. The council responded vigorously. On 11 February 1960 a letter from the NCC to the secretary of defense, Thomas S. Gates, Jr., described the introduction to the training manual as "a patent contradiction of the first amendment of the Constitution." In the face of mounting church protests, the secretary of the air force, Dudley C. Sharpe, wrote the council that the manual "has been withdrawn and action is being taken to prevent recurrence of the issuance of such material." A high-ranking FBI official stepped forward to affirm that the FBI believed the nation's Protestant churches were loyal and stated that blanket accusations against Protestant clergymen for alleged disloyalty were unjustified.

By way of summary, then, an assessment of four cases believed to be representative suggests that in the 1933 to 1963 period the council conceived its task relative to the national government as consisting primarily in fact-finding and institutional defense, though in the latter years of this period politically activist tendencies were becoming apparent, as will be seen shortly.

THE LYNCHING PROBLEM AND UNEASINESS OVER POLITICAL CRUSADING

While the council's behavior on controversial political issues in the years under discussion consisted largely in efforts to protect institutional stakes while avoiding overt involvement on broadly defined social issues, this is not the whole story. Minority sentiment for a more activist stance toward national policy questions existed and was gradually increasing in intensity. A useful index of this trend is the council's changing position on civil rights. This trend merits attention both for what it can reveal about the council in the pre-1963 period and also for the light it can shed on subsequent developments.

The council's Commission on Race Relations, founded in 1920, initially reflected the organization's overall educational approach to social problems. Its main emphasis was on convening conferences, publishing tracts and study lessons, and using other channels of communication in an effort to bring the problems of black Americans before church people for sympathetic attention. Perhaps the most characteristic feature of the commission's program was Race Relations Sunday, on which ministers were asked to preach on appropriate themes (suggested each year by the commission), white and black ministers exchanging pulpits. The council was thus prepared to condemn the grosser forms of injustice, to champion the need for good will and improved understanding, and to identify (within limits) with the black's desire for social uplift. The point is perhaps most clearly seen by observing the council's most advanced statement on race relations in this period, the "Revised Social Creed" of 1932:

> Relations between races have often been characterized by prejudice, antagonism, fear, cruelty, injustice, exploitation. But racial differences need have none of these consequences. The likenesses between races—the characteristics which the majority in each group have in common with those of other groups —are more numerous and more important than their differences. . . . [The situation requires] appreciation, . . . respect, . . . equality in educational, social and economic opportunities, . . . friendship, mutual goodwill and active cooperation among racial and national groups.[7]

But for a number of years the council was reluctant to identify itself in any explicit sense with black protest movements or campaigns to secure civil rights legislation. The struggle waged in the 1920s and '30s by a number of civil rights and civil liberties groups to secure legislation making lynching a federal crime, punishable by stiff penalties, may serve as an illustration of this point. The council had strongly condemned lynching as early as 1919; in 1934 its Executive Commitee (which occupied a position analogous to the General Board of the NCC) adopted a resolution favoring federal legislation to deal with the problem. Yet at no time did it endorse specific legislative proposals such as the Costigan-Wagner Bill.

Nor did endorsement of the principle of federal antilynching legislation lead the council to participate actively in the antilynching coalition. In the 1920s the NAACP, the American Civil Liberties Union, the Public Affairs Committee of the YWCA, and other groups engaged in a sustained, though ultimately unsuccessful, effort to secure passage of particular antilynching bills. The spearhead of the movement was the NAACP national secretary, Walter White, whose talents as a legislative strategist were considerable. The council lent this campaign its interest and sympathy, but little in the way of concrete support.[8] It was prepared to join others in official delegations to wait upon officials highly placed in the government, such as the delegation of six who confronted President Roosevelt in April 1938, yet it saw no need to make use of its own publicity resources for any sustained support of the legislative drive. During the crucial years of the campaign, 1937 to 1939, its official organ, the *Federal Council Bulletin,* contained not a single reference to lynching or proposed antilynching legislation. *Information Service,* the respected bulletin of the Department of Research and Survey, indexes one article on lynching in 1937 and one in 1940, but none for the other years. Even those publicity channels over which the race relations department presumably had direct control accorded the antilynching campaign only passing notice. Although in its 1936 annual report to the Federal Council the department referred to the resolution of the Executive Committee passed in 1934 in favor of national legislation on lynching, there was no mention of the matter in the annual reports of 1937 and 1938. In the department's annual suggestions for Race Relations Sunday programs during those years when the antilynching drive reached its peak, there was no mention of it.

That these were rather routine years for the department is suggested by the fact that its budget in the five-year period beginning in 1934 increased only a modest 6.7 percent (from $16,930 to $18,058), the same period during which the Federal Council's total budget increased by 29.4 percent. A reasonable conclusion would seem to be that the lobbying effort in behalf of antilynching legislation was regarded by council leaders as largely outside its area of primary concern.

CONTINUED COUNCIL HESITANCY IN AN ERA OF GROWING CIVIL RIGHTS FERMENT

While in the 1940s and '50s council statements reflected a more pronounced sense of urgency over the race issue, these were normally formulated not with a view toward influencing Congress or the president, but toward altering discriminatory practices prevalent among the federation's own member churches.* Significantly, it issued no pronouncements on the

---

* The following civil rights statements were adopted in the 1950s: "The

1957 or 1960 civil rights acts at the time these were pending in Congress; and it addressed itself to the Greensboro, North Carolina, lunch counter sit-ins and the "freedom rides" across the Deep South by turning down resolutions that would commend the actions of protesters, approving, instead, a resolution rather blandly endorsing the "principle of non-violence." According to one well-placed observer, prior to the establishment of the NCC Commission on Religion and Race in 1963, the Protestant "churches did not have a very good reputation among other parts of the Freedom Movement." [9] Even as late as January 1963, after several years of direct-action campaigns in the South, the NCC and the predominantly white churches were only perfunctorily represented at the widely publicized Conference on Race and Religion held in Chicago. One prominent Protestant leader did appear, NCC president J. Irwin Miller, but his address implicitly indicated that the churches had by no means made up their minds as to how best to relate to the changing temper of American race relations. The executive heads of the major Protestant denominations and top NCC staff personnel were not present at the meeting.

STEPS TOWARD CIVIL RIGHTS ACTIVISM

Without casting aside its long-standing preference for avoiding active commitment in reform political struggles, the council did in the 1940s and '50s make a series of moves that represented a departure from previous strategies toward greater involvement with public policy. One analyst, Louis C. Kesselman, ranked the council among the foremost groups pressing in the early 1940s for effective fair employment practices legislation, a major civil rights issue of that period:

> On June 13, 1941 the Federal Council issued the first of a long list of statements advocating church cooperation in bringing economic discrimination against minorities to an end. . . . The

---

Churches and Segregation" (11 June 1952), "A Guiding Principle for Meetings and Conventions (11 Mar. 1953), and "The Churches and Segregation" (5 Dec. 1957).

moral and religious issues involved in discrimination were given full play in the statements. . . . The Federal Council gave wholehearted support to the establishment of the President's Committee on Fair Employment Practices in 1941. It also was in the vanguard of the National Council for a Permanent FEPC in urging permanent legislation in this area.[10]

In the middle 1940s a number of churchmen active in the council carried on this concern with federal civil rights policy. Three of these, G. Bromley Oxnam, Henry Knox Sherrill, and Frederick Reisig, were especially active, one or another of them participating in President Truman's Committee on Civil Rights and later in the National Committee on Mob Violence. In December 1948 the organization went formally on record in its "Statement on Human Rights," supporting a broad list of demands for congressional and presidential action. The following year J. Oscar Lee, the director of the council's Department of Race Relations (successor to the Commission on Race Relations) was among those involved in organizing an emergency "mobilization" for civil rights legislation; and Lee was later to serve as the council's delegate to the Leadership Conference on Civil Rights, a permanent coordinating body dedicated to achieving major new legislation in this area.[11]

Moreover, this growing concern among a minority of council activists with securing major civil rights legislation found increasing support in the editorial content of leading religious periodicals of the period, especially in liberal Protestant publications. Though the periodicals actually bore no official connection with the council, their increasing concern with civil rights quite probably had an effect both on Protestant opinion generally and on those active in the organization.

Table 13 presents a tabulation of articles listed under the headings "Negro," "Christianity and Race," and "Church and Race" in the *Index to Religious Periodicals*. Some might question the significance of the demonstrated increase because volumes of the *Index* vary in the number of years they cover and also because the number of periodicals indexed increases substantially from 1949 to 1962. In an effort to hold constant the factor of increasing coverage, the author undertook a more dis-

Table 13 ARTICLES ON RACIAL MATTERS FOR ALL PROTESTANT
PUBLICATIONS, 1949–62 *

Year	Number of Articles	Articles per Year	Number of Issues Indexed	Articles per Periodical Indexed
1949–52	7	1.8	31	0.22
1953–54	0	0.0	30	0.00
1955–56	22	11.0	63	0.35
1957–59	54	18.0	58	0.93
1960–62	76	25.3	76	1.00

* Source: *Index to Religious Periodicals*, vols. 1–5 (1949–62). Figures represent the total number of items under "Negro" and "Christianity and Race." Inspection indicated that items listed under the one heading were not repeated under the other.

criminating tabulation, which focused on selected Protestant journals that were covered by the *Index* throughout the 1949 to 1962 period (table 14). Two of the periodicals selected were

Table 14 ARTICLES IN SELECTED PROTESTANT PUBLICATIONS ON RACIAL
MATTERS, 1949–62, BY YEAR AND PUBLICATION*

Year	Publication		
	Christianity and Crisis	Social Action	Five Scholarly Protestant Journals†
1949–52	1	0	0
1953–54	0	0	0
1955–56	4	2	14
1957–59	8	9	23
1960–62	15	14	14

* Items indexed under "Negro" and "Christianity and Race." (Source: *Index to Religious Periodicals*, vols. 1–5 [1949–62].)
† The five journals were *Journal of Religious Thought*, *Lutheran Quarterly*, *Review and Expositor* (Southern Baptist), *Union Seminary Review*, and *Theology Today*.

"journals of opinion" having a liberal outlook; five were of a scholarly nature. In this tabulation a pattern of increasing liberal Protestant attention to racial matters also is apparent.

The skeptic might still maintain that these findings lack importance on the grounds that *all* periodicals with an interest in public affairs, liberal Protestant and otherwise, were increasingly devoting attention to racial events over these years. Race, after all, made good copy. Did the Protestant journals simply mirror the general editorial mood in the mass media, or did their interest in race exceed the prevailing norm? A way of dealing with this question is to compare the attention given racial matters in the most widely circulated Protestant liberal journal, the *Christian Century*, with the largest mass circulation weekly news magazine, *Time*. A Protestant journal of opinion with *conservative* leanings, *Christianity Today*, is also surveyed. As table 15 indicates, all three publications did tend to increase

Table 15   ARTICLES ON RACIAL MATTERS IN SELECTED PROTESTANT AND NON-PROTESTANT PUBLICATIONS, 1949–62, BY YEAR AND PERIODICAL*

	Periodical		
Year	Christian Century	Time	Christianity Today
1949–50	80	90	†
1951–52	87	92	†
1953–54	109	63	†
1955–56	190	96	†
1957–58	156	74	9 (9/56–9/58)§
1959–60	103	79	10 (9/58–9/60)
1961–62	155	117	1 (9/60–9/62)

* For all these publications the number of annual issues remained constant throughout the period in question.
† Not published in these years.
§ The discrepancy in time periods covering the data for *Christianity Today* and that of the other two periodicals is due to the difference in periods covered by the annual indexes, from which these data were assembled.

their coverage of racial matters during times of dramatic events in the area of civil rights (1955, for example, was the year of the Montgomery, Alabama, bus boycott; 1963, of civil rights efforts in Washington and throughout the South). But whereas *Time* and *Christianity Today* devoted only passing attention to racial matters in years that lacked dramatic incidents, the *Christian Century* showed less fluctuation of racial coverage and a higher absolute level of interest in all years. The comparison between this latter publication and *Christianity Today* is of particular interest because it brings out the special saliency of the civil rights issue for liberal Protestantism. It appears, then, that the era immediately preceding the early 1960s saw a decided increase in liberal Protestant concern with race as a basic problem for churches and American society.

Moreover, there is evidence that the change in thinking also encompassed an increased willingness to reconsider council strategy toward the political system generally. On 13 September 1961 the Reverend R. H. Edwin Espy (American Baptist), the NCC associate general secretary who would be named general secretary the next year, delivered an important address on the topic of church political representation. Espy began by indicating that several factors were making this "a time to try men's souls." He pointed to three developments as specially important:

first, the nation and the world impinge on our lives in a degree unimagined two generations ago. On the domestic scene there is the massive presence of the military, which makes an impact on the lives of most Americans, and the participation of the majority of earning Americans in social security and other federal benefits. Numerous welfare institutions receive aid from the Federal government, raising important questions about the role of private agencies, including those of the churches. . . . Whether we like it or not, big government is with us and is here to stay.

second, there is a development that is perhaps anomalous, namely that at a time when the national government has penetrated our lives so deeply, we should be so reluctant as a people to share in determining its policies.

thirdly, the churches of the United States are in contact increasingly and inescapably with the federal government.

Espy then went on to endorse the view that the churches must stand prepared to bring to bear their moral judgment upon the state:

God is the ruler of both the church and the state, as of all the affairs of men. His voice must be heard by the state. Both as an individual and as churches we have a solemn responsibility to speak out and act as we feel God calls on us to do. While the church is not equated with God, it is expected by God to be a special instrument of his will. . . . There is evidence that many of our government leaders expect and desire the church to speak in this sense—from the high plane of Divine perspective insofar as this is humanly possible.

Espy then indicated that this responsibility obliged the church to take an interest in broad political issues, not merely those affecting the churches as institutions. Stands on public issues, he continued, could be expected to arouse controversy among church members, as had recently occurred in reaction to NCC pronouncements dealing with race relations, federal immigration laws, cessation of nuclear testing, exchange of persons, support of the United Nations, and the American foreign aid program. The address closed with the remark that "The church must skillfully and prophetically point its people to opportunities for Christian witness and service in the life of the community, both governmental and non-governmental." [12]

Also indicative of the change in thinking at the top level was a policy statement passed a little over two years later by the General Board that called upon members of the constituent churches of the NCC not to remain aloof from politics. It urged the Christian voter to exert his influence through all proper channels to elect candidates whose policies he believed best represented the ideals of the Judeo-Christian faith. This was not a statement likely to provoke controversy; it was nevertheless significant as one stage in a trend toward more overt NCC concern with national political matters.

CONCLUSIONS

The history of the council prior to 1963 was marked by a belief in the effectiveness of an educational strategy for dealing with major social issues. Such a policy had originally made sense, both with regard to the general climate of liberal opinion at the time of its formulation and in light of the particular constraints under which religious bodies must operate in the American system. Increasingly, however, events began to outpace the council's generally apolitical orientation. The organization early found it necessary to intervene directly in behalf of certain well-defined institutional stakes, including the need to safeguard the good name of Protestant and Orthodox churches in American life. Later, the force of external events caused council leaders (some of them referred to in this chapter, others in the latter section of chapter 2) to question the received wisdom and behave in ways that ran contrary to traditional strategies. This was most apparent in the civil rights area, but was indicated in other areas as well. The stage was set for even more dramatic changes about to occur.

9. Continuity and Change
in Racial Attitudes

Something happened in the early 1960s which marked a fairly radical departure. During the whole era of the Federal Council of Churches the emphasis was on changing the attitudes of individuals—set up social standards and get ministers to realize that these are part of their jobs, get educational materials dealing with social problems in the hands of children and young people. It was a favorite thing to quote the phrase in the 1908 Social Creed of the Churches: "the application of the law of love in social relations." But in the early 1960s it was realized that preaching, teaching and proclamations generally were not producing anything very definite in the way of social change; there was a loss of confidence in the efficacy of social education. It came to its sharpest focus in connection with race, but it also affected the attitude toward other social problems.[1]

The NCC's response to the race issue in the 1960s evidenced a profound alteration in basic strategies. Obviously, a change that was so fundamental required a shift in perspective among officials throughout the organization. Bearing this point in mind, it is nevertheless convenient to center the present discussion around the tumultuous four-year history of the Commission on Religion and Race (CORR), the immediate organizational response to Birmingham, whose brief existence reflected acutely the many cross-pressures that affected the council as a whole during this critical period in its history.

FORMATION OF CORR

Civil rights had existed as an issue for a considerable time before the council was prepared to accord it high priority. From a purely objective standpoint the events in Birmingham, Alabama, in spring 1963 were not in a class by themselves among the high points in the history of the civil rights movement. Of comparable importance were the 1954 Supreme Court school desegregation decision, the 1955 Montgomery bus boycott, the 1957 Little Rock crisis, and the 1960 to 1961 lunch counter sit-ins and "freedom rides." The difference in the organization's response in 1963, compared to earlier years, does not lie in the intrinsic character of the event so much as in the NCC's predispositions at the time. Had Birmingham occurred ten or twenty years previously the NCC would probably have responded less overtly and comprehensively.

Yet given the trend of thinking in the years leading up to this event, discussed in chapter 8, the council by 1963 was more than ever prepared to accept far-reaching changes in social action strategy. The Protestant churches' sense of shock over Birmingham, it is true, partook of the general national reaction, as many Americans (not the least the president of the United States) were made aware of the urgency of the situation and began to reassess their assumptions. Yet the response of churchmen was more intense than that of most persons who did not view events from a religious perspective; and in the case of the NCC, it may validly be said that the events of 1963 have constituted a major catalyst, which brought into focus and gave momentum to long-term changes heretofore only latent in the organization. As the following discussion will suggest in more detail, Birmingham was a major event in the life of the council for three reasons. First, it served to raise a single public policy issue to a level of transcendent importance and thus to subordinate other social concerns, something unique in the council's recent history. Second, it entailed significant changes in the federation's decision-making process, substituting for the decentralized, pluralistic structure implied by the constitution and by-laws one that was relatively centralized and vested significant discretionary powers in a few individuals. Third, it effectively pushed to one side those in the organization habituated to the social action strategy of earlier years by creating a staff unit with its own special mandate to act, its own source of emergency funds separate from the council's general operating budget, and its own staff recruited largely from persons who had never before been employed by the council.

What happened in Birmingham was briefly as follows. A series of civil rights protest demonstrations, at the outset like ones occurring in other southern cities, began to take on unique importance with the arrival on the scene of Martin Luther King, Jr., and Ralph Abernathy. On 6 April 1963, following the refusals of police commissioner "Bull" Conner to permit the picketing of stores where lunch counters had been closed because of the sit-ins, there occurred the first in a long series of street marches by black protesters. A few days later King, Abernathy, and 60 others were arrested for violating a court injunction prohibiting further demonstrations. While in jail, King was sent a letter by eight white Birmingham ministers, who professed sympathy for civil rights aims but challenged the need for the current demonstrations, questioned King's right to "intervene" in the situation, and called upon black citizens to withdraw their support from march leaders. King responded with an eloquent defense of his actions, "Letter from the Birmingham Jail," in which he expressed keen disappointment at the limited vision displayed by the authors of the letter. King's letter was widely circulated in areas outside the South and aroused a generally favorable reaction. Though he was released on bond after eight days in jail (following phone calls from the president of the United States and other government officials expressing concern over his safety), the street demonstrations continued. By early May the number of march participants had increased to from 2,500 to 3,000 and Commissioner Conner ordered the use of police dogs, fire hoses, and cattle prods to control and disperse demonstrators. Newsreels depicting this police action were flashed over television to a national audience.

More than any other single aspect of the situation, Dr. King's "Letter from the Birmingham Jail" stabbed the liberal Protestant conscience. It threw doubt upon a whole tradition of Protestant efforts to cope with social problems through campaigns of "social education." Not only had Protestant efforts failed to eliminate racial injustice, they had not even managed to create an atmosphere in which leading clergymen would feel embarrassed in using their prominent positions to cast aspersions on civil rights leaders, implicitly defending the racial status quo. Though NCC activists did not go so far as to hold liberal Protestantism "responsible" for Birmingham, they by no means exempted it from guilt; what certain observers had long stressed suddenly became painfully obvious, namely, that the Protestant churches in America had mostly served to sustain, not attack, racial discrimination.

But if Birmingham was the *ultimate* cause of the NCC's transformation of policy, three other factors were of *proximate* significance. The first was an action taken by one of the council's more active constituent churches, the United Presbyterian Church in the U.S.A. (Northern Presbyterian). During the third week in May, the Presbyterians held their annual General Assembly in Des Moines, Iowa, attended by more than 800 delegates ("commissioners"). The meeting had special significance since this was the first plenary meeting of an NCC member body since the Birmingham demonstrations. In his address to the assembly and in private conversations, the NCC president, J. Irwin Miller, an invited guest at the meeting, did not miss the opportunity to urge the strongest action on the civil rights front. In this he had the wholehearted support of Eugene Carson Blake, the denomination's highest full-time executive. Out of these meetings came a proposal to create an official Presbyterian Commission on Religion and Race, with instructions to fulfill its mandate, not on a narrow denominational basis, but ecumenically, through cooperation with other denominational civil rights agencies. The resolution carried a budgetary allocation of extraordinary size, $500,000. Without a single negative vote the assembly adopted the proposal on 20 May.

A second significant development was a meeting between NCC officials and several blacks who resided in New York and were active in the civil rights movement. This meeting grew out of an earlier "secret" meeting between a delegation of black leaders and Attorney General Robert Kennedy. The black notables, including actress Lena Horne, author James Baldwin, and playwright Lorraine Hansberry, had requested the meeting to voice concern over racial conditions in various parts of the country. The meeting went poorly, and Baldwin later declared that Kennedy "failed to understand the full extent of racial strife in the nation"; others in the delegation declared it a "flop." [2] Hopeful of generating a broader base of citizen support, one of their number contacted the National Council of Churches and a meeting was arranged the last week in May between these same blacks and a group of NCC leaders (R. H. Edwin Espy, general secretary; Jon Regier, Division of Home Missions; Arlid Olsen, Division of Christian Life and Work; and J. Oscar Lee, Department of Cultural and Racial Relations; among others). The NCC officials were deeply impressed with what they heard and were thereby convinced that the situation required of them truly unprecedented action. Shortly following this meeting, a working committee of four church officials (Regier, Robert W. Spike of the United Church of Christ's Division of Homeland Ministries, and two others) sat down and drafted a resolution for submission to the General Board, whose semiannual meeting was scheduled for 6 to 8 June.

A third important development occurred within 24 hours of the opening of the General Board's meeting. Eugene Carson Blake, drawing upon his prestige as leader in the United Presbyterian Church and his prominence as past president of the NCC (1954 to 1957), and co-author of a widely discussed plan of church union (the Blake-Pike proposal, 1960), placed telephone calls to the executive heads of the other leading liberal churches. Blake requested, and managed to secure, pledges of substantial financial support for an interdenominational NCC racial commission. Although the decision-making procedures in the churches were normally cumbersome, Blake was able to marshal substantial funds in a matter of a few hours.[3]

The full text of the resolution the Temporary Committee of Six on Race presented for the General Board's action on 7 June was rather lengthy, but a few excerpts may serve to indicate its broad outlines. It began with a statement setting forth the criterion by which actions of the churches were to be measured:

The Church of Jesus Christ can make no compromise with discrimination against or segregation of peoples on the basis of race, and still be faithful to her Master. God came to make his dwelling among men in the person of a man. He went to his death and rose again for every man.

Against such a standard the past actions of the churches were viewed as altogether inadequate:

It must be said that while many Christians have worked hard in this cause, the Church has not been free from sin in this serious issue. Many churches are closed to Negroes and other ethnic minorities; church institutions discriminate, and we have not taken vigorous enough action in the public domain. Up to now there always has seemed to be time for gradual change, and modest tokens of progress in racial justice were accepted as the best we could do. But now in the providence of God, the issue is being sharply focused in every corner of the nation.

It was felt that words were no longer sufficient; actions alone could demonstrate the depth of conviction:

The world watches to see how we will act—whether with courage or with fumbling expediency. In such a time the Church of Jesus Christ is called upon to put aside every lesser engagement, to confess her sins of omission and delay and to move forward to witness to her essential belief that every child of God is a brother to every other. Now is the time for action—even costly action that may jeopardize the organizational goals, and institutional structures of the Church, and may disrupt any fellowship that is less than fully obedient to the Lord of our Church. . . . Words and declarations are no longer useful in this struggle unless accompanied by sacrifice and commitment.

In order to most effectively focus concern, mobilize resources, and provide interdenominational liaison, the resolution proposed that the NCC General Board authorize its president to immediately appoint a Commission on Religion and Race:

The General Board authorizes the Commission to make commitments, call for actions, take risks in behalf of the National

Council of Churches which are required by the situation and are consistent [with previous actions and decisions in this area].[4]

The NCC churches pledged themselves to give the commission adequate staff and resources to accomplish its purposes. Until a permanent staff could be formed, Jon Regier was named to head an "emergency staff."

The atmosphere in the General Board meeting on 7 June as the document came up for consideration was one of deep anxiety:

> Throughout the meeting the atmosphere seemed taut with awareness of and concern over the current crisis. Repeatedly it was predicted that this summer the racial crisis will not only persist in the Southern states, but will spread into northern cities.[5]

The resolution was approved by the General Board substantially unchanged.

While the report as excerpted above speaks for itself, three of its facets merit special emphasis. First, the unprecedented scope of the mandate granted the commission is striking (". . . take risks in behalf of the National Council of Churches . . ."; "Now is the time for action—even costly action that may jeopardize the organizational goals . . . of the Church"). In substance, the Commission on Religion and Race was given carte blanche, subject only to the stipulation that it periodically report back to the General Board. Second, the status granted the commission in the council's organizational structure was unique. Instead of being grouped under one of the regular operating divisions, the commission was to enjoy direct access to the General Board. The usual hierarchical arrangements were short-circuited in order to insure the commission maximum freedom of maneuver and minimum bureaucratie interference. Third, the decision bypassed the existing Department of Cultural and Racial Relations. This was done in the belief that the situation required a more drastic change in strategy and approach than could reasonably be expected of a long-existing department with well-developed routines and procedures. The

Cultural and Racial Relations department continued to function as a subunit of the Division of Christian Life and Work for another two years before being disbanded. Its director, J. Oscar Lee, now joined the commission's staff and served until his departure in 1967. Having two race relations agencies in the council might detract from orderliness and procedural regularity, but those who proposed the new commission felt that this difficulty would be more than offset by having a new agency to carry out a crash program.

Late in June it was announced that Robert W. Spike, a staff executive in the United Church of Christ headquarters office, had been appointed to serve as executive secretary, and Arthur Lichtenberger, the presiding bishop of the Protestant Episcopal Church, as chairman of the commission. Eugene Carson Blake, stated clerk of the United Presbyterian Church, was named vice-chairman, becoming CORR chairman a few months later when Lichtenberger resigned because of illness. It should be noted that Blake, Spike, and the key denominational leaders to whom Blake turned in setting up the commission were all whites; this white bias was not mitigated by the facts that a black leader, B. Julian Smith, bishop of the Christian Methodist Episcopal Church, was named vice-chairman early in 1964 and that other blacks assumed staff positions. A number of prominent individuals, including Walter Reuther and Ralph McGill, agreed to the use of their names as commission members. The full commission seldom met, however, and there is every evidence that the crucial decisions were worked out between the chairman and his staff.

CORR IN THE SPIKE ERA

CORR was a relative latecomer to the civil rights movement and it was by no means clear in 1963 that other, more established groups in the movement were prepared to trust it. Nevertheless, the situation as they viewed it early in the summer of 1963 was sufficiently urgent for them to put aside whatever doubts they may have had about the depth of Protestant commitment. CORR succeeded in establishing itself in a few weeks as a leading element in the civil rights phalanx. With the issues already sharply defined, the weight the churches could add to the political muscle of the coalition proved to be an overriding consideration.

Immediately following the commission's first meeting on 28 June 1963, Blake announced that he was planning to attend a CORE-sponsored rally in Baltimore as the commission's representative. Less than a week later, on 4 July, he joined one Roman Catholic and two Episcopal bishops and a rabbi from Baltimore in leading an integrated delegation of protesters in a deliberate violation of a Maryland trespass law. The delegation chose as its target a privately owned Maryland amusement park. The exclusion of blacks from such public places was the subject of a key section of the Kennedy administration's civil rights act then pending in Congress. Blake was arrested by local police, and a photograph of him behind the bars of a paddy wagon being taken off to jail was given wide press circulation.

CORR was soon caught up in the effort to secure maximum Protestant involvement in the forthcoming March on Washington, planned by civil rights groups for 28 August. Although Blake was given prominent attention in the press for his role in the march, he and Spike appear not to have been a party to most of the key decisions, many of which had already been made. The commission's involvement, however, did affect the character of the march in one important respect: it changed what would otherwise have been an all-black demonstration into one with significant white representation. As Blake later commented in a March 1969 interview with the author, "We desegregated the March on Washington." Blake and Spike were instrumental in securing a place for the head of the National Catholic Interracial Council, Matthew Ahmann, in the leadership of the march. They also took steps to head off a last-minute withdrawal by a prominent Catholic figure, Patrick O'Boyle, archbishop of Washington, D.C. O'Boyle was provoked over a passage in a draft of a speech to be delivered by John Lewis of the Student Nonviolent Coordinating Committee (SNCC). The objectionable passage ridiculed the idea of new civil rights legislation and alleged that the Kennedy administration's bill offered nothing to the great majority of black people. Though

Blake and Spike were prepared to agree in the abstract that the pending bill fell drastically short of a solution to the problems of low-income black people, they insisted that a speech based on this premise would play into the hands of the opposition. From the outset CORR had made it a major point of strategy to open lines of access to the more militant wing of the civil rights movement, particularly SNCC. This in part accounts for Spike's and Blake's ability to get through to SNCC leaders and persuade them to modify the speech's objectionable passages. With this assurance, Archbishop O'Boyle took part in the ceremonies.

Relationships in the newly enlarged march coalition between the NCC and the more established civil rights organizations remained correct rather than cordial. In mid-July, Spike invited Anna Arnold Hedgeman, a black churchwoman active in New York politics and a former official in Mayor Robert F. Wagner's administration, to join the CORR staff as coordinator of special events. Her appointment coincided with the decision to enlarge the march committee to include Catholic, Jewish, white Protestant, and labor representation; and in the six weeks remaining until 28 August, she was assigned to help arrange mass Protestant participation. Hedgeman's work required her to be in regular contact with the "big six" on the march committee: A. Philip Randolph, Roy Wilkins, Martin Luther King, Jr., James Farmer, Whitney Young, and John Lewis. The experience was not always a pleasant one for her. According to Hedgeman's own account, there were several instances in which the original march leaders slighted the (predominantly) white newcomers:

> The [black] civil rights leaders were not always as considerate of these [newly found] allies as they should have been. There was a new undercurrent among Negroes generally that this was to be *their* protest to the nation and the world, and that allies were, after a fashion, appendages rather than equal participants.[6]

In addition to negotiating with other civil rights groups in advance of the march, the commission made strenuous efforts to secure maximum participation on the part of white church people. In this it enjoyed the active support of the Association of Council Secretaries (ACS), a body composed of paid executives in the roughly 300 state and local councils of churches employing paid staff. After passing a formal resolution concurring with the 7 June decision of the NCC General Board, the ACS took steps to establish local interracial councils in their constituent areas, both as a way of bringing pressure to bear on state and local governments and as a method of backing NCC lobbying efforts in Washington. Interracial groups of a religious character sprang up in such cities as New York, Pittsburgh, Raleigh, St. Louis, Detroit, and San Francisco. In view of the fact that several Protestant bodies were working to build support for the 28 August march, it would be an exaggeration to suggest that the commission alone was responsible for the impressive turnout of white churchmen, who constituted a large percentage of the roughly 40,000 white people taking part in the rally, along with approximately 160,000 blacks. But clearly CORR was the agency primarily responsible for the large white Protestant turnout.

During the remainder of 1963, action on the administration's civil rights proposal was mainly confined to top-level negotiations among administration officials and congressional leaders. The bill's chances were much improved by public revulsion over the death of four black children in a Birmingham church bombing early in September. Having concluded hearings early in August, a House judiciary subcommittee came forth with a bill that went far beyond the scope of the administration's original proposal. Though initially given little chance of passage and objected to by Attorney General Robert Kennedy because of its slim chances, the amended bill gained a new lease on life in the wake of the murder of President John F. Kennedy with the public's desire to pay tribute to his memory. The new president, Lyndon B. Johnson, used his position to translate the national mood of shock into increased support for Kennedy's entire legislative package. The NCC lost no time in voicing support for the bill. At its triennial meeting in December, the NCC General Assembly issued a statement calling

upon the Congress of the United States to take every step necessary to insure the earliest possible passage of the Civil Rights Act of 1963 [sic], including the immediate use of a discharge petition which will enable the House of Representatives to take action on the bill.

The General Assembly of the National Council of Churches also calls upon Christians across the Nation to urge their Representatives in Congress to sign such a petition when it is presented.[7]

The statement was reported in the press and later reprinted in the *Congressional Record*. With the threat of a discharge petition hanging over his head, House Rules Committee chairman Howard Smith agreed to allow the bill to come to the floor for a vote. The bill later passed the House by a 2–1 margin and was sent to the Senate for further action.

The question for civil rights forces now became whether the necessary two-thirds majority could be lined up to invoke cloture against the expected southern filibuster. The cloture rule had never been successfully applied against a civil rights filibuster, despite eleven attempts. Given the reluctance of many senators to vote for cloture, even if they disagreed with the position of the filibusters, it was evident that the well-established civil rights groups could hardly hope to overcome the southern effort on their own. The support of organized religion was thus particularly welcome.

Sunday, 28 April 1964, marked the beginning of a drive by the nation's churches and synagogues in support of civil rights legislation. Across the nation that day convocations, rallies, and worship services were held to emphasize the essential moral basis of civil rights. Scores of rallies were held, of which the following were fairly typical:

(1) In *Montpelier, Vermont*, some 500 Catholics, Protestants, and Jews met on the State House steps for a rally led by Governor Phillip Hoff and Mayor Manuel Canas. After several preliminary speeches, the governor and mayor led the assembled throng in a brass band parade to the city auditorium for an amplified telephone conversation with Vermont's senators, Winston Prouty and George D. Aiken (both Republicans) in Washington.

(2) In *Jefferson City, Missouri*, some 200 members of the three major faiths gathered at the state capitol rotunda to send telegrams to the state's senators, Stuart Symington and Edward V. Long.

(3) In *St. Paul, Minnesota,* 300 people met in the state capitol rotunda to pray for civil rights legislation and to set up a committee to coordinate trips to Washington for calls on senators.

(4) In *Detroit, Michigan,* an interreligious convocation mailed 250 letters to senators and established daily noon-hour meetings, which continued throughout the period of the senate filibuster.

(5) In *Red Bank, New Jersey,* church bells were rung throughout the city at noon and at 6:00 P.M. to remind citizens that the Senate had not yet passed the bill.

(6) In *Dayton, Ohio,* some 400 people filled the Westminster Presbyterian Church, and promptly at 11:00 A.M. marched en masse to the post office to mail letters to their senators. Elsewhere in the city numerous churches and synagogues held continuous meetings, lasting from 9:00 A.M. to 9:00 P.M., to discuss the civil rights bill and distribute civil rights propaganda.

(7) In *Lincoln, Nebraska,* Governor Frank B. Morrison led a tri-faith service in the state capitol. A committee from the worshipers was dispatched to Washington to call upon Senator Roman L. Hruska.

Meetings similar to these were held the same day in other communities throughout the country (except in the Deep South): Concord, New Hampshire; San Diego, California; Billings, South Dakota; Denver, Colorado; Fort Wayne, Evansville, and Indianapolis, Indiana; and many others.

The mass meetings at the state and local levels were timed to coincide with the Interreligious Convocation on Civil Rights, held the same day in Washington at Georgetown University. Attendance at the convocation was approximately 5,500. The principal Protestant speakers were Eugene Carson Blake and Bishop B. Julian Smith. Blake declared that civil rights legislation "must and will be enacted—and the time is now!" In addition to the overt opposition of the "intransigent Southern Senators," Blake identified as hindrances to the passage of legislation "those who see no clear moral or spiritual issues before the nation . . . who allow considerations of order, peace or profit to neutralize their too-general moral commitment to justice or freedom." Other speakers addressing the convocation were Archbishop Patrick O'Boyle, chairman of the meeting; Lawrence J. Shehan, Archbishop of Baltimore; and Rabbi Uri Miller, president of the Synagogue Council of America. The next day a delegation of 177 religious leaders representing the convocation were invited to the White House by President Johnson, who gave them his solemn pledge to see that civil rights legislation would be passed, even "if it takes all summer."

That same morning the Protestant and Orthodox participants under CORR auspices launched a series of prayer services held once a day, Monday through Saturday, at the Lutheran Church of the Reformation on Capitol Hill. There were 43 services in all during this "prayer vigil," which continued up to the day of the cloture vote in the Senate. Each morning, following worship, a briefing was held to bring the churchmen the latest information on the status of the legislation. Delegations and individuals numbering nearly 1,500 persons came to Washington by chartered bus or car at various times to visit their senators and make known their concern. On 18 May, the tenth anniversary of the Supreme Court school desegregation decision, 270 delegates representing councils of churches, denominational agencies, and United Church Women in 44 states came to Washington to worship at the Lutheran Church of the Reformation and to march in a procession to the steps of the Capitol, where they were welcomed by Senators Hubert Humphrey, Democrat, and Kenneth Keating, Republican, both leading proponents of the bill. The delegates then followed the usual procedure of calling upon the senators from their home states.

The "prayer vigil" in Washington was only the most visible part of the intense propaganda efforts being exerted by CORR. In addition to its own publications, the commission served as a conduit for information originating with its own leaders and allies in the struggle (such as the Leadership Conference on Civil Rights and friendly senators), which was aimed at stimulating grass roots pressure on senators known to be wavering on the cloture issue. Although information was mailed out to a variety of local sources, the primary channels for reaching local church people appear to have been the state and local councils of churches and the local judicatory offices of the various NCC denominations.

These efforts bore fruit. On 10 June the Senate voted cloture on the civil rights bill, 71–29; this was the first time the cloture rule (rule 22) had been successfully invoked on a civil rights measure since its adoption in 1917. The leader of the southern forces, Senator Richard B. Russell of Georgia, conceded just prior to the crucial vote that the cloture movement would never have gained headway had it not been for the pressure from the president and from much of the nation's clergy. In his Senate speech Russell stated,

> During the course of the debate, we have seen cardinals, bishops, elders, stated clerks, common preachers, priests and rabbis come to Washington to press for passage of this bill. They have sought to make its passage a great moral issue

although he himself insisted it was "strictly a political issue." [8] Coming from a leader of the opposition, Russell's remark is conclusive evidence of the power wielded by church groups on the measure.

Within a year of passage of the 1964 Civil Rights Act, CORR joined with other groups promoting a similar measure concerned with the matter of voting rights. While CORR's involvement in the 1965 campaign was by no means as significant as its 1964 actions, it went out of its way to manifest concern and support for the forces led by Martin Luther King, Jr., who had organized a series of mass demonstrations to protest discrimination in voter registration and other injustices in Selma, Alabama. Initially, CORR was not itself involved in the demonstrations, although Spike made his sympathies unmistakably clear when he publicly blasted the Hammermill Paper Company shortly after the beginning of the protests for the timing of its announcement of a plan to build a $30 million plant in Selma. Noting that the announcement made no mention of open hiring of black people, he remarked that it demonstrated "either the height of naïveté or the depth of racism." The company later admitted that the issue of open hiring had not been raised in its negotiations with the city of Selma.

The commission was drawn directly into the Selma situation in the aftermath of violence between demonstrators and state troopers occurring on Sunday, 7 March, at the Edmund Pettus Bridge. The morning following this bloody confrontation, in the words of a CORR newsletter, the "Commission's switchboard was buzzing before all the office lights were on with calls from clergymen in all parts of the country enquiring how they might best manifest concern." Later in the day a telegram arrived from King urging clergymen to join a ministers' march on the Alabama state capitol in Montgomery. From this point onward the commission was fully represented on the Selma scene, though it was careful to play a subordinate rather than a leadership role.

As events in Selma generated momentum for new civil rights legislation on the voting rights matter, CORR shifted its attention to Capitol Hill. On 12 March, within a week of the Pettus Bridge incident, the commission joined forces with Roman Catholic and Jewish groups to sponsor a large rally of 3,500 people at the Lutheran Church of the Reformation, scene of the "prayer vigil" a year earlier.

A few days later the Johnson administration submitted to Congress its voting rights proposal, and the commission lost no time in joining hands with representatives of the other two major faiths to voice organized religion's support. The following month Spike, sharing the rostrum with Vice-President Humphrey, addressed a dinner for congressional leaders. So great was the Johnson administration's congressional support at this time, and so effectively had King succeeded in mobilizing public sentiment, that the role of the NCC and other interest groups was modest. Nevertheless, the fact that the three faiths appeared before the House Judiciary Committee and otherwise made known their active concern probably helped to remove the issue from the realm of partisan controversy and make it possible for both Republican and Democratic members of Congress to support the measure on moral grounds, thereby avoiding charges of partisan opportunism.

Lobbying activity in Washington was not the only, or even necessarily the most important, expression of CORR concern with racial problems during the Spike era. One of CORR's most significant achievements was the launching of the NCC's Delta Ministry Project in the fall of 1964.

The Delta Ministry grew out of contacts between NCC leaders and Mississippi civil rights activists made at the June 1963 funeral of Medgar Evers, the slain leader of the National

Association for the Advancement of Colored People. Originally CORR's aim had been to act as a force for mediation and reconciliation between white and black Mississippian churchmen. Shortly after its founding, it had helped sponsor an interracial and interdenominational worship service in Clarksdale, Mississippi, from which a number of black people had gone to "kneel in" at local white churches. The white leadership of the city had sternly rebuffed the overtures of CORR and secured an injunction from a local judge forbidding any further activity, including the "kneel-ins." During the fall of 1963 and the winter and spring of 1964, the commission became involved in a variety of civil rights efforts in the Mississippi Delta, including voter registration, raising bond money for arrested civil rights workers, and developing community centers. It endeavored to avoid becoming embroiled in mass protest demonstrations and confrontations with constituted authority so as not to alienate moderate whites.

On the basis of these initial experiences, the CORR field staff became strongly committed to the idea of establishing "freedom schools" where black people could be taught their constitutional rights and instructed on how to realize their political potential. As a way of furthering this idea, CORR offered to sponsor a curriculum conference in New York in March 1964. In addition to CORR field workers and representatives of the Council of Federated Organizations (COFO), a Mississippi civil rights coalition, conference participants included leading social scientists, educational consultants, historians, and social workers. An agreement emerged out of the conference to organize a "freedom summer" in Mississippi, with CORR paying for the training and transportation of volunteers.

As the nature of the NCC's "freedom summer" commitment became more widely known, opposition began to mount, especially in Mississippi, where the local reaction was hostile and vitriolic. In remarks made on the floor of the U.S. Senate, John Stennis, Mississippi senator, charged,

The invasion of Mississippi this summer by outside racial agitators primarily under the so-called Mississippi summer project is sponsored by the Council of Federated Organizations—

COFO. The National Council of Churches has announced adoption of a tentative budget of $250,000 to support a task force which will come to Mississippi this summer.[9]

Stennis inserted in the *Congressional Record* an editorial from the *Shreveport* (La.) *Journal,* which read in part,

In its issue of March 11 the [Harvard] *Crimson* attributes to Claude Weaver, SNCC worker and Harvard student recently released from jail in Jackson, a statement that Negroes might start killing the white people in Mississippi pretty soon. "Yes," Weaver was quoted as saying, "if we wanted to get a small Mau Mau going, it wouldn't be difficult. Might be a nice summer project." In its editorial of March 12, the *Crimson* speculates upon the coming invasion of Mississippi as follows: "This summer will witness a massive, daring, probably bloody, assault on the racial barriers of Mississippi. The 1964 plan calls for an invasion of over 1,000 Peace Corps type volunteers, in order to shake Mississippi out of the middle ages. . . ." So there you have it. There is the explanation of why the National Council of Churches is lobbying alongside the NAACP for passage of the infamous civil rights bill. No longer content to sponsor such mild interracial activities as its annual observance of "Race Relations Sunday," the NCC now sponsors an integrationist movement which it expects to end in violence.[10]

Governor Paul Johnson of Mississippi, angered by what he believed was an impending invasion by "organized revolutionaries," requested funds from the legislature to increase the size of the state police force from 275 to 475 and authority to use the enlarged force for "unrestricted" enforcement purposes. The state senate considered, but later sidetracked, a bill requiring all schools to be licensed by the local county school superintendent and banning all schools supporting disobedience to the laws of Mississippi. Rumors circulated widely among Mississippians of planned mass assaults by black men on white women and of plots of black cooks to poison food. A Letter to the Editor of the *Jackson Daily News* reflected the thought in some circles:

It is incredibly criminal and cowardly for a group calling themselves the Council of Churches to send young students out to prepare a blood bath that would invite a death dealing shower of hot lead. Have these Marxist-mannered ministers who plan to flood our state with their guerrillas never heard of the scripture which warns "Whatsoever ye shall sow, that shall ye also reap"? We are glad that they served notice of their intention to bathe us with blood, otherwise we might not have been ready for our bath.[11]

Though white Mississippi was the center of the opposition to the "freedom summer" plans, opposition also came from outside the South. At the end of April, the original northern training site for NCC volunteers was unexpectedly canceled; and other church-related structures withdrew their support under threat of retaliation.

It is unnecessary to document the many facets of the "freedom summer" projects or assess their long-term significance. Briefly, the NCC was directly responsible for training some 800 (mostly white) recruits for the Mississippi "freedom schools." Any lingering optimism about the possibility of achieving changes peacefully was dissolved with the news that three of the first volunteers, Chaney, Schwerner, and Goodman, were reported missing, later to be found murdered. Even before this event council leaders had begun to have grave doubts over the willingness of white Mississippians to respond reasonably to the NCC effort. Despite its utmost attempts not to give offense, the NCC was perceived as a threat to the established order and its every move seemed to intensify suspicion. At the same time, NCC leaders became increasingly convinced that significant change would require a long-term commitment and the deemphasis of crash programs like "freedom summer." These were the factors that entered into the decision, announced on 1 September 1964, to found the NCC Delta Ministry Project as a separate administrative unit of the council, with its own staff and its own governing commission.

The Delta Ministry reflected the conviction, by this time widely shared among council leaders, that various social problems were not separable from one another, except, perhaps, for purposes of analysis. An action program, it was realized, could only be fully effective if it took account of the interconnectedness of issues. One observer, writing in 1965, summed up this interrelationship:

It is necessary to see the Delta Ministry's current activities in their relationship to the whole civil rights program, for they are carried on in context. For example, community leaders emerge through concern with local issues, as witness the work of the health committees. Voting rights means improved schools. A mill picket line means more jobs, more money. The promise of a job gives the illiterate the incentive to learn to read; thus increased employment is related to the literacy training program.[12]

The observer's statement indicates how much the NCC's action program in Mississippi had changed. What had begun early in the summer of 1963 as a series of narrowly focused, specific commitments in the areas of voter education, literacy training, and legal aid had become in two years' time an interlocking cluster of activities aimed at assisting local black people to become an effective force in Mississippi politics. The notion that the NCC might serve as a force for reconciling the black and white Protestant church people was not altogether abandoned, but in actual practice this goal gradually gave way to that of providing the more disadvantaged group with an institutional ally. By 1966 an NCC evaluation committee headed by Dr. A. Dale Fiers, executive head of the Christian Church (Disciples of Christ), and former Arkansas congressman Brooks Hayes concluded that "the Delta Ministry has become the number one civil rights organization in Mississippi . . . the best financed . . . [and has] produced results far beyond the gross activity of other civil rights groups." Despite continuing opposition to it among conservative churchmen, by 1969 the ministry had a field staff of 35 persons, 30 of whom were black and only 5 of whom were white.

CORR IN THE PAYTON ERA

It is always hazardous to fix a precise moment for a shift in an organization's strategy in dealing with a complex matter. While surface events can be dated with accuracy, underlying forces having their origins at indeterminate points in the past are more difficult to date. This caution is applicable to the shift in the NCC's approach to racial matters from that of the legislative-civil rights period (1963 to 1965) to one involving an emphasis on black people's social and economic needs. A change in focus had been emergent in CORR for some time. It became manifest in the six-month period of early June to early December 1965. In accounting for the strategy change, one must consider developments both external and internal to the NCC.

A change in the external environment was signaled by President Johnson's address, "To Fulfill These Rights," delivered at the Howard University commencement on 4 June 1965. In the speech Johnson called attention to the fact that for blacks "freedom is not enough" and advocated an attack on the special nature of black poverty and the "breakdown of the Negro family structure." The speech aroused much initially very positive comment. On 6 August the president put his signature to the 1965 Voting Rights Act, which many supporters hoped would help to take the struggle for equal justice off the streets and place it before legislative bodies and the courts.

Such hopes were dealt a rude blow less than a week later, when, on 12 August, the Watts Riot erupted in Los Angeles. Watts apparently helped crystallize backlash sentiment among many whites. Among civil rights leaders the riot tended to result in an abrupt shift of focus from the rural South to northern urban ghettos, where the issue, as leaders defined it, required urgent action to combat unemployment, police harassment, the dead-end nature of many jobs, and other factors that led to hopelessness and despair among the black population. Increasing stress was placed on the basic structure and character of the black urban community: its seething discontent, its pathologies (including family breakdown), its deprivation as compared to white communities.

These developments on the national scene were paralleled by internal changes in the NCC. Late in the summer of 1965, Eugene Carson Blake was offered the position of general secretary of the World Council of Churches. His decision, not announced publicly until several months later, was to accept. The new position would require Blake's leaving the country and taking up residence at the WCC's headquarters in Geneva, Switzerland, and his abrogating his official posts in American Protestantism, including the chairmanship of CORR. Knowledge of Blake's impending departure was evidently a factor in the thinking of others on the commission. About the same time Robert W. Spike was offered a highly attractive position as professor of social ethics at the University of Chicago Divinity School. Spike accepted the offer and left the council in mid-November.

This same period of August to October was one of special significance for Benjamin F. Payton, who would soon be selected as Spike's successor in CORR. At this time he was on the staff of the Protestant Council of the City of New York (since renamed the Council of Churches of New York City), where he had come following several years as a faculty member of Howard University. During the months of July and August, Payton had engaged in writing a critique of the so-called "Moynihan Report." Moynihan's central thesis was that a breakdown in the black family structure, produced in large part by the very high unemployment rate among black males, was creating a generation of black youths unable to compete effectively in American society. It was the contention of Daniel P. Moynihan, assistant secretary of labor, that the ascendancy of a *matriarchal* pattern in the black community was structurally incompatible with black effectiveness in the larger white society, the essential structure of which was *patriarchal*. In his critique Payton voiced his distress over what was, to his mind, a dangerously misplaced emphasis on family breakdown in the "Moynihan Report" and a tendency to give inadequate importance to joblessness in the ghetto, which was, as Payton saw it, the central issue. He endeavored to develop an "alternative framework" to the Moynihan thesis. Payton circulated copies of his critique to a wide circle of friends in the academic and social work communities, and his analysis quickly won acceptance among many black and some white leaders who, like Payton, had come to view the "Moynihan Report" as a slur on the black family.

Also about this same time the Johnson administration was preparing a White House Conference to be held in 1966 on the underlying causes of black disability, interest in which had been generated by President Johnson's Howard University speech. Just two weeks prior to Payton's appointment to the

NCC staff, he and Moynihan directly confronted each other at a public meeting in Washington called to lay plans for this conference. The two men, both of whom were participants on a panel dealing with "The Family: Resources for Change," squared off against each other in an impassioned verbal exchange. Moynihan was astonished that Payton's critique should have accused him of having played down the importance of social and economic remedies, since, in his mind, the issue of joblessness had been clearly set forth in the report as the root of the whole problem. Payton heatedly retorted that most readers of the report had failed to see it as calling for action on the job front. Though the exchange between the two men settled nothing, the growing support for Payton's position among black leaders present at the conference was the primary factor in striking the issue of the black family from the agenda of the White House Conference. The continuing bitterness Moynihan felt over the matter was reflected in an article written for a national magazine some months later, in which he characterized Payton's critique as "the apotheosis of the big lie" and deplored the nefarious influence of an "organized Protestant opposition" in scrapping the black family issue.[13]

The decision to appoint Payton, regarded as a controversial figure among both white liberals identified with the Johnson administration and some black leaders, would deny CORR some of the advantages enjoyed during Spike's tenure as director. At the time of his resignation, Spike enjoyed reasonably good White House contacts and a broad measure of support among the more liberal of the council's constituent bodies. His relationships with civil rights organizations were correct though rather distant; Spike was acknowledged as having some claim to be consulted prior to the announcement of major decisions, but was still on the periphery of the movement's leadership core.

Interviews conducted by Lee Rainwater and William L. Yancey shortly after Payton's appointment, but presumably before he had a chance to chart his own course, found that although civil rights leaders regarded the Commission on Religion and Race as useful to the movement as a source of "push, money and manpower," they did not wholly trust it, since

CORR members were alleged to be "on the make" and "trying to be more militant than anyone else." [14] Payton would face this same essential distrust but would enjoy few of the compensating advantages accruing from contacts with Protestant denomination leaders and the White House. Presumably Daniel Moynihan's high standing among officials in the Johnson administration would predispose them to accept his version of the dispute, despite the fact that Payton had gone to some lengths to direct his criticism solely at Moynihan's thesis and had repeatedly praised Johnson's Howard University speech as being constructive and timely. Payton's appointment also helped intensify doubts about CORR's intentions among moderate civil rights leaders like Whitney Young, Roy Wilkins, and Bayard Rustin. Quite apart from Payton's own personal views and temperament, his appointment came at an inopportune moment because it roughly coincided with a reduced interest in racial issues among executives and board members of NCC constituent denominations, upon which CORR ultimately depended for support. There was a growing feeling that race was a divisive issue and that poverty should now be given priority, although Payton's own work would not be overtly interfered with.

While he was thus regarded as controversial by the more moderate wing of the national civil rights movement, Payton's image within liberal Protestant churches could scarcely have been more favorable. Several persons close to his selection remarked in interviews with the author that Payton was an obvious choice, "a natural for the job," as Eugene Carson Blake put it in a March 1969 interview with the author. It was believed that as an ordained clergyman and a black, Payton could exploit his connections in the black churches to involve black churchmen more actively in the NCC's racial efforts, something that had been difficult to achieve as long as the commission's officials were mainly white. Second, he was accustomed to working in interdenominational Protestant agencies, having served as head of the New York Protestant council's race division, having had a hand in organizing the 1963 March on Washington, and, finally, having operated a training school for voter registration volunteers in the 1964 "freedom summer." Third,

he possessed outstanding academic qualifications, for he held
a Ph.D. in sociology from Yale. His critique of the "Moynihan
Report" had aroused favorable reactions among liberal Protestants generally, as witnessed by the treatment accorded his
views in the *Christian Century* and *Christianity and Crisis.*
Fourth, he was rather young, only 32 years of age, and this was
probably in his favor.

In the course of his dispute with Moynihan, Payton had
already indicated the general lines of policy he would follow as
CORR director: he would emphasize the need for a clear-cut
statement of *federal* priorities, a statement that should primarily
address itself to the interrelated problems of joblessness, low
income, and lack of comprehensive planning for metropolitan
areas; the pathologies afflicting black urban dwellers (of which
black family breakdown was perhaps one, but not the most
basic, causal factor); and, finally, the need to reassert the
dignity, pride, and self-respect of black people, particularly
against well-meaning whites who too often in the past had
usurped leadership from blacks.

A few weeks later he made it clear that this might require
the repudiation of policies long adhered to by the NCC that
were now looked upon by many black churchmen as evidence
of timidity and lack of genuine concern. He ridiculed Brotherhood Week, Race Relations Sunday, and other such ceremonial
expressions of interracial brotherhood as "little aspirins by
which we salve our consciences"; and he proposed their abandonment. The real test, he told the NCC's General Board
meeting in St. Louis, is "our ability to identify with the suffer-
ings of others." [15]

Payton's application of these general principles to a definition of specific programs was to emphasize ghetto community
organization for the purpose of lobbying Congress, community
self-development, and the fostering of group pride and self-
respect among black people. Payton's thinking on these matters
diverged from that of the Johnson administration and the
established civil rights organizations NAACP, Urban League,
and the A. Philip Randolph Institute. Though all parties were
inclined to favor massive economic aid to black inner-city
neighborhoods, Payton was not as optimistic as others about the

chances of obtaining such aid without first achieving some major changes in political priorities.

Payton's differences with the civil rights establishment were illustrated by the marked divergence of opinion over the 1966 "freedom budget" proposal. The "Freedom Budget for All Americans" was put forward by a group of civil rights leaders of which A. Philip Randolph, a venerable figure in the protest movement, was the spokesman. The budget advocated a federal commitment of $185 million over a ten-year period for raising millions of Americans above the poverty line. The original sponsors endeavored to enlarge their base of support by securing endorsements of the proposal from other groups. An effort was made to secure Payton's endorsement as the NCC spokesman on racial matters. When he failed to respond favorably to an initial contact, further efforts were made to reach him through high-level NCC officers, again to no avail. Payton's thinking on the matter, which owed a good deal to the ideas of Columbia University professor Seymour Melman (author of *Our Depleted Society*) was that a massive spending proposal must carry with it a commitment to a reordering of priorities such that the problems of the central cities took priority over the Vietnam War effort and military spending in general. Though realizing that a withdrawal from Vietnam was unlikely given the present political climate, Payton feared adding to the cynicism of ghetto residents caused by the fact that in the past far-reaching promises and proposals had not brought any basic improvements.

"Freedom Budget" advocates had a different view of the matter. Leon Keyserling, who had worked out its monetary concepts in conjunction with other leading economists, insisted that the budget would require neither new taxes nor a drastic cut in Vietnam War expenditures. Its entire cost, he maintained, could be met through the "economic growth dividend," which would accrue to the federal treasury from the rising yields on existing taxes.

In private conversations and other informal ways Payton pressed his objections to Keyserling's views with considerable force. He was reluctant, however, to air this "in-movement" dispute before the general public. The closest he came to doing so was in an article published in the United Church of Christ publication, *Social Action,* in which he put the matter in a somewhat veiled form: "the recently-published 'Freedom Budget' evades the fundamental moral issue of economic priorities and does not project a strategy by which the budget it projects can be gained." [16] In December 1966 he persuaded the NCC General Board to pass a resolution endorsing his notion of a "priority program" for cities and challenging the emphasis being placed by the Johnson administration on the war effort.

DEMISE OF CORR

A few weeks subsequent to the adoption of the General Board resolution, however, Benjamin F. Payton announced his decision to resign from the council. Though the offer of an attractive and challenging post as president of Benedict College, a black institution in Columbia, South Carolina, was presumably a factor in the timing of his decision, it is apparent that the job offer was only incidental to his resignation from the council scarcely 18 months after his appointment.

Four factors have been set forth by Payton's associates as helping to account for his decision. First, Eugene Carson Blake's resignation in the spring of 1966 and departure from the country that fall tended to isolate Payton in efforts to win compliance for his views. In a March 1969 interview Blake willingly accepted personal responsibility for the frustrations Payton had encountered: ". . . we let him down—we failed to provide the backup he needed to do an effective job." Moreover, in October 1966, Robert W. Spike, still a supporter of CORR's work from his position on the University of Chicago Divinity School faculty, was murdered while attending a conference at Athens, Ohio. (The person responsible for Spike's death has never been brought to trial. There is no direct evidence to suggest that his death is attributable to his controversial civil rights activities.) Without Spike's and Blake's support, there was really no one closely identified with the commission who commanded sufficient prestige in the NCC constituent churches to shield it effectively from its well-placed critics.

Second, there was Payton's rift with the moderate civil rights leaders, especially Whitney Young, Roy Wilkins, and Bayard Rustin, over the "freedom budget." This apparently aroused doubts among some in the council who were inclined toward the moderate position.

Third, there was a growing struggle in each of the member denominations between those who wanted the "religion and race budget" sustained and those who wanted a cutback in this area and who opposed the separate racial programs (counterparts to CORR) for the cities. The counterpart agencies within the larger liberal denominations were themselves placed on the defensive at this time, and this indirectly weakened CORR.

Fourth, one must take account of Payton's inability to get wholehearted support for his *economic* approach to city problems, even though he managed to secure "formal" approval for this strategy at all decision-making stages in the council. Payton was never explicitly rebuffed, but he was made conscious of growing uneasiness.

It is worth noting that on all the focuses of dispute above (the second, third, and fourth factors), Payton enjoyed the unstinting support of the other black executives on the commission, James Breeden, Anna Arnold Hedgeman, and J. Oscar Lee. It was not accidental that Payton and the three others all left the council at about the same time, Breeden in March and Lee, Hedgeman, and Payton in the summer of 1967.

Payton's departure coincided with a decision to reorganize the commission, to reduce its budget drastically, and, in effect, to downgrade it bureaucratically. In its new form the commission became the Office of Religion and Race within the newly created Department of Social Justice, whose other constituent offices dealt with religious liberty, economic life, social welfare, ministry to migrants, and poverty. It was not initially made explicit whether this reorganization meant that the Religion and Race office could continue to enjoy the special mandate granted CORR by the NCC General Board in June 1963, but it later became apparent that the mandate indeed had lapsed. On the other hand, by 1970 the council had filled the posts of director and assistant director of Racial Justice, and these persons continued to carry forward the traditions begun by Spike and Payton.

CONCLUSIONS

The implication is clear that the Commission on Religion and Race enjoyed a broad mandate in the council and a substantial measure of constituency support only as long as the issues with which it concerned itself were mainly focused on the South, especially in those areas of the South where the NCC had never enjoyed a great deal of support among local ecclesiastical leaders. Though actions focusing on these areas might be controversial among local residents, they did not prove to be particularly disruptive in the council's own internal affairs. When the focus of the "freedom revolution" shifted to the northern urban areas, however, the tendency to define urban problems as being primarily ones of race was less acceptable. CORR's activities now became controversial within the organization, in part because churchmen, who in many cases had supported the council over the years, now perceived its work as threatening, in part because a number of persons concerned with the problems of low-income people, both urban and rural, felt that the time had come to deemphasize "race" in order to forge a more effective coalition among the poor and disadvantaged of all racial and ethnic backgrounds.

Events inside the council thus paralleled, in an interesting way, the trend in alliances and cleavages that occurred in the U.S. Congress. When racial injustice was seen there as being essentially a southern phenomenon, controversy tended to fall along sectional lines, with an embattled southern minority opposed by a much larger and increasingly determined alliance of northern and western interests. As the civil rights issue became national in scope, however, the sectional nature of the struggle faded. The race issue now became a divisive issue among the parties to the previously dominant congressional coalition. In neither the case of Congress nor the NCC did the nationalizing of civil rights result in an abandonment of positions previously taken; but it did result in an increasing reluctance to follow black leaders in their calls for still more drastic steps, a point to be developed at greater length in the following chapter.

Yet despite his evident frustration on larger issues, Benjamin F. Payton's efforts to reorient council thinking toward the structural defects in the American social and economic system were not without their effect. Late in the 1960s the council's General Board endorsed a federally guaranteed annual income for all citizens and a program to involve local churches in a united effort to improve living conditions in depressed inner-city areas. CORR's early concern with the problems of black ghettos found expression only a few weeks subsequent to Payton's departure in the formation of the Interreligious Federation for Community Organization (IFCO), an agency to be analyzed in greater depth in the following chapter. Finally, and not the least important, the Committee of Negro Churchmen, which Payton had helped found, continued to be extremely active under its new name, the National Committee of Black Churchmen. If CORR is then to be viewed a "post facto" embodiment of NCC concern with the civil rights crisis of the late 1950s and early '60s, it must also be regarded as itself having influenced the parent body to assume a more activist, economically aware, and power-conscious approach to social problems.

10. James Forman and the "Black Manifesto"

The demise of the Commission on Religion and Race marked an important turning point for the NCC, for it signified that the race issue, once considered an emergency problem to be dealt with by an ad hoc agency functioning in large part outside regular channels, was now an essential organizational concern and accordingly would be assigned to an already constituted unit of the NCC, the Division of Christian Life and Mission. This involved no necessary retreat from the racial activism of the CORR era, but it did involve a rechanneling of organizational energies.

Yet there was an important measure of continuity in the events preceding and those following Benjamin F. Payton's 1967 departure from the council. Payton's stress on the importance of institutional racism and economic exploitation of minority groups was carried forward in the months subsequent to his departure, especially by the even more articulate caucuses of black churchmen. Late in the 1960s there was an increasing belief that the major, predominantly white denominations, in view of their earlier support of CORR and other civil rights programs and their continued openness on racial issues, might be moved to make contributions to the redress of black grievances on an unprecedented scale. As this mood of expectancy became widespread among black church activists, there was a growing cleavage and antagonism betwen militant blacks and moderate-to-liberal whites. This interesting period is best discussed in relation to the actions of James Forman, whose "Black Manifesto" and call for "reparations" was accorded much attention in the mass media and whose militancy constituted a major issue for NCC leaders.

EVENTS OF MAY–JUNE 1969

Briefly stated, the particulars of James Forman's confrontation with the NCC are as follows: On Sunday, 4 May 1969, Forman, a leader of the Student Nonviolent Coordinating Committee (SNCC), led a delegation of black militants in disrupting an 11:00 A.M. communion service at New York's Riverside Church, located on Riverside Drive immediately across a side street from the Inter-Church Center, national headquarters for the National Council of Churches and several of its constituent denominational bodies. Forman had previously contacted the pastor, the Reverend Ernest T. Campbell, expressing a desire to appear in the church to read the "Black Manifesto," a list of demands recently approved at a national meeting of black leaders in Detroit (see pp. 191–93). Campbell had granted this somewhat unusual request, stipulating only that Forman not interfere with the communion service. When Forman chose to ignore the stipulation and rose to deliver his message in the middle of the service, Campbell, the associate ministers of the church, the choir, and several score of the 1,500 people in the congregation walked out, returning only after Forman had finished reading the manifesto and, along with his cohorts, had left the church. Photographs of Campbell's departure from the church and accounts of the event were given prominent attention by the national wire services and television networks, and by nightfall the news was the subject of anxious discussion across the country. On subsequent Sundays allies of Forman interrupted services in leading local churches in other cities in order to read the manifesto and demand that churches contribute the sum of $500 million to establish a "black development fund."

Coinciding with their demands to be heard by local congregations, the militants launched a series of demonstrations at the national headquarters of the major Protestant denominations. Though Forman had on 1 May presented his list of demands to the Episcopal Church (chiefly for $60 million), the demand for funds from denominational bodies received little attention until after the Riverside Church confrontation three days later. On 14 May the Forman forces turned their attention to denominational headquarters located in the Inter-Church Center, on this occasion "liberating" some of the offices of the United Presbyterian Church. Staying for various lengths of time, the militants took over certain offices of the United Methodist Church on 22 May, the Reformed Church in America on 5 June (remaining there 5 days), and the executive offices of the National Council of Churches and, again, briefly, the offices of the United Presbyterians on 6 June. On 9 June, Forman called a strike against all 19 stories of the Inter-Church Center. Though his claim that the occupation was 80 percent successful is perhaps exaggerated, there is no question that for several days the militants succeeded in drastically disrupting the work of the 28 organizations in the center, which employs around 2,200 persons. Picketing was at all times peaceful, and no effort was made to physically interfere with those who wished to enter the building; but several organizations chose to shut down their operations rather than have their black employees cross picket lines where signs were being carried denouncing any black entering the building as "house niggers."

On 17 June the Board of Trustees of the Inter-Church Center went into court and obtained an injunction barring Forman and his followers from engaging in further disruptive tactics at the center. In response Forman called a news conference, at which he denounced "the racist Christians" and dared them to try to enforce the injunction. He went on to call upon "those so-called 'brave Christians' who were eager to march in Mississippi, to interpose their bodies between the police and me," and advocated a "splintering of the Church between those willing to fight racism and the Church bosses who perpetuate it." [1] Despite the defiant oratory, however, Forman ordered his followers to withdraw, and there were no arrests. Nevertheless, he vowed to continue his campaign of disruption until the money he demanded as "reparations" for centuries of white injustice against black people was provided him. Yet by mid-August his group had raised only about $20,000, three-quarters of which was from a local Methodist church in New York.

Having thus described the events that transpired at Riverside Church and the Inter-Church Center, let us consider their significance, both for the NCC member bodies and for the Forman forces.

BACKGROUND TO THE EVENTS OF MAY–JUNE 1969

A convenient date to begin a discussion of the Forman movement is with the founding of the Interreligious Federation for Community Organization in September 1967. IFCO was created as a vehicle by which the three major religious faiths in the United States (Protestant, Catholic, and Jewish) could pool their funds in order to achieve a coordinated effort in the field of community organization, especially in inner-city ghetto areas. By the spring of 1969 its membership included 13 Protestant denominations (11 of which had paid the prescribed $1,000 membership fee) and representatives of the Catholic and Jewish faiths. The 40-member board consisted of 22 blacks, 2 Roman Catholics, 1 Spanish-American, the remainder being Jews and white Protestants. In its first 18 months IFCO spent around $1.5 million. Protestant churches had provided almost all of this sum (96.4 percent); and the Jews and Roman Catholics, only token amounts (3.4 percent and 0.2 percent, respectively).

Though the board and staff were racially integrated from the outset, the work of IFCO made it particularly receptive to the growing mood of black self-consciousness and separatism. It was thus not surprising that when it decided to schedule a conference for late April 1969 for the purpose of exploring the relationship between community organization and the broad question of economic development for millions of blacks, the invitations to attend the meeting should be extended to blacks only. Known as the National Black Economic Development Conference, the meeting was held in Detroit and was attended by more than 500 delegates. An early decision was to exclude white reporters.

James Forman, who was one of those invited to the meeting, chose to gamble on the willingness of the other participants "to be taken over." [2] On 26 April he introduced, and requested his fellow delegates to approve, a "Black Manifesto," the central theme of which was that the predominantly white churches and synagogues of America shared in the guilt of centuries of racism in America and that they therefore owed the black people "reparations." The figure Forman arrived at was $500 million ("$15 per nigger"), but this was raised to $3 billion subsequent to the conference. The manifesto was quite detailed concerning how the money would be used: a southern land bank to secure land for black farmers, black-controlled publishing and broadcast enterprises, research and training centers devoted to the needs of black people, organizations to uphold the rights of welfare recipients and workers who strike to protest racist working conditions, a fund to develop cooperative business in the United States and Africa, and the establishment of a black university to be located "in the South." The manifesto also proposed the creation of a National Black Economic Development Conference (NBEDC) to serve as a steering committee for the expenditure of the funds.

Of equal significance to the program of the manifesto were the contents of Forman's impassioned introductory speech, "Total Control as the Only Solution to the Problems of Black People." [3] In it Forman identified the freedom struggle of American blacks with the suffering of oppressed peoples in other lands, in particular Africa, Santo Domingo, Latin America, and Asia, all of whom, he maintained, were "being tricked by the power structure of the U.S. which is dominating the world today." He spoke of the need for a revolution "which will be an armed confrontation and long years of guerrilla warfare inside this country" and of a solution involving "total control." This term meant "a society where the total means of production are taken from the hands of the rich people and placed in the hands of the state for the welfare of all the people." Since black people have been the most exploited group in the U.S., Forman reasoned, they should "move to protect their black interest by assuming leadership inside of the United States of everything that exists." He ended by declaring that "we" have the "revolutionary right" to seize power at the conference based on the program of the manifesto.

The debate at the conference following Forman's address was not over its rhetoric, but over whether Forman's specific proposals were radical enough. The manifesto was approved overwhelmingly, 187–63 (the fact that over 100 delegates abstained is presumably significant). In effect, the conference abandoned its IFCO parentage.

The National Black Economic Development Conference began to take shape at once, and by July a twenty-six member steering committee had been named. Of the six clergymen on the committee (all black), five at the time were identified with one of the predominantly white denominations; the one exception, the Reverend Calvin B. Marshall, a member of the African Methodist Episcopal Church and its steering committee chairman, until recently had been a member of the predominantly white Episcopal Church, which he served as a deacon. This is a significant point and it will be returned to in a moment. Up to the present writing the conference had no separate staff or office facilities and instead relied on facilities made available by black staff members of the NCC.

IMPACT OF THE FORMAN "CONFRONTATIONS" ON ECCLESIASTICAL STRUCTURES

Forman's "revolutionary" step at Detroit and his disruption of services at Riverside Church a week thereafter precipitated an immediate crisis in IFCO and had a significant, though less dramatic, impact on the racial strategies of its member denominations. Several publicly repudiated it when its board failed to denounce the "Black Manifesto." The American Jewish Committee forthwith withdrew from membership. The Synagogue Council of America and the National Jewish Community's Relations Advisory Council issued a joint statement denouncing the manifesto's demands and the related tactics as "objectionable on both moral and practical grounds." Though some influential Catholic journals of opinion, such as *Ave Maria,* were

inclined toward the view that the church had been implicated
in the exploitation of blacks and should manifest an attitude
of contrition, the leaders of the Catholic hierarchy who took
the trouble to comment were vehement in their criticism: the
official publication of the Archdiocese of Baltimore labeled
the proponents of the manifesto "ideological stunt men"; the
Archdiocese of New York flatly rejected the demand that it give
NBEDC $200 million.

The National Council of Churches found its own constituency sharply split on the matter, with certain of its supporters
inclined to enter into conversation with NBEDC, or in some
cases to increase their contributions to IFCO as an indirect
consequence of Forman's appeal for funds, while other churches
were inclined to reject altogether Forman's diagnosis of the
problem as well as his proposed solution.

It was the more liberal members of the council's constituencies who proved themselves the more sympathetic, though
none were prepared to go along with the concept of reparations. A leading Methodist official commented to a reporter for
the *New York Times,* "The controversy has 'unglued our bureaucracies' and made it possible for us to shift priorities away
from traditional projects like elementary schools and concentrate on community organization and other work with the
disadvantaged." [4] The agency vested with responsibility for
arranging the 181st General Assembly of the United Presbyterian Church invited Forman to address the delegates assembled at San Antonio, Texas. Subsequent to the address the
General Assembly voted to appropriate $100,000 toward meet-
ing IFCO's needs, a substantial increase over its previous donations to that body. The newly elected Presbyterian Church
moderator, George E. Sweazey, later commented that Forman's
address at San Antonio showed him to be "the most disturbing
critic of the churches from the militant point of view" and
affirmed that "We need to hear him, to listen thoughtfully to
him, to try to understand what he represents." [5] The Executive
Council of the Episcopal Church voted to give $25,000 to an
Episcopal Black Caucus of Clergy and Laity and also made
available office space in the Episcopal Church headquarters in
New York. There is evidence that another organization exer-

cising an influence on NCC thinking in racial matters, even though it was not, strictly speaking, a member organization, the National Committee of Black Churchmen (NCBC), felt a profound identification with Forman's activities and that its thinking became more radical as a result. The Reverend J. Metz Rollins, NCBC executive director, told an interviewer, "There's no question that Jim Forman's actions have forced us into a more unified and radical stance." [6] The NCBC national board released a statement referring to Forman as "a modern prophet" and supported increased funding for ghetto community organization.

In the case of IFCO itself, the events in question were an embarrassment, since it had provided Forman with the forum he needed and now found itself in direct competition with him for funds. On the other hand, Forman's actions also appear to have benefited it by adding a new sense of urgency to its requests. Thus, while IFCO took certain steps to demarcate the line separating it from the Forman-backed NBEDC, it was evidently with Forman's actions in mind that IFCO's executive director became more outspoken: "The church isn't yet convinced in its very guts that a crisis exists," he told the NCC General Board early in May; "The churches are playing with the crisis, and while they are playing with it, it has gained momentum!" He went on to refer caustically to the "meager" funds allocated the IFCO in the budgets of most NCC churches.[7]

The more conservative NCC denominations, however, were decidedly unfriendly to Forman's actions. The president of the National Baptist Convention, the nation's largest black religious body, compared the manifesto to Marx's "Communist Manifesto" of 1848 and unequivocally declared that his denomination would "neither share in nor contribute to the fund that the NBEDC is seeking to share." [8] (The word *share* was an allusion to the fact that the NBEDC was proposing to serve as a conduit between donating white churches and recipient black groups.) The executive head of the Christian Church (Disciples of Christ), Dr. A. Dale Fiers, made public his belief that the NBEDC was a "movement which is admittedly Marxist and subversive in character" and urged his constituency to write the NCC opposing the manifesto.[9] Only somewhat less pointed was the criticism implicit in statements released by John F. Anderson, executive secretary of the Board of National Ministries of the Presbyterian Church in the U.S. (Southern Presbyterian) and by Edwin H. Tuller, general secretary of the American Baptist Convention.

While these statements were not voiced publicly until mid-summer, it is clear that a diversity of opinion had begun to develop among NCC leaders as early as a few days after the Detroit conference. The NCC General Board was unable to reach consensus on the matter at its regular meeting of 1 to 2 May. The pro-Forman forces at the meeting emphasized what one official termed the "blatant injustice" of the contemporary American racial situation and called upon the NCC to maintain its traditional role as a leader on social issues by extending Forman the hand of friendship. Yet other leaders, including some who had recently been deeply involved in the council's racial program, emphasized the danger of a revolt among the rank and file if action were taken in any way favorable to Forman. As an interim move a resolution was agreed upon in which the board cautiously affirmed that it "shared in the aspirations of the black people of this country" and requested the NCC Executive Committee to consider more specific action at its next meeting, scheduled for 23 June, more than seven weeks away.

In view of all that went on during the intervening seven weeks (for example, Forman's "confrontations" at Riverside Church and the Inter-Church Center and evidence of restiveness against him among constituent churchmen), one might have expected the Executive Committee to have taken an uncompromising stand against the manifesto and its adherents. In all likelihood this would have been the response if the opinions of Protestant church people at the grass roots level had been the decisive factor. A Gallup poll conducted in June revealed that more than 90 percent of the American people rejected the notion that the churches and synagogues owed black people $500 million in reparations. The NCC received a flood of mail from constituents critical of Forman.

Instead, however, the Executive Committee passed a resolution that was quite conciliatory, though not endorsing the manifesto outright. The statement referred to "the great injustices done to the black and brown man by Christian white men throughout the entire history of our country" and expressed concern over "the increasing race gap between white liberals and the new black movements." The resolution alluded to "the need for penitence and a readiness to make recompense," adding, "we confess that we have no right to appear before the altar of God so long as this priority has not taken possession of us or in any moment of time when we have renounced it." [10] In what was the closest any official organ of American Protestantism had come to recognizing the NBEDC, the Executive Committee went on to call for the member churches "to develop, in cooperation with the yet-to-be-established National Black Economic Development Corporation, programs of mutual interest and concern." It was also voted to appoint a delegation of 16 churchmen to "enter into consultation with" NBEDC for the purpose of recommending program proposals for the NCC, reporting back on its proposals by 14 July. The initial NBEDC response to this gesture was negative, as has been its continuing response to NCC funding proposals over the last several years.

Though the factors contributing to the Executive Committee's surprisingly conciliatory response have not been spelled out in published accounts, three factors may well have had an important bearing on it. First, Forman himself had in several ways shown himself to be what NCC leaders might have construed as reasonable. For example, he had reappeared at Riverside Church a week after his initial 4 May confrontation and had at that time refrained from disrupting services; for the moment at least, he seemed prepared to accept a statement from the church's elders indicating that some of his demands might be met, though others were rejected as being "unrealistic." In addition, despite the revolutionary slogans and sweeping denunciations of the "white racist establishment" that had accompanied his occupation of the Inter-Church Center early in June, since then Forman had restrained his forces from actions that might have rendered further negotiation impossible. On 16 June, just after issuance of the injunction banning further picketing of the center, he had dismissed his assistants from the "liberated" sixteenth floor (the United Church of Christ's Board of Homeland Ministries), thus keeping them from being arrested, and had announced later in the day that the floor was being returned to its original occupants. In view of the tradition in the civil rights movement of willingly accepting jail sentences when necessary to accomplish strategic goals, Forman's restraint seems to indicate a desire not to push his advantage too far.

A second factor that may have entered into the decision was evidence of restiveness among Inter-Church Center personnel over the decision to seek a court injunction. At what must have been an extraordinary meeting on 18 June, the NCC staff voted to urge its general secretary, R. H. Edwin Espy, to seek a reversal of the injunction request. The staff members also decided to form an Ad Hoc Committee of Center Employees, whose purpose was to act as "a humanizing force between the polarizing opinions at the Center." [11] There was known to be considerable adverse feeling among the staff over the fact that when officials of the center were deliberating on whether to seek an injunction, no black was drawn into the discussion.[12] Creation of the ad hoc committee presumably put the Executive Committee on notice that decisions in the sensitive area of racial policy would henceforth have to take into account the possibility of a "palace" revolt by headquarters personnel if black militant demands were not accommodated to some degree.

A third factor, though more indirect than the other two, was the fact that those churches identified as liberal in chapter 3 enjoyed a clear majority (13) of the 22 members present at the Executive Committee meeting. Among the member churches with a pronounced conservative bias, on the other hand, only two delegates were present, one each from the National Baptist Convention and the Syrian Antiochian Orthodox Church. Delegates from middle-of-the-road churches made up the balance. Since, as suggested above, most liberal denominations were more receptive to the NBEDC than the more moderate and conservative churches, the greater liberal representation at the meeting was a factor contributing to the decision reached.

ANALYSIS OF STRATEGY

It is paradoxical that James Forman and the other black militants, in their desire to focus on the alleged "institutionalized racism" of American society and in seeking substantial financial aid, should see fit to confront, almost as a first priority, the nation's main line Protestant churches. Protestantism had not, after all, shown itself unresponsive to the black "freedom revolution," at least not since June 1963. The singling out of Riverside Church for the first major confrontation also at first seems ironic, in view of the fact that it had for a number of years maintained a more than tokenly integrated staff and Sunday school enrollment and had taken the lead, through its FM radio station, WRVR, in focusing on the needs of black citizens in New York.

Yet on closer examination these considerations can be shown to miss an essential point. It was not the fact that main line northern Protestantism had proved itself indifferent to the needs of black Americans that made it such an ideal target, but rather the fact that the churches' efforts (inadequate as they were) has served to arouse higher black expectations of the churches than of other structures in society. If the churches could take one step in the "right" direction on the basis of their own consciences, some black leaders reasoned, might they not now be induced to take several more, given a little pressure?

In relative terms the sum the Forman forces asked for was not as unreasonable as some whites at the time suggested. "The real wealth of American churches," one writer remarked, "runs into tens of billions of dollars in property, deposits and investment portfolios. Religious organizations take in $6.5 billion a year in members' contributions." [13] Viewed in this perspective, Forman's demands might even appear to have been somewhat modest! Disregarding his more incendiary *statements* and his Marxist *rhetoric* (which implied that the churches were beyond redemption), Forman's *behavior* was consistent with the view that the churches, although not the "enemy," were, as long as they failed to identify completely with the cause of black liberation, nevertheless "racist." Since racism is a grave sin, which the churches presumably wished to expiate, the pressure of Forman's militants was designed to capitalize upon white Protestant guilt. In strategic terms, the white church leaders had to be confronted with the issue and given an opportunity to come to terms with their own consciences. Thus, "liberating" the Board of Homeland Ministries of the United Church of Christ, the offices of the NCC, or any of the other church agencies had a somewhat different tactical purpose than the civil rights demonstrations had had early in the 1960s in the South. In the southern case the county sheriff and local white power structure had typically been assumed to be impervious to direct pressure; but they could be moved, it had been thought, if civil rights demonstrations could induce the intervention of a powerful third party, the national government. The southern strategy, then, had been to provoke the sheriff into extreme actions. In the 1969 case, however, there is no evidence that any such outside intervention was sought, nor was it essential to success. A certain measure of sympathy was assumed on the part of the opponent, and the aim was to goad the white churchmen into doing "right."

Assessed in these terms, Forman's tactics can be termed a partial, but by no means unqualified, success. Some of his actions were decidedly counterproductive. His extravagant rhetoric at the Detroit conference, tinged with overtones of class warfare and black supremacy, alienated a number of potentially sympathetic white church leaders whose good will would be necessary in drawing open the denominational purse strings. More importantly, Forman's extremism allowed churchmen to slip off the hook of their consciences and reject his proposals out of hand. The statements apparently appealed to the blacks in his immediate audience, many of whom might not have responded so enthusiastically had he been more temperate, and Forman doubtless had this consideration in mind when he delivered his Detroit speech. It is also unclear what strategic purpose was served by the NBEDC's swift rejection of the NCC Executive Committee's 23 June resolution. It is possible, of course, that the black militants, after weeks of effort, had begun to despair of success and were inclined to interpret conciliatory words as mere lip service, but assuming they still hoped for financial aid, the rejection scarcely makes sense.

Yet, whatever one's judgment on these specific points, there can be little question that Forman's strategic situation was an unusually difficult one, one that even the most gifted strategist might have found perplexing. In the first place, his power base was less than secure. The largest black denominational body implacably opposed him, and the thinking of the other all-black denominations probably ran roughly parallel. Forman could count on the support of the various black caucuses (largely composed of local pastors) in the predominantly white denominations, and he received some backing from the National Committee of Black Churchmen.

Yet lacking a staff of his own, he also had to consider the views of the black staff personnel in the NCC who came to his aid. Since the salaries of these men were ultimately derived from the budgets of the major white churches, which mainly supported the NCC, this part of his constituency could scarcely be regarded as fully in the Forman camp. If Forman was too *successful* in generating trouble for the churches, the level of white financial support was likely to decrease and many of the more vulnerable staff positions were likely to be eliminated. In a small way such a decrease in financial and bureaucratic support was soon to occur. By August 1969 the National Council of Churches made public the fact that it would not be able to meet its projected $25 million budget and was thus forced to reduce staff in six program areas. Substantial cuts were made in the programs of the Department of Social Justice and the Department of Church Renewal. Those in the NCC interviewed by a *New York Times* reporter gave Forman's activities as a major contributing factor in the financial stringency.

In view of these considerations, Forman's ongoing confrontation tactics may indeed succeed in drawing attention to black demands, but only in a manner that does injury to many of the blacks with a stake in the predominantly white churches and in the NCC. Also, NBEDC success in raising funds in Protestant churches is quite likely to be at least partially at the expense of the black-oriented community-action programs that Protestant churches are now funding and in which blacks have long since been accorded the main leadership role. Forman himself alluded to this problem during the Inter-Church Center sit-in, when at one point he criticized the churches for their alleged willingness to give money to their own black administrators as a way of sidestepping the NBEDC. The relationship between the Forman forces and civil rights activists on the NCC headquarters staff might thus be characterized as one of antagonistic symbiosis, in which both sides need the other (in their common desire to exert pressure on the assemblies and chief executive officers of the main line churches), but in which neither side can altogether trust the other, since the success of one may be at the expense of the other.

Though the Interreligious Federation for Community Organization has become the broker between the white liberals and black radicals, this role is likely to be difficult to fulfill to the satisfaction of all parties concerned. Black strategists are no longer decisive as to exactly what staff level of representation they should seek within the NCC.[14] Until this is decided, no stable patterning of roles is likely to emerge.

NBEDC AFTER ONE YEAR

As of the spring of 1970, a year after the manifesto's appearance, the National Black Economic Development Conference was still a going concern. While its total income for the 12 months, $300,000, amounted to only a small fraction of the sum initially requested, the agency was nevertheless in a position to employ a staff of 30 persons and to carry on programs in Philadelphia, Detroit, Cleveland, and Chicago. Its Black Star Press, located in Detroit, and its printing arm in Philadelphia were publishing black newspapers and periodicals for the four cities. At an Inter-Church Center ceremony called to recognize the first anniversary of the confrontation, James Forman and the Reverend Calvin Marshall, conference chairman, renewed earlier calls for church reparations and expressed confidence in the continuation of progress.[15]

But relationships between the NBEDC and the main line churches remained uneasy. One observer, writing in an official United Presbyterian publication, reported his skepticism about and dejection over the possibility of church acceptance of the basic issues raised by the manifesto: "I have heard many pejorative adjectives and much ad hominem snarling about the manifesto and its authors," he wrote, "and a minuscule bit of serious examination and discussion. . . . The manifesto's demand for reparations has met massive resistance."[16] Recent months had produced a "crisis of trust" between black caucuses and denominational establishments, he added. He cited the case of the presbytery of Philadelphia, which, when presented with an NBEDC demand for $50,000, voted to give nothing to the demanding group, offering instead the sum of $60,000 to a caucus of black Presbyterian clergymen, an offer which the latter group summarily rejected on the grounds that the original request should have been met.[17]

It was also a matter of concern that fully two-thirds of conference income the first year had come from a single source, the Episcopal Church, and that opposition within that body to further funding was mounting. In the summer of 1970, top officials of the United Presbyterian Church, a body whose social views generally parallel the NCC's, rejected the concept of reparations, noting that while churchmen "have particular obligations to those whom we have treated unjustly and from whose oppression we benefit, . . . no amount of money can make amends for the wrongs blacks (and other minority groups) have suffered in this nation, and to assume that we could fulfill our obligations through the mere payment of reparations would be a mistake." The churches could be most effective, the leaders maintained, by using their influence to wring concessions favorable to blacks from government agencies, labor unions, private foundations, and so forth.[18] At roughly the same moment the Board of Christian Education of the Presbyterian Church in the U.S. (Southern Presbyterian) voted to withdraw from membership in IFCO, though other large denominations continued to support it.

CONCLUSIONS

The relationship between the National Council of Churches and the National Black Economic Development Conference resembles in its competition for leadership that existing between the council and leaders of the civil rights movement from 1963 to 1965, as analyzed in chapter 9. As a predominantly white body, the motives of the NCC in involving itself in the race issue are, and were, suspect among many blacks. Yet the impressive resources the Protestant churches can make available (including money, political leverage, bureaucratic resources, and access to communication media) make it unlikely that the black leadership will fail to find some place for white Protestantism in their strategic planning. In 1969, as in the earlier period, the difficulty in the choice facing the National Council of Churches lay not primarily in the question of whether to identify with the black "freedom revolution," but rather in the question of which of several competing black leadership groups was the most valid spokesman for the black community.

It is plausible to suggest that the NCC's continuing difficulty in dealing with black militant groups arises more out of differences in style than in matters of substance, though, of course, substantive differences also exist. The style of the black protest leader is not that of the white liberal activist. The protest leader appears uncompromising, inflammatory, receptive to strategies of overt conflict, even of violence, and is critical of those within his constituency who would seek accommodation within the political system. Were he to deviate from such a style, at least before securing a firm organizational base, he might weaken his credibility among blacks and be outflanked by some would-be leader even more militant than he is. Yet, while an inflammatory style may be initially helpful to the black militant leader in fending off rivals, it may prove a hindrance if later he is obliged to turn to white liberals for help in meeting expenses. Liberals are prone to take the rhetoric at face value and become alarmed over its implications.

Since the NCC's constituency is predominantly white, negotiations between its leaders and black militants have a considerable capacity to generate controversy in the council. In the

1960s it proved possible to contain such controversy, thus to prevent its disrupting the organization; whether it can be similarly contained in the 1970s is an open question. One reason it is likely to be a more troublesome problem in the future is that black churchmen are no longer as prepared to defer to white Protestant leaders on racial matters as they once were. It will be recalled that the decision to involve the Protestant churches in the civil rights struggle was urged by *white* liberals. Although the council at the time had a race relations office (with a black executive) and for many years had black churches among its constituent bodies, the formulation of the resolution adopted by the General Board on 6 June 1963 involved blacks only indirectly. In addition, the churchmen subsequently appointed to direct the civil rights effort in the 1963 to 1965 period were in almost all cases white. It was felt, rightly or wrongly, that the blacks in executive positions in the NCC and in the major black churches were not likely to break with their well-defined style of action, viewed by some as accommodationist and dated, in order to relate positively to the mood of extreme impatience that had recently come to the fore in the area of civil rights.

In more recent years black churchmen, especially those identified with the predominantly white churches, have coalesced and begun demanding concessions. All main line Protestant churches with a significant number of black members have witnessed the organization of black caucuses. This change in mood doubtless owes something to the growing list of black leaders who achieved martyrdom in the mid-1960s, especially Martin Luther King, Jr., and Malcolm X. In response to this pressure and the growing emphasis on racial pride in the black community, the predominantly white churches have recently begun channeling funds into IFCO and other black-led community-action groups. In one or two cases, the American Baptist Convention most particularly, denominations that had not been especially active in the NCC's civil rights efforts in the early '60s but have a significant percentage of black members have begun to commit substantial funds to racial action programs.

James Forman became the common point of reference for

the various black caucuses. The fact that he had good credentials as a protest leader yet was not an ordained clergyman and had not been actively involved in church affairs probably helped him win support. His success could not be construed as a victory for any one faction of black churchmen, thus it did not provoke jealousy. In a larger sense, one may anticipate that Forman's ascendancy will be looked back upon in future years as having marked the point at which leading white churchmen were obliged to assign a larger role to black churchmen in planning action programs, not just in the area of race (narrowly conceived), but in the whole field of social action. Forman himself may not continue to fulfill this catalytic role for any lengthy period of time, especially in view of his fragile base of support; but a single spokesman appears to be a functional necessity if the various black caucuses are to avoid working at cross-purposes. Were Forman to falter, one can anticipate that some other black leader would step forward to assume his role.

II. The NCC and National Educational Policy

*A*s noted in the preceding chapter, the motivation for Protestant-Orthodox involvement in reform causes stems in part from a biblically founded imperative to seek social justice and in part from a desire to project a strong, forceful image to the nation. While this interplay between transcendent moral principle and institutional self-protection was apparent to some degree in the area of civil rights, it was even more visible in the area of national educational policy. While the Protestant-Orthodox churches for many years found it possible to accord racial issues low priority, not until recently becoming intensely embroiled in civil rights affairs, no such period of indifference has marked their attitude toward education. The churches' stake in the education of young people has always been relatively large, and they have seen to it that their views have been made known to those making the crucial decisions.

Efforts for many years remained at the state and municipal level, since the national government lacked a major educational role. In the past quarter-century, however, educational matters have increasingly become an object of federal government attention, and this has contributed to the NCC's growing involvement. Beginning in the early 1940s and continuing in every session of Congress throughout the '50s and early '60s, bills have been introduced by education-minded lawmakers that proposed general federal aid for primary and secondary schools.

In the same years the federal courts were increasingly involved in deciding cases raising the question of the proper relationship between the principles of religious freedom and secular education. For a time it was possible for the council to avoid coming to grips with the more complex aspects of these policy questions. But in the '60s it was obliged finally to choose between two conflicting positions, each of them strongly supported by vocal and influential churchmen. On the one hand, there were those who insisted on the need for a "wall of separation" between church and state and were prepared to sacrifice, if necessary, federal aid to public education if such aid could be obtained only by agreeing to give some funds (directly or indirectly) to parochial schools. On the other hand, there were those who insisted that church-state separation should not be made absolute, that a "flexible" position was the wisest course from both a principled and a practical standpoint. In the present chapter the discussion will focus on how the council's increasingly self-conscious progressivism found expression in this difficult and controversial area.

ROOTS OF PROTESTANT CONCERN WITH EDUCATION

Prior to the Civil War the stake Protestant churches felt themselves to have in the area of primary and secondary education was highly manifest and action in its behalf was overt, since in many areas of the country, including the larger population centers, common schools were run under church auspices. As the movement for free compulsory, universal, and secular education gained headway after 1865, the churches gradually yielded this direct administrative involvement. Yet neither a cessation of active concern with the schools nor a decline in influence was involved. It was not accidental that in many communities schools were pervaded by a kind of nondenominational Protestantism, apparent not only in such obvious ways as Christmas pageants and daily recitations from the King James Version of the Bible, but also in more subtle ways, in the manner in which history and society were interpreted to students. Even in areas with large non-Protestant populations, school boards were often overwhelmingly Protestant; and the presence of Protestant clergymen on them was by no means rare.

It is scarcely surprising that the Protestant churches should wield their influence in this way. In the absence of an established religion in this country, churches must rely on voluntary support, which will not be forthcoming unless young people receive early religious indoctrination. Though it is customary to place primary stress on the Sunday schools and family as the chief vehicles of religious instruction in twentieth-century America, it is widely recognized that the public schools have important consequences for children's religious beliefs, a consideration that has led Roman Catholics and, in some regions, Lutherans to establish and support their own sectarian schools. Though most main line Protestant bodies have not taken this route, one senses a concern among them that public secular education may inculcate attitudes of indifference, or even antipathy, toward organized religion.

Protestantism has been ambivalent about the movement to strip away the last vestiges of religious instruction from local school systems. It supports the principle of separation of church and state, yet at the same time it affirms that public schools should interpret America's religious heritage in a sympathetic light. Thus, in 1953 the National Council of Churches, in one of its first pronouncements following the merger, had this to say:

> We believe that the public school has a responsibility with respect to the religious foundations of our national culture. It can declare, as the state itself declares, that the nation subsists under the governance of God and that it is not morally autonomous. It can acknowledge, furthermore, that human ethical and moral values have their ground and sanction in God.[1]

Another indication of the NCC's concern is the support it has given, albeit qualified, to the establishment of religious schools where local conditions seem to require it. In a statement issued at the time of the 1961 struggle over the Kennedy administration's school bill, the organization reaffirmed the Protestant view that no government funds should be made available to help defray the operating expenses of religious schools. But the statement went on to affirm, "as Christians . . . [we support] the right of all parents, all citizens, and all churches to establish and maintain non-public schools whose ethos and curriculum differ from that of the community as a whole." The statement even suggested that religious schools were to be encouraged "where the ethos of the public school system is or becomes basically inimical to the Christian education of our children." [2]

These views place the NCC in the middle of most struggles over government aid to sectarian schools. It is unwilling to accept the official Catholic view that government funds should be made available to sectarian schools on the grounds that these institutions help perform a necessary public function and thus deserve equal treatment when it comes to doling out federal school funds. It has been equally reluctant, however, to side with the militant separationists, who would absolutely bar any form of government aid, however indirect, to sectarian schools. Nor can the council afford the luxury of standing apart from the fray, leaving the settlement of disputes to the other contestants—the stakes are too high for this. Given Protestantism's relatively high status in American society and its ambivalent stance on the religious school aid issue, the NCC finds itself placed at the focal point of cross-pressures. On the one hand, the Protestant churches are called upon to be flexible and supportive of a more cooperative atmosphere between Protestants and Roman Catholics; on the other, they are urged by conservatives not to compromise basic doctrinal and constitutional principles for the sake of expediency. The tension between these two conflicting demands as they were felt in the 1963 to 1964 struggle over the proposed Becker Amendment and the 1964 to 1965 battle over the administration's Primary and Secondary School Act is the central theme of the following discussion.

NCC SCHOOL AID STANDS IN THE ERA
OF SECTARIAN RIVALRY (1945–60)

Educational controversy centered around church-state issues has taken a variety of forms. There have been the problem of whether the schools have the right to compel Jehovah's Witnesses to salute the flag, the question of the constitutionality of New York's Released Time Act, and numerous disputes over the holding of Christmas pageants in public schools. Though these issues have been important at the local and state levels, the issue that has most consistently engaged the attention of the National Council of Churches has been the proposed use of federal tax revenues to relieve the tax burden on parochial schools. Generally this issue has arisen in connection with bills proposing to give federal aid to the nation's public schools; though Catholic schoolmen have not been opposed in principle to public school aid, they have consistently asked for corresponding benefits for their schools. For a number of years militant Protestant groups joined hands with fiscal conservatives, the champions of local control of schools, and segregationist southern congressmen to defeat general school aid proposals. Such measures gained considerable favor in the Senate in the quarter-century after 1940 and passed that body in six separate sessions. Prior to 1965, however, the House of Representatives proved itself a legislative graveyard for bills of this type. It is true, of course, that prior to 1965 some federal school aid proposals did pass Congress (the "federally impacted areas" program, the National Defense Education Act, and so forth); but these were directed at specific, narrowly defined categories of need. The really controversial issue, then, was *general* federal aid to local school systems.

The council's position on this matter had once been highly receptive; but as sectarian considerations became central to the issue, its position became increasingly equivocal. When the issue was first extensively discussed in the late 1940s, the Federal Council of Churches took a straightforward stance. In a 1947 resolution it expressed support for federal school aid, stipulating only that it be restricted to "such schools as the constitution or statutes of the several states make eligible for State support." The position was similar to the compromise proposed by Senator Robert A. Taft of Ohio to leave the decision on aid to religious schools to the school authorities in each state pursuant to the state's own constitution and laws. Under Taft's plan, in other words, federal funds might reach parochial schools in certain of the states. But this did not for long remain the council's position:

> Under pressure the Federal Council reconsidered its position. The 1949 hearings on the Barden bill [a federal school aid proposal] came and went without the Council's participation. Late in the year the Executive Committee of the Council approved a new formulation of policy, hardly less equivocal than the old. The Federal Council's new position called for a separation of programs involving aid to schools from programs supplying welfare services to children. Each, the Council suggested, should be considered on its merits, but no aid should be given to parochial schools.[3]

While this Executive Council policy precluded the council's agreeing to direct aid to sectarian schools, it left open the question of what might constitute aid to the child and "services to children." The ambiguities implicit in this notion first became apparent in connection with the demands in many local communities to provide public bus transportation for parochial school children. The agency appointed to speak for the council on such matters, the Committee on Religion and Public Education, was for a time agreeable to using public money for this purpose when a majority of local citizens desired it; but in 1958 the committee changed its mind and decided to oppose public busing of parochial school children. In the opinion of R. L. Hunt, the executive director of the NCC's Department of Religion and Education and the committee's spokesman, the basic objection to this proposal was not primarily the possible infringement of church-state separation, but a more immediately practical concern: that such bussing might tend, unwisely, to extend the "welfare state," pave the way for state interference in religious schools (from which Catholics might suffer as much as Protestants), and compromise religious freedom by making the church schools excessively dependent on outside aid. As of 1958, therefore, the National Council of Churches had yet to spell out what, if anything, might qualify as acceptable under the "child benefit theory," which it had implicitly adopted in 1949. It rejected bus transportation and all other types of support for parochial school children on either constitutional or practical grounds.

The NCC's opposition to direct state aid to sectarian schooling presumably helped reinforce and increase the legitimacy of other, more militant Protestant groups adamantly opposed to even indirect state aid to religious schools. Groups such as the Church League of America, the Supreme Council of the Scottist Rite Order, the American Protestant Defense League, the National Association of Evangelicals, and, especially, Protestants and Other Americans United for Separation of Church and State testified in favor of absolute prohibitions on the use of federal funds to relieve parochial school burdens. The Protestant organizations, allied with the leading public educational groups (NEA, PTA National Congress, and so forth), comprised a potent veto group, which, through the end of the 1950s, successfully defeated all efforts to provide federal aid to religious schools. Since Catholic groups were opposed to legislation that failed to provide benefits to parochial schools, the net result was a stalemate.

PERIOD OF TRANSITION

After ten years in which bills providing for federal aid to primary and secondary schools were defeated in Congress, the chances of securing such legislation seemed to improve following sweeping Democratic victories in the 1958 off-year elections and the election of a Democratic president, John F. Kennedy, in 1960. On 20 February 1961, Kennedy sent his "Message on Education" to Congress, and the matter was a major item on the congressional agenda for a period extending up to the early summer. The Kennedy bill was a comprehensive educational package, including measures designed to benefit higher education (public and private), an extension of the soon-to-expire "federally impacted areas" program, and, most controversial, a three-year program of general federal assistance for *public* elementary and secondary classroom construction and teachers' salaries. Catholic criticism of the program for having excluded the parochial schools was quick in coming. On 1 March the administrative board of the National Catholic Welfare Conference issued a statement vigorously criticizing what it called "discrimination" against Catholic school children embodied in the administration's proposal.

At his 8 March press conference the subject of possible loans for parochial schools took up almost a third of the president's time. Though reiterating his view that across-the-board loans to parochial schools would be unconstitutional judging by his reading of the Supreme Court's 1947 decision in the *Everson* v. *New Jersey* case, the president nevertheless indicated that

> there have been some kinds of loans to non public schools which have been supported by the Congress and signed by the President and about which no constitutional objection has been raised, and the National Defense Education Act is the best example.

It also was significant that the administration's floor manager for the education bill in the Senate was Wayne Morse, who was not only a staunch federal aid supporter, but who was known to feel that some forms of aid for nonpublic schools would be acceptable. Thus, although the bill actually submitted and discussed was strictly confined to the needs of public schools, Protestant spokesmen became alarmed over what they regarded as an implicit threat to the strict separationist stance.

Some people active in the National Council of Churches advocated that it adopt a distinctly "Protestant" (separationist) position and vigorously protest the Roman Catholic statements being made as to the bill's true impact and meaning. Others, however, saw no need to take exception to Catholic statements, since these had not found their way into the language of the bill, which on constitutional grounds was unexceptionable. It was also pointed out that a hard-line stance would involve the Protestant churches in an inconsistency, since many Protestant colleges and universities accepted, indeed solicited, federal aid without fear of censure from denominational leaders. Taking the hard line would also conflict with the emerging spirit of ecumenism, now beginning to dissolve ancient barriers dividing

Protestants and Catholics and would thus threaten the atmosphere of fraternal goodwill.

Late in February 1961 the National Council of Churches endorsed federal aid to public schools, but reiterated its stand against grants out of public funds for nonpublic schools. In response to questioning before House and Senate subcommittees, the NCC witness, Gerald Knoff, spokesman for the NCC Committee on Public Education, expressed the view that the NCC General Board would also probably oppose nonpublic school aid in the form of loans, although thus far it had not acted on the matter. Another NCC spokesman, President Eisenhower's former secretary of health, education, and welfare, Arthur Flemming, however, refused to regard the bill as threatening to church-state separation because it made no explicit provision for parochial schools.

THEOLOGICAL DEVELOPMENTS

Although in testimony before Congress and in other public statements there appeared to be no significant changes in NCC attitudes on educational and church-state matters, important developments were occurring offstage. Among staff and elected officials in the NCC and main line Protestant church headquarters, long-standing antagonisms to the Roman Catholic church were undergoing a significant, if subtle, softening process. According to one informed observer, ". . . the past five years [1959 to 1964] have witnessed a slowly but gradually changing attitude toward Roman Catholicism among Protestant spokesmen and denominational officials. . . ." [4]

This development reflected a change in viewpoint among leading Protestant theologians as to how churches ought to relate themselves to the state. Since the time of the Reformation, Protestant authorities had endorsed either the "Lutheran" or the "Anabaptist and Mennonite" approach to how church and state should be related. Basically, both approaches conceived church and state to be morally autonomous from each other, neither within its proper "sphere" entitled to stand in judgment upon the other. Even a tyrannical government, it was believed, upholds God's will and must be obeyed. These traditional doctrines, essentially European in origin, were strongly reinforced by the experience of most Protestant churches during the American colonial period. Since all the colonies with the exception of Pennsylvania had an established church at one time or another, many of the Protestant sects came to the conclusion that while the establishment of one's own religion might be preferred in principle, not having an established church was preferable to having another, "heretical" church in an established position, which would enable it to support itself out of tax funds and persecute nonconformists. The experience of Roger Williams, who was ostracized from the Massachusetts Bay Colony in the seventeenth century, was prototypical. The decision to disestablish religion and strictly separate church and state, once regarded as the lesser alternative by Protestant leaders, came to be viewed by the end of the eighteenth century as reasonable and proper. The First Amendment to the United States Constitution embodied this notion.

With the growing political strength of Roman Catholicism in the nineteenth and twentieth centuries, Protestant support for strict church-state separation took on renewed strength as a way of minimizing Catholic political influence. By the 1940s secular humanists such as Paul Blanshard could find common ground with many Protestant churchmen in guarding "American Freedom" against "Catholic Power." [5]

By the late 1950s, however, separationist doctrine, though still the dominant tendency, began to be seriously reevaluated in leading Protestant seminaries, especially Union Theological Seminary and Yale Divinity School. A new approach known as "transformationism" was put forward as an alternative formulation. The transformationists argued that one cannot hold as absolute for all time the New Testament outlook on the state ("Render unto Caesar that which is Caesar's. . . . My Kingdom is not of this world"). The ultimate criterion of the church-state relationship should not be scriptural absolutes, but a more flexible and relative one that seeks to

> guarantee the freedom and integrity of political and religious institutions amid many overlapping concerns and issues. . . .
> It recognizes the influence of the church upon the state as a fundamental element of Protestantism, without which Pro-

testantism would be truncated, individualistic, and altar bound, without moral influence upon the important institutions of society.

Of particular importance for the present discussion is the fact that transformationism embodies a willingness to criticize Protestant misrepresentations of Roman Catholicism and stresses the need to avoid using Catholicism as a scapegoat or to regard it as, by definition, a threat to freedom.[6]

By the late 1950s and early '60s transformationism had begun to have a pronounced impact beyond the cloistered setting of Protestant seminaries. Individual denominations began to hold special study conferences to reexamine church-state issues (Congregationalists held such a conference in 1950, United Presbyterians in 1959, and Methodists in 1960). By 1964 nearly all major denominations had manifested an interest in fundamental church-state questions; "in most cases the development [was] from no consistent thought [on the subject] or from separationism toward transformationism."[7] At all stages the staff of the National Council of Churches was significantly involved. The Department of Religious Liberty, under the leadership of the Reverend Dean M. Kelley (Methodist) sponsored a coordinated national study conference on church and state in 1964 and a series of smaller study conferences early in the 1960s. It would be misleading to suggest that Protestant churchmen in large numbers were converted from separationism and suspicion of Roman Catholic intentions. Nevertheless, the rise of transformationist thought did serve in the mid-1960s to challenge the prevailing Protestant consensus on the church-state question and did give intellectual support to the growing minority that was anxious to explore new directions.

Reinforcing this trend was a parallel change in Catholic thought and attitudes. One observer has suggested that 25 December 1961, when Pope John XXIII officially convoked Vatican Council II for the following year, was the turning point in the Catholic stance.[8] As an outgrowth of the new mood generated by Vatican II and particularly in response to the "Decree on Ecumenism" of 21 November 1964, a series of "working groups," comprising Catholic bishops and major non-Catholic denominational bodies (Presbyterian, Episcopal,

Methodist, and Orthodox) were launched in 1965 under the auspices of the World Council of Churches and the Vatican's secretariat for christian unity. Working groups continued to meet through 1967 and helped engender a new era of dialogue and mutual respect. In July 1966 a Jesuit priest, Father David J. Bowman, became associate director of "Faith and Order" studies on the staff of the National Council of Churches, the first Roman Catholic to serve on the administrative staff.

Changes on both the Catholic and Protestant sides of the fence were thus clearly evident by 1964. While neither side was prepared to depart from positions previously adopted regarding the church-state issue, there was a new mood present that fostered a desire to interpret earlier statements flexibly so as to mitigate as much as possible the previous atmosphere of sectarian rivalry.

CRYSTALLIZATION OF A NEW CONSENSUS (1964–65)

Books and articles published by seasoned observers as late as 1964 predicted that it was unlikely that church-state separation would ever be compromised or that federal aid to education could be passed in the decade or so immediately ahead. Coupled with the intractableness of the church-state issue were other serious political obstacles: the insistence of civil rights groups upon a proviso stipulating a willingness to desegregate as a precondition to receiving federal aid, a condition unacceptable to southern congressmen and senators; the issue of federal control, viewed as a threat to the autonomy of local school boards; and the interminable disputes over the formula to be employed in the distribution of funds. Thus, federal aid to education was viewed not as a single conflict, but as a multiplicity of conflicts; and to two informed observers it seemed "plausible that the difficulties faced by a federal aid bill have multiplied within the past few years and seem likely to increase in the immediate future." [9]

The passage of the Elementary and Secondary School Act of 1965 was soon to demonstrate that such a conclusion was excessively pessimistic, for the obstacles to general aid to education were in fact becoming less potent in the early 1960s. It is not the purpose of the present discussion to enter into an exhaustive or comprehensive analysis of the 1965 act, or even to offer a full-fledged exposition of the church-state settlement implicit in it, since these topics have been covered in other works. Rather, the analysis will focus on changes in Protestant church thinking as these were reflected in behavior leading up to passage of the bill.

The passage of general school aid legislation in 1965, after a quarter-century of effort during which school aid supporters had frequently despaired of success, required not only the committed support of a strong president, but also the removal of certain major roadblocks. Of these, two were of critical importance: first, the refusal of the southern congressional bloc to go along with legislation making school aid contingent upon the willingness of southern schools to desegregate (originally known as the Powell Amendment); and second, the church-state question arising out of the determination of Catholic leaders to see to it that the proposed measure offered significant benefits to parochial schools.

The first of these two problems was dissolved by the electorate in the 1964 presidential and congressional elections. In defeating Senator Barry Goldwater President Johnson accumulated 61.0 percent of the total vote, a landslide victory of devastating proportions, which slightly exceeded even Roosevelt's 60.7 percent margin in 1936. Whereas the impact of FDR's 1936 victory had been mitigated by the increased power of the southern conservative bloc in Congress also resulting from the 1936 elections, Johnson's victory was coupled by a great increase in liberal congressional strength, especially in the House of Representatives, which in recent years had tended to be the more conservative of the two houses. In the election the Democrats picked up 38 House and 2 Senate seats, giving the president's party a majority of 295–140 in the House and 68–32 in the Senate. With majorities of this magnitude, it would no longer be possible for southern congressmen to find sufficient northern Republican support to defeat social welfare measures to which the president was committed.

Like no other before it, the Eighty-ninth Congress was dominated by northern urban Democrats. A school bill with school desegregation "teeth" in it could now be pushed through, no matter how strongly the southerners protested. Related to these developments was the fact that Adam Clayton Powell, a strong supporter of federal school aid, by virtue of seniority now assumed the chairmanship of the House Education and Labor Committee, where the liberals were also firmly in the majority. In short, the Democratic landslide demolished for the moment the veto power of the southern Democratic-Republican coalition. This left only the troublesome church-state issue as an obstacle to federal school aid legislation.

Immediately after the election, the president asked the commissioner of education, Francis Keppel, for an education bill that would avoid a church-state fight. Earlier in the year the president had appointed a task force on education headed by John Gardner, then president of the Carnegie Foundation, whose report (submitted in mid-November), although informative concerning leading educators' insistence upon the need for federal aid, was of little help in resolving the delicate matter of federal aid to private and parochial schools. The heart of the process that resolved the church-state issue lay in a series of meetings and informal negotiations late in 1964 involving principal groups and forces that had in the past contended over federal aid. In particular these included representatives of the National Catholic Welfare Conference; the National Education Association; key congressional leaders like Carl Perkins, chairman of the educational subcommittee of the House Education and Labor Committee; and two other highly respected members of that committee, congressmen John Brademas and Hugh Carey. (Carey represented the position of the Roman Catholic hierarchy on aid to education.) The National Council of Churches, though not as regular a participant as some other groups, was represented at all critical sessions by Dean M. Kelley. Though details of the legislation to be introduced by the administration were never systematically discussed at these meetings, the participants did have a chance to weigh and evaluate their respective positions; and the fact that none of the key groups involved (the National Catholic Conference, the NCC, the NEA) subsequently came out in opposition to the proposal was one of the major results.

Despite the work of the Gardner task force and the informal consultations with group leaders late in 1964, the bill as presented to Congress by the president on 12 January 1965 contained a number of novel provisions, on which many large organizations, the NCC included, had not yet made up their minds. The contents of the bill were not made known to concerned groups until the day the president sent it to Congress. Hearings before the General Subcommittee on Education were scheduled for 22 January, only ten days later, and the committee leadership deliberately rushed them by holding Saturday sessions. Hearings thus came peremptorily to an end only 18 working days after the bill's proposal, on 2 February. This haste was apparently a deliberate attempt to forestall controversy (a successful strategy as it turned out). The Senate hearings were more leisurely but less important, since all the major issues had been decided in the House. The stringent time pressures resulting from the manner of the bill's introduction and handling by administration floor leaders significantly affected the ability of NCC leaders to provide for adequate representations, a matter to be taken up later.

Compared to previous school aid bills, the terms of the proposed legislation were unique and represented the most serious effort to date to arrive at a formula that would sidestep the church-state issue. At no time did the administration propose direct aid to parochial schools; instead it accepted the alternative of directing the aid to the child ("child benefit theory"), an approach Justice Department lawyers were willing to certify as constitutional. The particular application of the "child benefit theory" that had received greatest attention in recent years was the concept of dual school enrollment, or "shared time," as it is sometimes called. Under this arrangement a child attending a private school is allowed to take part of his courses in a public school, thus permitting the student the best of both public and religious education. The religious school receives no public funds directly, but it can save money by eliminating some subjects or some services.

Although some anxiety was felt by the National Council of Churches over what seemed "unprecedented and dangerous" federal control involved in Title I (the details of which need not concern us here), the deepest fears were aroused by Titles II and III. Title II provided $100 million for the purchase of library resources and other instructional materials "for the use of children and teachers in public and non-profit private elementary and secondary schools." Under this section public school officials were required to approve all books and materials purchased through the program, thus eliminating the danger of having public funds used for direct indoctrination. Once this requirement was met, the materials usually became a permanent part of the parochial schools' resources. Early in the hearings an administration witness conceded that the White House's intention was to make grants directly to parochial schools under this title, at least in the 32 states where the state constitution did not proscribe federal aid to parochial schools. Furthermore, in those states with constitutions prohibiting such aid, the bill specifically authorized the U.S. commissioner of education to provide library and instructional resources directly, thus bypassing state agencies and constitutions. If state constitutions were to be so circumvented, the NCC and its allies queried, what was to prevent the U.S. Office of Education from doing so every time an education act aiding parochial schools was passed?

There were also constitutional objections raised against Title III of the bill, which provided $100 million in grants to initiate a system of federally supported educational centers and services. To encourage innovation and to avoid the educationally dated influence of certain local public school establishments, the bill provided that Title III aid be channeled through an administrative system consisting of a "consortium" or partnership. The language of the bill made it possible for grants to go to any agency in a community, public or private, secular or religious, as long as one public school was represented in the consortium. The NCC staff regarded this as "a significant departure from traditional church-state relationships." [10]

In summary, the National Council of Churches was receptive to the legislation insofar as it offered real help to the nation's public schools. It was prepared to accept federal aid that would indirectly assist parochial schools provided that such aid clearly followed the "child benefit theory." Although the

General Board did not explicitly endorse the "child benefit" approach until its meeting of 26 February (which issued a statement that was simultaneously adopted, with only slight variations, by the American Jewish Committee), it had been generally open to this approach for some years. The NCC's most serious objections were aroused by provisions in the act (especially in Titles II and III) whose rationale was not the "child benefit theory," but necessity for direct aid to parochial schools, and that, inadvertently or not, opened up a number of church-state problems. On these points the NCC was not prepared to compromise. The American Civil Liberties Union and certain interested Jewish groups expressed similar views.

Given the time pressure, the witnesses had more latitude to offer their own interpretation of their organizations' position at the House and Senate hearings than might have been the case had there been more time for internal consultation. It was thus of some significance that the man chosen to represent the NCC, Arthur Flemming, was identified with the movement for federal aid to education. Then the NCC's first vice-president (later to become president), Flemming was president of the University of Oregon and a former secretary of HEW. In testifying before the Congressional Subcommittee, he reiterated the official views of the NCC as laid down in prior years, including opposition to grants to private schools, acceptance of publicly supplied "distinctly welfare services" for private school children, and receptiveness to "experimenting" with dual school enrollment. Yet he refused to see these as obstacles to the present bill. Flemming closed his opening statement with a plea for accommodation and compromise on the church-state issue:

> The church-state issue . . . has been one of the principal roadblocks standing in the way of constructive federal legislation in the areas of elementary and secondary education. It has likewise been a decisive factor in the life of our nation. I hope that all concerned will analyze HR 2362 [the bill pending] with the end in view of doing everything possible to make it an instrument of reconciliation. I believe that it can be. . . . The National Council of Churches is prepared to do anything it can to make HR 2362 such an instrument of reconciliation. The time for action in the area of federal financial assistance to elementary and secondary education is long overdue.[11]

Flemming was subjected to lengthy questioning by the committee. Many of the questions concerned aspects of the bill on which the NCC had no precise stand, and on these he could only communicate his own views and how he thought the General Board might decide. Though lacking the full sanction of the NCC, his response apparently carried considerable weight with the committee. In part this was because other Protestant churches, with the exception of the Baptist and Lutheran, were either inadequately prepared or poorly represented:

The United Church of Christ apparently had no relevant policy. The Methodists had some policy, but it was presented in such a way that the aspects of policy that were emphasized were those of the testifier alone and not those of the Methodist Church. The Episcopalians had just passed a policy but turned over the job of testifying to a local Episcopalian minister who had no political experience, but whose testimony was not only factually incorrect, but certainly conflicted with the views of the presiding Bishop on these issues.[12]

Flemming's impact on the committee was also due to his relative flexibility of approach, which had such a marked effect on the committee members that the amendments later proposed came to be known on Capitol Hill as the "Flemming Amendments." While insisting on public ownership of Title III centers, he was quite willing to permit subcontracting with private schools to provide services. He also accepted, though reluctantly, the concept of public school teachers teaching in parochial schools under Title I. At the very least such flexibility helped offset the views of more doctrinaire Protestant witnesses appearing before the committee. Some of these, like C. Emmanuel Carlson of the Baptist Joint Committee on Public Affairs and Philip Johnson of the National Lutheran Council, were willing to go along with dual enrollment but drew the line at certain provisions Flemming was prepared to accept. Others, like those representing the National Association of Evangelicals and the Unitarian-Universalist Association, were opposed to all the provisions in the bill dealing with parochial school students.

Flemming's flexibility and willingness to consider other points of view had its parallel in a new sense of generosity on the part of Roman Catholic spokesmen. Monsignor Frederick G. Hochwalt, director of the Department of Education of the National Catholic Welfare Conference, the principal Catholic witness, stressed the new concept of partnership between public and private schools and implied a willingness to consider compromises in the working of the bill as long as these were consistent with the "child benefit theory."

The hearings before the House Education and Labor Committee came to a close on 2 February, and the committee then adjourned to executive session to amend the measure so as to make it more acceptable to the various groups. The task was not impossible. The original decision of the Johnson administration to center the education bill around the "child benefit theory" had itself been an accommodation to liberal Protestants and Jews and to civil libertarians who in prior years had objected to grants (or loans) to parochial schools as such. While some groups continued to reject the bill on the grounds that the proposal was only a subterfuge designed to accomplish *indirectly* what was clearly unconstitutional if done *directly,* the fact that the National Council of Churches, the leading Jewish organizations, and the American Civil Liberties Union were receptive to the approach helped to remove the matter from the arena of sectarian religious controversy. The committee made several stipulations that took account of specific objections raised: that property ownership and administration of Title I projects should remain in public hands; that ownership of library resources, instructional materials, and other tangibles to be furnished under Title II should be vested in a public agency only; and, finally, that educational facilities constructed under Title III should be wholly publicly owned. The committee heeded the protests against the consortium concept by placing sole administrative responsibility in public school boards.[13] In this form and without substantial changes the measure was passed by the House and Senate and signed into law by the president.

AFTERMATH OF THE STRUGGLE

It is a debatable point whether the NCC's qualified endorsement of the Johnson administration's 1965 school bill, which rested upon the "child benefit theory," represented a change in policy or simply a logical extension of earlier positions. It does seem significant that the NCC did not go out of its way to find grounds to reject the 1965 bill; had it been so inclined, it could easily have rationalized a stand in opposition, as several Protestant groups in fact did.

Though enactment represented a new peak in mutual understanding among America's three major faiths, the flexibility displayed by council spokesmen did exact the price of increasing factional strife within the NCC. Congresswoman Edith Green, an active supporter of federal school aid in earlier years but a staunch foe of the 1965 measure, broke with the NCC and "went after them tooth and nail" for supporting the bill.[14] Previous to this Green, a highly influential person in educational policy, had been a warm NCC supporter and had involved herself to some extent in its affairs. Also there were to be continuing problems in explaining the complex 1965 settlement to rank-and-file Protestant church people, especially since the act, as reported in the national press (*Time* and *Newsweek* in particular) gave somewhat misleading accounts of the church-state settlement involved, which could be construed as suggesting a sellout to the Roman Catholic position.

Not to have supported the measure, however, would almost certainly have seriously embarrassed the NCC's long-term position in the area of national educational policy. The dilemma confronting the National Education Association (NEA) as described by Eugene Eidenberg and Roy D. Morey was broadly analogous to the situation faced by the NCC:

The [NEA's previously] firm ["rigid" was an adjective used by people in the Office of Education] stand in opposition to aid to parochial schools was leading some people in the Office of Education to see the NEA as an obstacle to compromise on the delicate church-state question. Fear of possible exclusion from the policy making process helped persuade the NEA to go along with an aid formula that would see some funds channeled into the hands of private and parochial schools. In 1965, to be on the side of a minority when education legislation got passed would have left the NEA without influence during the critical period following passage. . . .[15]

Though education obviously is not as centrally important to the NCC as to the NEA, the Protestant churches do have, as noted at the outset of this chapter, a well-defined stake in educational matters and in part share the NEA's need for access to educational officials. Furthermore, in the 1965 issue the NCC had an additional incentive resulting from its increasing identification with the ecumenical movement and its rapprochement with Roman Catholicism. To have opposed the 1965 school act on grounds that aid to parochial school children violated church-state separation might have made the NCC's avowed interest in ecumenism less credible to Catholics, a heavy price to pay. Finally, while the legislative struggle resulted in a few defections from the growing coalition between liberal Protestants, liberal Catholics, and Jews, the general effect seems to have been to strengthen the coalition. It was without precedent for liberal groups like the American Jewish Committee, the National Catholic Welfare Conference, and the National Council of Churches to line up side by side in endorsing the same education bill. In terms of the NCC's desire to remain relevant to contemporary political conditions in the United States and, more basically, to protect Protestantism's good name in American society, its decision to go along with the 1965 education act can be looked upon as both prudent and farsighted.

SEPARATIONIST DOCTRINE AND THE SCHOOL PRAYER ISSUE

The decision of NCC executives reached late in 1964 to endorse rather than oppose a general school aid bill that incorporated some indirect aid to sectarian schooling might suggest that the organization was beginning to weaken in its ideological commitment to church-state separation. Notwithstanding what the council at the time claimed to be the fundamental assumptions on which it acted, some observers have construed its actions as expressing a sympathy toward increased amalgamation of the religious realm and the political order. One can test the correctness or falsehood of this impression by examining NCC behavior on another education issue that came to a head in 1964: the issue of prayer in the public schools.

In 1962 the United States Supreme Court, in the case of *Engle* v. *Vitale*, struck down the so-called Regents' Prayer, a theistic (though nonsectarian) prayer prepared at the behest of New York educational officials and recommended by them for recitation in the public schools of that state. Although the Regents' Prayer was defeated on rather narrow grounds (the court majority was not against school prayers per se, but objected to the fact that an agency of government had taken upon itself the task of formulating a prayer), it was believed that the *Engle* decision foretold an even more sweeping decision by the court on the then-pending cases challenging Bible reading and recitation of the Lord's Prayer, as permitted in the laws of numerous states. A case challenging the state of Maryland Bible-reading statute was pending and was expected to be decided by the court in its 1963 term.

Alarmed by what he believed the Regents' Prayer decision portended, Congressman Frank Becker filed a proposed constitutional amendment the day after *Engle* v. *Vitale* was announced. The Becker Amendment was worded simply: "Prayers may be offered in the course of any program in any public school or other public place in the United States." The amendment aroused immediate support, not only from conservatives, but also from some liberals such as Professor Reinhold Niebuhr and Bishop James A. Pike. Pike maintained that in the *Engle* decision "the Supreme Court has just de-consecrated the nation." On 3 July 1962 the Conference of State Governors passed a resolution without a dissenting vote approving the Becker proposal. There were but a few Protestant churchmen willing to voice support for the court's action. Senator James O. Eastland of Mississippi scheduled a hearing of his Senate judiciary subcommittee, which gave ample opportunity for Becker Amendment supporters to voice their opinions and endeavor to build public support. In the absence of support among congressional floor leaders, however, the proposal made little legislative headway for the balance of the 1962 and early 1963 sessions of Congress.

In June 1963, however, the Supreme Court handed down its long-awaited Lord's Prayer and Bible-reading decision, *School District* v. *Schempp*. The court held against religious recitations in school as a violation of the "establishment" clause of the First Amendment. Although the public response to *Schempp* on the whole was rather mild compared to the earlier reaction to *Engle* (partly because the former decision was anticipated), the reaction of one strategically placed body, the organized county and state public school officers, was highly adverse and vocal. It was estimated that the Bible was read in 76 percent of the southern schools, 67 percent of the schools in the Northeast, and 42 percent of the schools in the nation as a whole. School officials bore the responsibility for implementation of the school prayer edict, and many were antagonistic to it. Congressman Becker, having decided not to seek reelection in 1964, wholeheartedly dedicated himself to mobilizing public support against the decisions and achieved significant results. Congress was inundated with pro-Becker Amendment mail. In August 1963 a group of six congressmen who shared Becker's views on the school prayer cases got together and redrafted the amendment, and it was this revised measure that was before Congress when the struggle reached its climax in 1964.

Congressman Emanuel Celler of New York, chairman of the House Judiciary Committee, was a strong opponent of the amendment movement. At first Celler attempted to defeat the measure by exercising his prerogative as chairman to refuse holding hearings. But as his opposition began to marshal support behind a discharge petition, the effect of which would have been to remove the proposal from his committee's jurisdiction and bring it directly to a House vote, Celler finally consented to hold hearings, scheduling them for late April.

Up to this point no particular effort had been made to build a coalition of liberal forces in support of the Supreme Court's school prayer rulings, since the Becker Amendment had not seemed likely of passage. Given the growing manifestations of public support for the Becker proposal, however, a group of liberal leaders (Protestant, Jewish, and civil libertarian) met on

St. Patrick's Day, 1964, and organized themselves into an ad
hoc committee. It was believed that the proposed school prayer
amendment would easily gain House approval if it reached the
floor during the first flush of public enthusiasm, so the anti-
amendment forces decided upon an all-out campaign to insure
that the measure did not leave committee. The ad hoc committee members named one of their number, Dean M. Kelley
from the NCC's Department of Religious Liberty, to serve as
coordinator. The choice of a Protestant for this key post was
significant, since the Jewish community was more unanimous
and vocal on the issue than were the Protestant churches and
a Jew might have seemed the logical choice. But Jewish
leaders were acutely sensitive to the opposition's effort to minimize the importance of anti-school-prayer sentiment by defam-
ing opponents as "Jews, atheists, and Communists." Kelley, a
Protestant clergyman, would help deflect such criticism.

In subsequent weeks Kelley served as the channel through
which pressure was applied to the Judiciary Committee. This
pressure originated not only at the grass roots level, but among
opposition congressmen otherwise silenced by the charge of
proamendment forces that only antireligious people opposed
the measure (no congressman wished to appear antireligious).
Through Kelley's office these congressman were "amazed to
learn of the existence of others among their colleagues with
parallel views, and this gave them encouragement to take a
more forthright stand."

The Kelley Committee's immediate goal was to attempt to
reach uncommitted members of the committee through personal visits in the hope of reversing the balance of committee
sentiment. This involved visiting congressmen's offices and making arrangements for articulate and highly esteemed witnesses,
Protestant, Catholic, and Jewish, to testify in opposition to the
proposal before the committee. Perhaps the most significant of
these witnesses was a group of Protestant clergymen: Eugene
Carson Blake, stated clerk of the United Presbyterian Church;
Arthur Lichtenberger, presiding bishop of the Protestant Episcopal Church; John Wesley Lord, Methodist bishop of Washington, D.C.; Edwin Tuller, general secretary of the American
Baptist Convention; and Frederick Schiotz, president of the

American Lutheran Church. Their appearance had a profound impact on the Senate Judiciary Committee because congressmen had previously taken it for granted that Protestant leaders were friendly to continuance of prayers in the public schools. The Kelley Committee also helped arrange for the testimony of a group of prominent constitutional scholars, including professors from Harvard, Columbia, and Michigan and esteemed Catholic jurists from Boston College and Georgetown. The cooperation of prominent Catholics was particularly important, both from the standpoint of the outcome of this particular struggle and as evidence of the NCC's increasing willingness to forge coalitions with liberal Catholics on matters of common concern.

There is little doubt that the Kelley Committee had a dramatic impact. One indication was the changing contents of congressional mail. Overwhelmingly proamendment at the outset, the mail in April, May, and June began to lean decidedly in the opposite direction. The testimony at the committee's hearings, especially that of prominent clergymen, also made its weight felt. At the beginning of the hearings, members of the Kelley Committee had estimated that the Becker Amendment would easily win approval; but by the time the hearings closed, the *Wall Street Journal* estimated that not even 8 of the 35 Senate Judiciary Committee members still supported the proposal. Members' views altered almost exclusively toward opposition. Failing to win approval, the Becker Amendment died, and while efforts were made in subsequent years by Senator Everett Dirksen and others to revive the proposal, the proprayer movement no longer had the momentum it once had and the issue appeared to be a dead letter.

CONCLUSIONS

A comparison of NCC behavior on two major educational issues in the 1960s leads to the conclusion that its endorsement of the "child benefit theory" incorporated in the 1965 education act in no way involved a weakening of its long-standing commitment to the doctrine of church-state separation. On the issue of prayer in the public schools, viewed by council leaders as posing the church-state question in unambiguous form, the organization was fully prepared to commit resources, mobilize constituents, and even take risks in order to defend what it conceived to be basic First Amendment guarantees of religious liberty.

Though not wholly unrelated, the school aid and school prayer issues were thought by council leaders to involve two fundamentally different issues. On the question of school aid, NCC leaders formed a coalition with the Johnson administration and other groups to endorse, basically in the New Deal tradition, increased federal spending to aid deprived and needy persons. Though initially distressed over certain details of the administration's proposals, the council had little difficulty in accepting them in the spirit of the "child benefit" concept once these troublesome matters had been eliminated and the church-state specter laid to rest. On the school prayer issue, however, the New Deal coalition tended to fragment (one reason why the Kennedy and Johnson administrations avoided commitment on the issue), and the council found itself allied with civil libertarians and militant church-state separationists, while opposed, not only to self-proclaimed conservatives, but also to some New Deal liberals (for example, some Jewish and Roman Catholic spokesmen having a pronounced stake in sectarian schooling).

These findings clarify the fundamental assumptions informing the council's behavior in the 1960s. These were "liberal" in the New Deal tradition on matters relating to social welfare and human dignity, "libertarian" on matters relating to personal and religious freedom and to the "establishment" clause of the First Amendment to the Constitution.

12. The Problem of Internal Cohesion

*N*o aspect of the council's involvement in national policy disputes in the 1960s is more arresting than the fact that its activism was not accompanied by serious internal schism or defections by major constituent denominations. This is surprising inasmuch as organizations with a federal structure typically experience difficulty in reaching consensus on major issues. "Federated structures tend to have much less cohesion," David B. Truman has observed, "especially with respect to functions whose importance increases after the distribution of powers is agreed upon." [1] V. O. Key has made a similar point with respect to the United States Chamber of Commerce, also having a federated structure. [2] Federations frequently endeavor to minimize the danger of internal strife by avoiding controversial issues and by confining their representations before courts, legislatures, and administrative bodies to the defense of clearly defined institutional stakes.

If the maintenance of internal harmony had been an overriding consideration for the council in the 1960s, it presumably would have adhered to a cautious civil rights stance and avoided other controversial involvements. The moral imperatives were viewed as too great for this, however, and in 1963 the NCC leaders acted with full knowledge that the internal consequences of what they were proposing might prove severe. In the wake of their actions, defections by one or more large member bodies would have been expectable. Between 1909 and 1933, it may be recalled, no less than nine of the denominations that at one time or another had affiliated with the old Federal Council had voted to withdraw out of dissatisfaction with its views. Yet, with one very minor exception (to be discussed later in the chapter), there were no member-body defections in this, the most socially activist period in council history, notwithstanding considerable unrest at the grass roots level.

While calling attention to the factional strife that did occur, the present chapter takes up the problem of accounting for the council's ability to undergo a fundamental change in strategy without engendering large-scale defections.

CONSERVATIVE RESPONSE TO NCC ACTIVISM

Opposition to council activity in the 1960s on the part of self-proclaimed conservatives was apparent on almost every front: denominational assemblies, church publications, the NCC's own assemblies and boards. The best source of a reasonable sampling of conservative arguments against the council, however, are congressional committee hearings. Such hearings have particular value for three reasons: first, as an indication of the views of Protestant conservatives generally; second, for the clues they provide toward a fuller understanding of congressional floor struggles over proposed new legislation and fiscal appropriations relevant to church interests; and third, as a means of gaining insight into how council leaders undertake to cope with conservative onslaughts against NCC views and policies.

Conservative Criticism of the NCC from Members of Congress. One of the persistent themes in congressional hearings where NCC witnesses appear to testify is the dispute over whether the council is in fact representative of its rank-and-file constituents. NCC spokesmen have learned to be extremely wary of claiming that its stands on major issues in fact represent a cross-section of thinking among the more than 42 million persons who comprise its member bodies. The council has cautiously claimed only the right to speak *to* the churches, not *for* them, on key issues. But conservative congressmen are inclined to object when NCC spokesmen even so much as allude to their enormous aggregate membership, which is, after all, nearly a quarter of the entire U.S. population, a larger dues-paying membership than that of any other private organization. The following interchange, involving a southern senator and Benjamin F. Payton during consideration of a 1966 open-occupancy housing bill, is rather typical of challenges to the council's representative character:

> Senator [Sam] Ervin (Democrat, North Carolina): Dr. Payton, I notice you speak for the National Council of Churches and you state you speak for the 30 major religious bodies from the Protestant and Orthodox churches. You do not claim, however, that you are speaking in behalf of all of the people that are affiliated with those various churches, do you?
>
> Dr. [Benjamin F.] Payton (CORR, NCC): Obviously, Mr. Chairman, no organization can claim to say that its policies are agreed to by every single individual. But I must say this, that in the National Council of Churches, there is a process whereby the denominations and their leaders themselves are the ones who are finally responsible for our policy. It is not just a bureaucracy where bureaucrats make decisions. It is an organization in which the denominational leaders themselves bring forth policy and exercise it.
>
> Senator Ervin: I happen to be a member of one of the churches which is affiliated with the National Council of Churches. I will have to say that in my church one-half of the voting power belongs to the clergy, and the other half belongs to the members. The members are not used to attending church meetings; therefore, they are inexperienced and have difficulty in expressing their views. But I must say in my opinion at least 95 per cent of them are opposed to legislation of this type [i.e., civil rights]. Therefore, I feel that while you have some authority to speak for the National Council, you are not speaking for the majority of the members of my church when you support legislation of this type, even though it is affiliated with the National Council. . . .[3]

This mode of attack was repeated in August 1966 in another Senate hearing room, this time during testimony concerned with a proposed school prayer amendment:

Senator [Roman L.] Hruska (Republican, Nebraska):   . . . is
there an implication by reference and by use of that figure
[56.7 million as the total number of people embraced by NCC
member churches] that they did approve and do approve the
position of the leaders of the National Council? If there is, I
would like to know it.

Dr. [David R.] Hunter (associate general secretary, NCC):
The number was supplied solely to indicate the number of
people who looked to these leaders whom I have quoted here
for spiritual leadership.

Senator [Birch] Bayh (Democrat, Indiana):   If our witness
will permit me, and if the Senator will yield just momentarily—

Senator Hruska: Yes.

Senator Bayh: I gathered from our colloquy a moment ago
that Dr. Hunter was of the opinion that the membership of
the bodies which were represented were predominantly in support of the position.

Dr. Hunter: Correct, predominantly.

Senator Bayh: Which would tend to answer the question of
the Senator from Nebraska.

Dr. Hunter: Predominantly in support, so when these leaders
meet in plenary session these leaders were sustained, but apparently what I said, and it was not necessary to say it, obviously these 56 million American people do not have a mono-
chrome view on this.

Senator Hruska: It is not a monolithic view which would be
represented.

Dr. Hunter: No. But the majority apparently through their
representatives at least in the plenary bodies, do support these
leaders.

Senator Hruska: . . . at the outset of my questions I said I
was very intrigued by this game of numbers here. . . . You do
use numbers, and I think one of the ways that we here in Congress, in judging the desirability of the necessity of proposing
a constitutional amendment, find how much support there is
for the opportunity to use the amending process of the Constitution [is also to use numbers]. So you make it your effort
to find out what is good policy. We in the political scene make
what you make in the religious scene, you see. As I suggested
a little bit ago, *we politicians think we know something about*

the mind of the people. We have first hand and daily and other contacts with that very proposition [italics my own].

Dr. Hunter: I am sure you do.[4]

Finally, the same theme appeared in a House hearing earlier that summer (this time, skepticism was affirmed with decided intensity of feeling on the part of a conservative congressman):

Representative [Robert] Griffin (Republican, Michigan): Has the National Council of Churches ever polled the members of the member churches on this issue? [repeal of section 14(b) of the Taft-Hartley Act, which permits states to pass laws outlawing the closed shop in industry]?

Reverend [J. Edward] Carothers (Department of the Church and Economic Life, NCC): No; we don't proceed that way. Perhaps I can briefly outline our procedure. The General Board is made up of persons elected or designated by the denominations. The denominations designate or elect these persons— they have different ways of doing it themselves—to the General Board.

When a position or policy statement is being prepared it is with the understanding that the General Board is speaking as the General Board of the National Council of Churches and the persons who are there to make the decision obviously are representing their own point of view, although they are sent there by their denominations. In that sense it is a representative body and it does not, any more than the average state or county or even the Federal Government, go back to the citizens for a mandate on every issue.

Representative Griffin: But as a representative board it would be the intention and purpose of the Board to try to reflect the views of the membership that they represent. Wouldn't that be true?

Reverend Carothers: Not necessarily. I think there would be some times when persons after long study, and in this case it was two years, experienced a change of mind and actually knew that their constituency would differ with them. Yet they would vote for it, and this constitutes some problems for the representatives from denominations. Many times they have great difficulty explaining what took place in the two year period.

Representative Griffin: You mentioned of course that there are 40 million people.

Reverend Carothers: That is right.

Representative Griffin: This is a very impressive statement. You don't purport to represent that the Board reflects their views or even tries to; is that right?

Reverend Carothers: I tried to be very specific Mr. Griffin and I want to be very specific [referring to his prior statement]: "Obviously we make no claim to be speaking for each of these member churches individually nor for all the members in any one communion." And we want that to be very clear. It is a delegated group. It couldn't possibly claim to speak for the 40 million and has never attempted to say so.

Representative Griffin: Reverend Carothers, I am a member of a church that is affiliated with the National Council of Churches and I want to say on the record that I bitterly resent the fact that the National Council of Churches is involving itself in an issue such as this, which is not a moral issue as such, but which is a legislative issue, particularly when you are taking a position which is demonstrably in opposition to the views of a majority of the member churches of the National Council of Churches!

Reverend Carothers: I don't think it is so obvious, Mr. Griffin.

Representative Griffin: Would you take a poll of your members and see whether that statement is true?

Reverend Carothers: I don't know whether it is. I just say it is not obvious. Something that is obvious must be demonstrable. This is not demonstrable.[5]

What is chiefly remarkable about these interchanges between council spokesmen and conservative members of Congress is not the fact that the council's representative character should have been challenged. This sort of cross-examination is rather routine when individuals who purport to represent a certain constituency appear before Congress. AFL-CIO spokesmen are accustomed to being told that labor's official line does not reflect the thinking of all union members; the AMA, that all doctors are not in accord with the views of the "medical lobby"; and so forth. Congressmen are by nature skeptical about statements that imply, or are construed as implying, unanimity of sentiment among large groups of people. Also, the effort to weaken the impact of testimony by inquiring whether the membership has been polled on the issue at hand is a standard tactic, and in some instances the answer has yielded useful information to Congress. The crucial difference between the barrage faced by NCC spokesmen and that to which other groups are subjected was the conviction then of many conservative congressmen (whether or not well founded) that the NCC not only was exaggerating the extent of constituency agreement with its statements, but beyond this that a poll of constituents would have revealed a solid majority of people on the *opposite* side of the fence. One is struck by the intensity with which conservatives tend to challenge NCC statements, no doubt related in part to the fact that many conservative congressmen are life-long members of NCC-affiliated churches and thus feel themselves in possession of knowledge about grass roots Protestant sentiment that is not being reflected in NCC policy.

The claim that the council does not accurately reflect the views of its constituents on major social and political issues is widely pervasive among conservatives. To a certain degree the very existence of such broadly based rival organizations as the National Association of Evangelicals testifies to the effort to dramatize and capitalize upon the extent of anti-NCC sentiment in certain sections of the country and among certain groups in the population.

On one occasion, at least, an effort was made to demonstrate statistically the actual extent of such disagreement with official NCC views on a particular issue. The incident grew out of a 22 February 1966 General Board resolution favoring U.S. diplomatic recognition of mainland China and suggesting that serious consideration be given to lending American support for the admission of the People's Republic of China to the UN. Shortly thereafter, a group labeling itself the Emergency Committee on China, headed by the Reverend Daniel A. Poling, chairman of the board of *Christian Herald* (a conservative publication), was organized to voice objection to this suggestion. Former congressman Walter Judd, a well-known anti-Communist orator, was among its members. On 19 September 1966 the committee took out a full-page advertisement in the *New York Times* to announce the results of a poll, consisting of questionnaires purportedly sent to 65 percent of the nation's Protestant clergymen, 30,000 of whom responded. The results of the poll, the validity of which was later sharply challenged by the NCC, showed that "71.4 per cent of Protestant clergymen were opposed to U.S. diplomatic recognition of the Peiping regime" and that "72.9 per cent were opposed to admission of Communist China to the United Nations." [6] These results, though not the NCC objections thereto, were entered into the *Congressional Record* by Senator Thomas Dodd, Democrat from Connecticut. On the basis of the poll, Poling affirmed that "it is now clear that [the NCC leaders] speak only for themselves and not for the Protestant community." [7] While the comment was directed specifically against the mainland China stand, it seems reasonable to suppose that Poling would have drawn the same conclusion regarding the NCC's positions on a number of other issues. Two years later the same committee, now renamed the Clergymen's Committee on China, again purchased a full-page advertisement in the *Times* to publicize its dissatisfaction with NCC proposals for halting the bombing of North Vietnam and deescalating the war. The NCC's political activities generally were called into question.

A second theme that has recurred in conservative criticism is that the council's political involvement has been on faulty ground theologically because it has misrepresented the nature of the Christian Gospel and falsely construed the true nature of the church. An impression of this line of reasoning can be gained from the same committee hearings quoted above. On the bill proposing open-occupancy housing:

> Senator Ervin: . . . I would say that some of the people who opposed this legislation are pretty close to the teaching of [true] religion. In other words, I think some of us who oppose legislation of this kind believe that these problems can only be solved by the persuasive power of religion and not by the coercive power of law. . . . Perhaps we are closer to the real spirit of the church than some of those who indicate that they have more faith in the coercive power of man-made laws than they do in the persuasive power of religion.
>
> Dr. Payton: Mr. Chairman, I would not want to engage in

a theological debate, but I think that it is precisely at this point of the Gospel that we take our stand here, for the Gospel is the good news, and it is mainly the good news of God's deliverance of men from bondage. This is precisely what we are speaking for here.

Senator Ervin: If I understand anything about the Bible from one end to the other, it teaches freedom.

Dr. Payton: Oh, yes.

Senator Ervin: It says every person has a right to be free. He even has the right to do wrong and go to Hell instead of going to Heaven if he wants to. I think certain things should be left to the decision of the individual. If the Government is going to undertake to make decisions on what it conceives to be morally right and impose upon us the Government's idea of what is morally right, the Government is going to destroy our freedom.

Dr. Payton: Do you think, Mr. Chairman, that those Southern states which imposed upon Negroes segregationist statutes, do you feel they were infringing the freedom of Negroes?

Senator Ervin: I would say if those statutes were invalid or bad, then statutes that bring about compulsory desegregation are equally bad, because both of them deny people the right of freedom of association.

Dr. Payton: But do you agree that segregationist statutes are bad?

Senator Ervin: I agree that compulsory integrationist statutes are bad.

Dr. Payton: But do you agree that compulsory segregationist statutes are?

Senator Ervin: I believe that is a question for local solution and not for national solution. Such statutes were adjudged constitutional from 1896 to 1954. This was in accord with the history of the 14th Amendment and all the cases interpreting it.

Dr. Payton: But you just said, Mr. Chairman, that you believe in freedom. I simply commend to your attention the fact that millions of Negroes, mainly in the South, have never been free. They have not been free precisely because of the laws of segregation in the South.[8]

Like congressmen at congressional hearings conservatives

have attacked the NCC, alleging that the organization presumes to speak for its constituents on controversial social questions and endeavors to impose its official "line" on them. From time to time this basic point of opposition has been couched in terms of the conservative view concerning the indefeasible nature of private rights over against the council leaders' belief in the validity of positions officially adopted by a majority of voting delegates. In a House hearing concerning the proposed repeal of section 14b of the Taft-Hartley Act one conservative congressman attempted to get an NCC witness to agree that a man has an inalienable right to refuse to join a union as a condition of employment in a particular firm. Implicit in his mode of argumentation was the conservative principle of the sovereignty of the individual:

> Representative Griffin: Unions today are collecting union dues as a condition of employment and contributing it directly to candidates in elections for State and Local offices. They are contributing money to the Americans for Democratic Action, legally, because there is nothing in the law to prohibit it. Do you approve of that?

> Reverend Carothers: The point is not whether I approve of that or whether I don't approve of it; the point I wish to make here in this statement is that when it comes to the decision as to the union shop agreement we believe it should not be enacted by law. We believe it should be an issue settled in collective bargaining in the interest of a wider latitude of choice and democratic action. . . .

> Representative Griffin: . . . You are advocating compulsory unionism. You are advocating the repeal of 14(b) which will permit compulsory unionism, compulsory payment of dues, as a condition of employment. Isn't there a basic American right here that is involved so far as citizenship rights are concerned [namely, for the individual to be protected in certain essential rights and, in connection with such rights, not to be subject to majority vote]? *

> Reverend Carothers: . . . I am subject to the vote of the majority in almost everything I do.

> Representative Griffin: . . . how about the right to your own

---

* The section in brackets is a paraphrasing intended to bring out clearly the essential thrust of the congressman's argument.

religious convictions? Are you going to put that to a majority vote too or is that going to be different?

Reverend Carothers: Interestingly enough, I am under a great many compulsions in my relationships with my fellowman religiously. I have to consent to many things in my relationships.

Representative Griffin: Isn't your association with your church voluntary?

Reverend Carothers: So far as I hold my membership this is voluntary.

Representative Griffin: That is the crucial point, Reverend. Let's not keep getting away from that. . . .

I am trying to pin you down. There are some fundamental individual rights that are not subject to majority control and religious thought is one of them.

Reverend Carothers: I am not going to be pinned down to consent that there is an absolute principle that governs all human relations.

Representative Griffin: Once we start with the first one I am going to move to the second one and that is: Is there any individual right insofar as your support of an individual citizenship right [i.e., which takes precedence over majority opinion] regarding candidates, political causes, political parties of your own choosing. . . .

First of all you will agree with me that the matter of religious affiliation is an individual right that is not subject to majority control?

Reverend Carothers: That is right, that is entrance into the group. You must meet their requirements as you enter.

Representative Griffin: Oh absolutely. But the entrance is voluntary, right?

Reverend Carothers: It is voluntary, but not on your own terms.

· · · · · · · · · · · · · · · · ·

Reverend Carothers: I can't think of anything in our country, where the individual has absolute freedom, because—

Representative Griffin: He has absolute freedom not to be in a church.

Reverend Carothers: He has that freedom, but he does not have the absolute freedom to join on his own terms.

Representative Griffin: That has nothing to do with it! The point is he doesn't have to join. . . .

Reverend Carothers: . . . The absolute freedom to refrain is quite another matter from the absolute freedom to do. It has long been known that absolute freedom to refrain sometimes has been resorted to. People go to jail, or let themselves be burned at the stake, but the absolute freedom to do is almost rare. It is always limited. . . . The absolute freedom to join a church on your own terms doesn't exist.

Representative Griffin: Reverend, let me see if I can get the point across another way. . . .[9]

These congressional hearings are introduced at this point not to document NCC relations with an outside institution, but to indicate the kinds of problems encountered by NCC leaders in their dealings with conservative churchmen, most of whom are active in the federation's own constituent churches, although some do occupy seats in Congress. The views presented above have constituted an organizational problem in the sense that they have served to rationalize factionalism, thus adversely affecting NCC internal cohesion. The extent of such conservative factionalism among NCC member bodies is the topic of the following section.

Conservative Criticism from Constituent Bodies. Criticism of NCC policies voiced by conservatives is potentially more disruptive when it is voiced not by individual laymen and clergymen (as in the preceding cases), but in the name of an NCC constituent communion. It must be kept in mind that the NCC is a federation, the members of which are denominations, and that it is to these constituent denominations that the council is, strictly speaking, accountable. Member-church criticism, embodied in officially adopted resolutions, must thus be taken seriously, as this directly affects the council's principal source of income and ultimately its legitimacy. Every church has had its minority who were hostile to the NCC; but until the NCC became involved in the legislative politics of civil rights, such criticism seldom gained official recognition. The involvement in civil rights clearly changed the balance of forces in the churches: conservatives became more outspoken in their criticism while civil rights advocates generated support for increased political involvement.

The extent of internal dissension was brought to the attention of the General Board at its meeting in Portland, Oregon, in March 1965. There it was reported that in the year preceding the NCC had received some 10,000 critical letters, most of which presumably were centered on the race issue. The board was also given official notice of the decision of the council's smallest member body, the Unity of the Brethren Church, a Moravian denomination centered mainly in Texas and numbering 6,030 members, to withdraw from membership. The UBC's decision was actually reached at its May 1964 meeting, in the midst of the most intensive period of the NCC's civil rights activity. In its resolution addressed to the Council the UBC avoided any direct mention of civil rights, though it evidently had this in mind when it voiced "disapproval of some of the trends indicated in some of the actions of the NCC." [10] This was the first withdrawal from the council in 20 years, and up to the present writing it has been the last.

During its sixty-first General Convention meeting in St. Louis in October 1964, the Protestant Episcopal Church devoted considerable time to discussing resolutions critical of the NCC. The House of Deputies (composed equally of clerical and lay delegates) considered but soundly defeated a resolution calling for Episcopal Church withdrawal from the NCC until it had assumed "responsibility for actions and pronouncements of all its various agencies," closed its Washington Office, and ceased "activity on political issues in a partisan manner." [11] While this particular resolution was voted down by a large majority, the House of Deputies did vote to join with the House of Bishops (the coequal branch of the General Convention) in a resolution instructing NCC Episcopal delegates to seek to restrain the NCC and its member departments and agencies from efforts to influence specific legislation. In 1965 and 1966 the Vestry Committee of St. Mark's Episcopal Church, Shreveport, Louisiana, gained a good deal of national publicity for a study prepared under its auspices concluding that the NCC exceeded its rightful role when it spoke out on controversial issues and that it had become an aid to the Communist conspiracy.

About the same time the General Assembly of the Presbyterian Church in the U.S. (Southern Presbyterian) asked the NCC to amend its rules to provide that at least half the General Board members be present before a policy statement could be enacted. The assembly defeated a strong minority movement to have the Southern Presbyterians withdraw from membership. Also, a number of local congregations, mostly but not exclusively in the South, announced disapproval of the NCC and specified that none of the pledges to their own denominations be used to help support it.

NCC Response to Conservative Criticism. The initial NCC response to criticism from the conservative right was for the most part to ignore it, a strategy that had proved reasonably successful in prior years in dealing with the hysterical charges leveled against it by "right-wing extremist" groups. Toward the end of 1964, however, NCC leaders evidenced some doubts over whether silence was still the best approach. "Everywhere I go in this country," Bishop Reuben Mueller, NCC's president, reported at the time of the 1964 Triennial Assembly, "I find people saying that 'These accusations must be so, for no one representing the NCC gives answers to these criticisms and charges.'" [12] The best approach, it was apparently decided, was to deal directly and explicitly with accusations of an hysterical and extremist nature and to respond favorably to those demands that appeared reasonable and did not require a drastic break with prior commitments.

The task of dealing with the more hysterical accusations was assumed by the council's top elective and appointive officials, the president and general secretary, respectively. In a series of addresses in Des Moines, Iowa, at the time of the 1964 Triennial Assembly, President Mueller denounced as "absolutely unfounded" accusations that the council had Communist leanings. He labeled critics of the NCC as:

> men and organizations whose religion is pugnacious and narrow, and whose patriotism is measured by the dollars that gullible people send them to fatten their bank accounts. . . .

This kind not only makes the NCC its favorite whipping boy, but practices Hitler's theory of the Big Lie. . . .[13]

Certain critics were spreading "malicious falsehoods," he contended; the NCC had become "the favorite whipping boy of those who oppose it for selfish reasons." [14] The general secretary, the Reverend R. H. Edwin Espy, concerned himself with what the mood was doing to the internal life of the churches:

> The tactic increasingly is to invade the churches, usually bypassing ministers, confusing and dividing local congregations, calling into question national leadership and policies, undermining denominational programs by urging withholding of financial support, and calling for investigation of the National Council of Churches.

The aim was not limited to changing policies, he continued, but extended to efforts to undermine

> the present religious establishment as represented in the main line Protestant and Orthodox communions. . . . It is the ecumenical orientation of these communions with all that ecumenicity carries with it that the attackers seek to destroy.[15]

As evidence of what he saw to be a "profound polarization" between clergy and laity, Espy pointed out that donations to the council from "individuals, business organizations, foundations, etc." were currently running roughly ten percent behind projected revenues.

Not all criticism of the council's actions was ignored or condemned, however. On a number of procedural points the leadership was prepared to give ground. As noted above, the General Assembly of the Presbyterian Church in the U.S. had requested it to amend its rules to provide that at least half the General Board members must be present in order to transact business or adopt policies. Criticism along these lines had appeared repeatedly in the pages of conservative publications like *Christianity Today;* the critics pointed out that votes on a number of issues had been taken with less than a quorum present. The vote on the highly controversial proposal to repeal section 14(b) of Taft-Hartley, for example, had found barely 100 out of a total General Board membership of 250 in attendance. (The vote on this issue was 77 for and 16 against the resolution endorsing repeal, with 7 abstentions.) In response to these criticisms, the NCC voted to amend its bylaws so that a majority of voting members had to be in attendance for business to be transacted. The new policy was invoked for the first time at the General Board's meeting in February 1967, which President Flemming adjourned after two days when the number of those in attendance had fallen below half.

There are also some scraps of evidence that the NCC staff was exerting itself to deemphasize those General Board policy statements that might prove internally disruptive. Thus, the Washington Office advised against the NCC's offering testimony on the matter of repeal of section 14(b) of Taft-Hartley because of its awareness that the National Right to Work Committee was eagerly awaiting the opportunity to publicize the event to the council's detriment.[16]

The able leadership of top officials, employing a combination of judicious silence, rhetorical parrying, and affirmative responses to constructive criticism from assemblies that might otherwise have turned hostile, must be credited with helping to blunt the efforts of some to undercut the council's base of denominational support. Despite one member-church's decision to withdraw from participation, the more typical pattern was for denominational resolutions calling for denunciation of the NCC to be voted down, usually by wide margins. Even among denominations with pronounced conservative traditions, withdrawal motions were usually rejected decisively. The Southern Presbyterian Church, for example, defeated a motion critical of the NCC introduced at its 1965 General Assembly by a 318–120 margin.

CRITICISM OF THE NCC POLICY
FROM "MILITANT LIBERALS"

A second line of criticism against NCC policy in the mid-1960s came from a group within the community of liberal churchmen. The thinking of this group was shaped in large measure by the violence in northern black ghettos in the period 1965 to 1968, and one must delve briefly into the frame of mind of black intellectuals and militant leaders in this period in order to adequately comprehend their outlook.

By 1966 black militant leaders had come to the conclusion that the real significance of the Watts Riot was that violence, or at least the threat of violence, which up to now they had rejected, might in fact be advantageous in exacting concessions from powerful whites. The change was reflected when in that year SNCC voted to replace John Lewis, who stood for non-violence as a matter of deep personal commitment, with Stokely Carmichael, who was willing to embrace violence, and also when CORE elected Floyd McKissick, who had moved some distance to the left in his refusal to denounce categorically the Watts Riot. Though the summer of 1966 passed without major disorders, the rhetoric of the militants became increasingly inflammatory. By the time of the 1967 Detroit and Newark Riots, the words of the militants and the observable events began to mesh. Though it was possible to discount some of the more extravagent rhetoric of Carmichael and his SNCC successor, H. Rap Brown, the gist of their oratory succeeded in capturing white attention and persuading many influential whites that the riots could not be written off as the work of hoodlums and lawbreakers, that they were sympathetic of a pervasive social evil. It was this mutual reinforcement of the violence of a fair number of blacks (though not a majority, even in the riot areas) and the incendiary rhetoric of a handful of black theoreticians that served to compel the nation's political leadership to pay attention, as moderate blacks apparently could not do. Violence, and more especially the *threat* of violence, began to appear as a viable method of gaining political leverage.

The importance of this shift in sentiment was immediately sensed by those on the national staffs of the Protestant churches most closely in touch with the black community. Though all denominational staffs were presumably aware of the change, there is reason to think that its full significance was most quickly comprehended among staff personnel in the Board of Homeland Ministries of the United Church of Christ. In a Letter to the Editor of the *New York Times* in August 1967, the Reverend Willis E. Elliott of that office put the issue in terms that were at once coolly analytical and emotionally committed:

Negroes in America have been making progress through non-violence, threats of violence, and violence. All three strategies are essential to future progress. . . . Further progress will depend on the intelligent use of all three strategies, including strategic terror. At the present time there is no evidence that the present Negro leadership—if "leadership" is not too strong a term—has the organizing capacity to pass from mindless ghetto explosions to selective destruction of the property of those in whose hands are the levers of power.[17]

In the fall of the same year a group of 700 activist clergymen and laymen participated in a Conference on Church and Society, held in Detroit under NCC auspices. Though reports and position papers flowing out of the conference would have had no official status, they would presumably have had some influence. Significantly, one of the conference panels considered a position paper setting forth "The Role of Violence in Social Change," which proposed criteria by which "justified" violence might be distinguished from "unjustified" violence and a methodology of effective "justified" violence:

One criterion for judging violence is whether or not the violence seeks to preserve privilege or injustice or to redress wrongs. The former is unjustified. The latter can be justified. . . . [Violence] to be effective needs objectives, strategy, disciplined effort, action troops, people willing to sacrifice life, and a high degree of secrecy.[18]

This appeal for a more militant role for churches was vigorously disputed by Protestant churchmen in the liberal mainstream. James Y. Holloway, a leader in the liberal Committee of Southern Churchmen, took sharp exception to what he called the emergent "cult of violence":

There is . . . some evidence suggesting that the study of violence and its morality is the next detour that the intellectuals and the theologians will travel. Insofar as Christians are concerned, it is necessary to recall our own witness to and about violence: by and large, since the third century, we celebrate it, make a cult of it, because we Christians have exercised a preponderance of it in Western Culture. But when violence occasionally threatens our property we condemn it—in all forms. Today, to retain full membership in the Crisis-of-the-Month Club, there is every prospect that our theologians shall begin to inquire into the "anatomy of violence," to write papers and conduct seminars on "theology and violence" or even the "theology *of* violence." We may expect to be instructed in the linguistic distinction in the Old and New Testaments between "to kill" and "to murder," just as we have been told about the obvious distinction between "just" and "unjust wars." But like most detours of the great god Relevance, it is a dead-end.[19]

The long-simmering dispute finally reached the official attention of the NCC General Board at its meeting in New York in June 1968. Dr. Truman B. Douglass, head of the staff of the Board of Homeland Ministries of the United Church of Christ, presented for the board's ratification a policy statement on civil disobedience, which, in a carefully worded and somewhat indirect manner, suggested that violence could never be categorically rejected as a means of voicing disapproval of governmental actions. The statement alluded to the fact that in seeking to obey God's will, men have taken a variety of actions, even extreme ones, such as revolution. More particularly, it stated that "When justice cannot be secured either through action within existing structures or through civil disobedience, an increasing number of Christians may feel called upon to seek justice through violence or revolution."[20] The wording avoided explicitly approving violence, but seemed to leave the way open to it. Peter Day, a prominent journalist and author, who was among the Episcopal delegates on the General Board, rose to protest and moved that the "revolutionary" section be removed from the resolution because it was likely to contribute to the current atmosphere of violence. Day's remarks were sharply countered by several of the black churchmen present, and his amendment was at last voted down by a vote of 81–6, with 15 abstentions. It was reported that the opponents and abstainers consisted heavily of Episcopal and Eastern Orthodox delegates.

Thus, "militant liberal" critics of NCC policy would have had it identify itself more explicitly with minority group grievances and advocated a militant strategy in which violence and "strategic terror" would take their place alongside certain other acceptable tactics, the right of civil disobedience being the rationale. While agreeing with the prevailing NCC view that "political" strategies clearly had a place in church efforts to confront social issues, these critics differed with NCC liberals over the extent to which the regular political channels (courts, legislatures, political parties, and so forth) were responsive to the needs of oppressed blacks. On this point they were decidedly pessimistic.

"SELECTIVE" INCENTIVES AND CONTINUED CONSERVATIVE INVOLVEMENT

No amount of NCC leadership adroitness could have insured the continued support of churches inclined to differ with the federation's social action priorities and strategy if these bodies had not found compelling reasons of their own to justify membership. Leadership can be highly significant at the margins; but its effectiveness depends on an ability to relate to the long-term member-body interests that transcend the immediate situation or crisis. Without discounting the possibility that those identified with a militant left position may someday pose a serious threat to NCC internal cohesion, it is clear that in the 1960s and for several decades previous, the most persistent challenge came from those with rightist political leanings. Vocal conservatives, though often small numerically, have typically posed a threat to existing priorities because they are well organized, articulate, and fully aware of the leverage they gain by threatening to withhold pledges.

The question raised at the outset of the chapter—namely, how to account for the refusal of large member denominations to accede to repeated conservative demands for withdrawal from the NCC until such time as that body abandoned or drastically altered its political activity—has still to be discussed. Mancur Olson, Jr.'s, analysis of several large interest groups in *The Logic of Collective Action* (1965) offers a theoretical framework within which this question can be answered. Contrary to the beliefs of some earlier theorists, Olson asserts, the rational individual will not join a large lobbying organization simply because his interests are in jeopardy and the organization embodies a set of social and political goals that are useful to him (nor will he be motivated to form such an organization). Such an individual, along with others of the same inclination, helps to comprise, in Olson's terminology, a "latent group," a large, amorphous, but potentially organizable aggregate of persons with common interests. Yet the individual, simply by virtue of his being a latent group member, is unlikely to act in its behalf, since "by definition [he] cannot make a noticeable contribution to any group effort, and since no one in the group will react if he makes no contribution, he has no incentive to contribute." Mere membership in a latent group does not offer the individual

> any incentive to pay dues to any organization working in the latent group's interest, or to bear in any other way any of the costs of the necessary collective actions. *Only a separate and "selective" incentive will stimulate a rational individual in a latent group to act in a group-oriented way* [italics my own].[21]

Among organizations large voluntary associations have a particularly difficult time in marshaling the needed selective incentives, since they, unlike small and primary groups, are usually unable to make use of social sanctions and social rewards through which "the recalcitrant individual can be ostracized, and the cooperative individual invited into the center of the charmed circle." [22] Social sanctions may work reasonably well in groups marked by extensive face-to-face contact. Within latent groups (out of which the large voluntary association arises), however, there always exist more people than can possibly know each other; hence, such a group "is not likely to develop social pressures that would help it to satisfy its interest in a collective good." [23]

This leads Olson to the following fundamental proposition: while not all latent groups succeed in organizing themselves, those that do succeed have one important characteristic in common—namely, that their political activity is only a by-product of other, "bread and butter" functions, that they in fact "obtain their strength and support because they perform

some function in addition to lobbying for collective goods." [24]
Large voluntary organizations can acquire the needed selective
incentives only if they have either the authority and capacity
to be informally coercive or positive inducements to offer the
individual.

Olson's prime targets of analysis are the "largest economic
pressure groups in the United States." [25] He shows that a combination of positive inducements and informal coercion is a
major factor in membership support for such diverse economic
interests as business associations, labor unions, and professional societies. While believing his theory to help illuminate
the behavior of economic interest groups, in regard to which
rational calculation of personal gain is obviously an important
motivation for individual participation, Olson is dubious of his
theory's applicability to most noneconomic groups.* "In phil-

* Olson would exclude not only religious institutions per se, but also most
lobbying organizations with close ties to such institutions. Thus, he maintains
that the Anti-Saloon League, which successfully lobbied to secure a national
prohibition amendment, is not adequately explainable in terms of the "by-
product theory" because religious institutions (in this case Protestant churches)
were its main source of support (*Logic of Collective Action*, p. 161, n. 92).

anthropic and religious lobbies," he maintains, "the relationships between the purposes and interests of the individual
member, and the purposes and interests of the organization,
may be so obscure that a theory of the sort developed here
cannot provide much insight." [26]

Olson's disclaimers notwithstanding, it does seem that
lobbying organizations identified with organized religion lend
themselves in part to the kind of analysis Olson has proposed.
While it may be true that in regard to churches *as such*,
rational economic considerations are of minimal importance in
accounting for member loyalty, it does not follow that rational
factors are equally insignificant in accounting for the affiliation
of constituent members of a *federation* of churches, especially
one that makes a point of stressing the value and importance
of the benefits it provides members.

The FCC/NCC provides a convenient case for testing the
proposition that Olson's theory can help account for member
support even among noneconomic groups. Assuming that selec-

tive incentives can be shown to exist in the case of the FCC/ NCC, one would expect to find a correlation between their number and relative importance and membership loyalty. In recent years, when the leaders have been relatively successful in thwarting threatened defections and in attracting new member bodies, selective incentives should be numerous. In an earlier era, when certain eligible churches were reluctant to join and there was a significant number of defections, they should have been less numerous. This is not to deny that various nonrational factors have contributed to the council's survival. Yet it is scarcely unique in this respect; Olson himself points out that nonrational considerations are at least a secondary consideration in the survival of most large associations, even ones that he regards as most amenable to his theory.

To validate this hypothesis one may begin by noting that in the early stage of the FCC, when benefits to members were modest in the extreme, there was considerable internal antagonism to FCC social activism. In 1913, five years after its founding, the federation's total income was only $32,480, a paltry sum for a national organization, even in those years of non-inflated dollars, especially in view of the considerable wealth represented among its member denominations. The fact that the prominent and influential Protestant Episcopal Church (later to become one of the council's most consistent supporters) refused in these years to accept formal membership, preferring instead a nebulous "affiliated" status, and the fact that the involvement of the Presbyterian Church in the U.S. (Southern Presbyterian) was exceedingly tenuous testify to the council's original difficulty in appealing to churches that entertained the slightest qualms over the federation's theological and social views. The FCC may have had an important symbolic value to some members; but its *tangible* selective incentives were necessarily few in number.

Half a century later the situation had altered fundamentally. The council, in comparison to what it had been in its first decade, had grown to a veritable colossus: its budget by 1965 exceeded $21 million and its staff, both at the New York headquarters and in scattered field offices, numbered in the hundreds. The great majority of these resources were devoted to providing services of direct benefit to member churches. As one leading authority, Samuel McCrea Cavert, has put it:

> Probably most people think of the National Council as constantly involved in public affairs. . . . the churches are convinced that they cannot fulfill their mission in the world without wrestling with such critical issues as justice between the races, world peace in an era of atomic power, and poverty in the midst of affluence. . . . naturally enough it is these activities that attract the most attention.

But he warns against the danger of failing to view these activities in proper perspective: "Most of the Council's program has to do with little publicized operations of the churches in their day-to-day ministries in evangelism, education, pastoral work, missions and social services." [27] These operations, he recounts, involve an almost endless variety of direct service benefits to members: conferences, workshops, studies and research, major publication projects like the Revised Standard Version of the Bible, overseas relief, coordination of overseas missionary activity, and so forth.

It would be overstating the point to suggest that these services are absolutely indispensable to the members, since obviously some churches eligible for membership, the Southern Baptists, for example, manage well enough without them. The services do, nevertheless, constitute incentives for those denominations having once elected to join to remain.

Their importance is further attested by statements prepared by member bodies justifying to interested constituents their continued involvement in the federation. Typical of a number of such documents are two mailed out of the Valley Forge, Pennsylvania, headquarters of the American Baptist Convention. One, entitled *A Baptist Church Looks At the NCC*, is a reprint from the March 1969 issue of the Baptist periodical *Mission* summarizing a report prepared under the auspices of the Fifth Avenue Baptist Church of Huntington, West Virginia. After several descriptive paragraphs intended to answer the charge that the NCC is a "super church," the statement continues:

FACT TWO: Contrary to the critics, *the ministries of the National Council of Churches far exceed making pronouncements on public issues.* Of the Council's annual budget of $19 million in 1968, 60 per cent was spent to minister overseas through evangelism, education, healing, community development and relief to those in need; 12 per cent to translate the Gospel into action in everyday life across the United States . . . [italics my own].

The document further tries to minimize the importance of NCC social and political activities by discussing last the Division of Christian Life and Mission, the unit charged with such matters, after commenting on the work of the three other NCC divisions, and by emphasizing DCLM programs such as chaplaincy training, valuable to member churches, over such efforts as the religion and race program, from which member churches gain at most only indirect benefits. A similar emphasis is apparent in *American Baptists and the Wider Fellowship,* a document prepared by Willis H. Porter, the ABC's associate general secretary. There Porter justifies American Baptist involvement in both the National and World Councils of Churches by an exhaustive cataloging of services rendered to the Baptist Convention and other communions, but scarcely mentions council activity on complex social and political questions.

Conservative denominational spokesmen do not go so far as to suggest that NCC social action lacks a scriptural basis, but they do not generally employ scriptural passages as a sufficient or even as a primary justification for the continuation of their church's affiliation with the NCC. Moreover, the NCC, in its own accounting to members, takes pains to stress the value of its services and to underscore the fact that expenses involved in political activity never exceed five percent of its total budget.

The council was far more an object of conservative criticism in the 1960s than it had been half a century previous, when its priorities were not as well developed or as well known. Nevertheless, in the latter era criticism of its policies, though more vocal, appears to have had a lesser impact. In accounting for this paradox, we have underscored the enormous growth in council services to member churches, which countervailed the criticism of conservative churchmen. Denominational officials and bureaucrats, whatever their views regarding individual stands or programs bearing the NCC imprint, see genuine advantages in remaining in the federation and numerous and serious costs in withdrawing from it.

Assuming that this line of reasoning is valid, it should help not only to explain the behavior of denominations in remaining in the council, but also that of the one body, the Unity of the Brethren, which did not. While observers have no doubt been correct in attributing this defection in part to displeasure over council civil rights stands on the part of a communion with a white southern constituency, one also suspects that this church, whose congregations are situated in a region remote from NCC headquarters and field offices, was conspicuously lacking in the service linkages that tie most other denominations closely to the work of the council. There are no direct data to test this proposition, but it is a highly plausible hypothesis, given the known facts.

It should also be stressed that the council was offering selective incentives to member bodies at a time when the members had not yet begun to donate to the federation in amounts approximating the value of services received. Contributions from member churches did not become the largest source of federation income until the late 1940s, the largest single source prior to this time having been the category "individuals, foundations, and other nonchurch sources" (see table 2, p. 51). (A single individual, John D. Rockefeller, donated larger sums than several member churches in the early years.) Apparently, the member churches gradually came to regard these FCC benefits as quite useful, in some cases even essential, to their well-being and survival, and this awareness in turn came to be reflected in their level of contributions. It cannot be said, then, that the council's selective incentives were simply an outgrowth of the leaders' prior effort to solicit as members those churches believed likely to make large budgetary contributions. The time sequence was the reverse of this: selective incentives were made available first, and member-church donations of roughly comparable value were only much later reciprocated.

Olson's "by-product theory" also can contribute toward a

better understanding of the factors underlying council political involvement in the 1960s. Above a certain minimum level it is not necessary for a federation to continue increasing the level of services to members. One may speak of the spread between member needs and federation income as constituting an organizational "profit." As the size of this "profit" increases, as it did in the council's case in the 1950s and '60s, it becomes increasingly feasible, without risking member-body defections, for the leaders to hire staff, print and distribute informational literature, and otherwise act to influence national policy decisions. This is not to say that the profit *must* be spent in this manner, but it is a distinct possibility that it will be.

CONCLUSIONS

The dissent present within many of the NCC constituent churches and among conservative critics in the U.S. Congress was effectively countered by a strategy alternating between prudent silence and strenuous advocacy, depending on the circumstances. One reason why dissenting opinion could be contained is apparently that the dissidents, instead of being concentrated in one or a few member bodies, the defection of any one of which would have proved highly embarrassing, were scattered about among a number of denominational bodies. Thus, the internal life of many of the constituent churches in the years after 1964 has been more disrupted than has the council's own General Assembly or General Board, to which the dissidents had difficulty gaining access.

The significance of skillful leadership should not be overgeneralized. The council's federated structure does serve to constrain the organization's behavior, as Key and Truman have suggested is typical of federations. It would be misleading to claim that the factors causing its defensive posture in the 1950s were entirely removed in the wake of Birmingham and Selma. Yet, while council leaders may be obliged to modify the extent and intensity of their involvement in national policy struggles so as to take account of the changing balance of forces among constituents, the federation's survival as an organization and the persistence of its progressive stand on social issues appears not to have been jeopardized by the backlash response to its strategy shifts of the 1960s. By introducing Mancur Olson, Jr.'s, selective incentives concept, it has been possible to account for the rather high level of NCC cohesion in the face of major strategic change and the continued affiliation of most member bodies, even those that, on the basis of their social views alone, would seem most prone to defection.

Returning to the problem raised in the introduction to part 3, it is clear that the council did not back away from national policy struggles at the first opportunity after Birmingham. The evidence assembled in the last three chapters indicates that it continued to adhere to an activist, explicitly political strategy, despite the risks entailed of internal controversy and adverse reactions among external bodies in a position to affect the council.

13. Conclusion: *Toward a Theory of Interest Group Activism*

*I*n this concluding chapter the overall argument of this work will be briefly summarized. Then, a comparative survey will be undertaken to determine the extent to which the NCC's growing political consciousness parallels that of other voluntary organizations resembling it both structurally and environmentally. In this way the contribution of the present study to the general problem of interest group behavior will become more apparent.

THE PROCESS OF BECOMING POLITICALLY AWARE

The NCC's self-conscious and activist political stance is a recent development in the 60-year life of the organization. This is not to say that it had altogether been lacking in political interests in previous periods or that it had not from time to time endeavored to mobilize political resources in behalf of reform goals. But national politics had seldom, if ever, engaged the attention of the leaders for more than brief intervals, whereas in the present era at least some top officials have taken a continuing interest in the governmental process.

Previous to this present stage it is convenient to divide the council's emergent concern with politics into two periods. Bearing in mind a certain amount of overlapping between periods, it could be said that its first quarter-century (1908 to 1933) represented an initial stage of concern over social issues. During this period, the "high noon of the Social Gospel," the majority of member churches were prepared to go along with the council's adopting an outspoken stance on controversial issues of the day, though not all of them were equally supportive and some actually balked. Acting through its relatively autonomous commissions and with meager staff resources, the council identified itself before World War I with the progressive movement and with world peace, disarmament, and, especially, organized labor. Despite the secession of several smaller and more pietistic bodies, the organization continued to enjoy substantial backing from its constituents, including many conservative churchmen who found much to approve of in its stands, even though they objected to certain policies. The FCC's image of being controversial acquired in this period was not so firmly fixed nor so strongly endorsed by activist churchmen as to preclude later adoption of a more moderate stance should circumstances so require.

The inauguration of President Franklin D. Roosevelt in 1933 roughly coincided with commencement of the second stage in the council's development. Under the impact of the New Deal, programs that had set the organization apart in previous years now became less and less controversial and divisive. Prompt repeal of Prohibition and the refusal of the Republicans to turn this action into a partisan issue effectively removed the liquor question from the realm of national politics, much as the council would have liked to have seen it kept before the public. The coming to power of Hitler in Germany and the mounting evidence of his unlimited aggression helped nullify the council's earlier hostility to American rearmament and military preparedness. (This was especially the case since grass roots sentiment for intervention on the side of the Allies after 1939 was strongest in the urban East, a traditional center of council strength.) Finally, the passage of numerous domestic measures under FDR's leadership neutralized many social reforms as sources of factional strife, especially those concerned with the passage of bills relating to child labor, union rights, and social security. While the council might claim a certain measure of credit for fostering these domestic programs in the years prior to Roosevelt's taking office, their enactment as national policy and subsequent indirect massive public endorsement in the 1936 election made them innocuous issues, except among a small band of ultraconservatives on the extreme right.

Council leaders seized upon this opportunity to put the organization on a more moderate course with respect to national issues. Speaking broadly of the period 1933 to 1963, one must frankly acknowledge the difficulty of characterizing the organization's behavior on any one-dimensional scale; a variety of social impulses were reflected, even some anticipating the more activist and explicitly political era to follow. In general, however, the NCC treated highly controversial questions with caution and softened the old reformist zeal in an effort to define itself as protector of the status and good name of the main line Protestant and Orthodox churches. This institutional defensiveness was reinforced by several factors: the decline in church membership and religious fervor during the Great Depression, which resulted in pressure to organize an evangelical counterattack; the rise of a self-confident and articulate antisocialist, promarketplace viewpoint among businessmen and industrialists, many of whom directly challenged the council's Social Gospel traditions; the McCarthy era hysteria, involving accusations that the Protestant and Orthodox churches were riddled with Communists; and the increasing sectarian rivalry of the period, which aroused grass roots Protestant anxiety over alleged Roman Catholic threats to American freedom.

In confronting these issues the council came to function as a Protestant "defense group." Coalitions with non-Protestant organizations in behalf of broadly defined social goals were mostly avoided, even though individual officers and staff did lend their support to such causes on occasion. Staff personnel assigned to the sphere of social action often encountered stout internal opposition (for example, from J. Howard Pew's National Lay Committee) when they proposed action on controversial social questions, and at such times their morale usually suffered. Though there were exceptions, staff posts in an organization with these priorities did not hold much attraction for young men deeply concerned about social problems.

The present stage of social concern has its roots in the early months of the Kennedy administration and crystallized in 1963 to 1965 as a result of the events in Birmingham and Selma, Alabama, and the introduction of the 1965 Elementary and Secondary School bill. To view the change as simply a response to an emergency situation would be misleading, however. Already in the late 1950s a new mood was evident among men recently out of seminary. For them, Martin Luther King, Jr.'s, 1955 Birmingham bus boycott and his subsequent emergence as a black protest leader, the rising level of inner-city decay and unemployment, and growing black discontent caused by increasing frustration and despair had already made them skeptical about the utility of the old strategies and formulas for social action. A handful of such men (drawn from a larger number of "new breed" American churchmen) joined the staff of the NCC in the late '50s and began raising questions about the accepted "educational strategy." The emergent crisis atmosphere of the early '60s, created by circumstances to which their liberal analysis seemed appropriate, served to enhance their influence in the organization. Their standing was also augmented by support received from older and more prominent churchmen, especially Eugene Carson Blake, J. Irwin Miller, and Arthur Flemming.

Whereas prior to the 1950s staff had been predominantly recruited from among clergymen, now they were drawn from these liberally inclined seminarians bent on a bureaucratic career. This professionalization of staff, which increased the NCC's capacity to deal with complex social issues, also made it possible to relate more effectively to national governmental officials and to staff personnel serving in other private voluntary organizations. The NCC's early thrust into the political arena in 1960 to 1963 on the issues of migrant worker and civil rights were followed by its involvement in a larger number of complex issues: poverty, housing, general and voter education, community organization, and black economic development. While it would be misleading to attribute this expansion of political goals entirely to the paid professional staff (thus neglecting the importance of actors not holding staff positions), the data stipulate this group of persons as an important sponsor of change.

Another factor that attests to the staff's special significance is the fact that successful passage of meaningful civil rights legislation in the 1963 to 1965 period did not find the council reverting to its former pattern of relative political quiescence. In the post-1965 era it remained insistent that major social issues be confronted by the churches. Coalitions forged at the height of the civil rights era were for the most part maintained, and new coalitions, particularly with black militant groups and liberal elements in the Roman Catholic and Jewish communities, were formed.

Never before was pressure group activity aimed at social reform goals pursued as systematically and with as much sophistication as it was in the decade of the '60s. The organization's receptiveness to the view that the national government should play an increased role in solving social problems represented a break with its own traditions and aroused opposition among certain constituents, conservatives in particular. Unlike the 1910s and '20s, when dissension chiefly followed denominational lines (pietist versus modernist churches), the controversy of the 1960s was characterized by the attacks of conservatives, whatever their denomination, on the organization's liberal activism. Yet, while member churches with marked conservative tendencies were participants in the federation, their influence did not significantly disrupt the liberal consensus. An explanation for this has been found in the relatively higher rates of liberal church involvement, as measured by delegate attendance at board meetings, faithfulness in meeting budgetary quotas, and encouragement of members to seek elective and appointive office in the organization. The merger of 1950, discussed in chapter 2, also contributed to the liberal consensus, since social problems were now viewed in more comprehensive terms; thus, more comprehensive and radical solutions were proposed.

One would not anticipate any drastic changes in predisposition as long as NCC liberalism is supported by its more actively involved member bodies. True, there are numerous conservative churchmen in these same denominations; but their opposition has not succeeded in reordering priorities. Their impotency is partially attributable to the skill of council leaders in countering criticism and isolating opponents, as discussed in the preceding chapter. Though concrete evidence is lacking, it would also seem that within each member body liberals are more attracted to high-level staff posts than conservatives and are thus in a good strategic position to counter any conservative moves against the NCC.

PARALLELS WITH OTHER REFORM
ORGANIZATIONS

An important question the present study has raised is this: Under what conditions do mature organizations that are committed to broad social objectives undergo a reorientation in strategy such as the one described in the present work? The NCC has been our case study. In order to move to the level of generalization of the question raised, it is necessary to compare it with other organizations like it. Does the NCC's reorientation in the 1960s find its counterpart in other reform organizations; and if so, are common causal factors identifiable to account for the behavioral similarities?

It has already been shown that the NCC's stance toward domestic political issues can be classified into a threefold sequence. First, there was the stage prior to the New Deal era, when its reform goals were pursued through essentially private, nongovernmental channels. Though Federal Council leaders met with high government officials from time to time, they generally regarded increased government intervention as neither prudent nor wise. Second, the period beginning in the middle '30s was one in which council leaders, though clinging essentially to an apolitical stance, addressed themselves from time to time to important political questions, most especially to ones involving a threat to Protestant-Orthodox institutional status, but also, though more limitedly, to issues of broader social significance. Third, in the stage beginning in the early 1960s, the old anxiety over governmental intervention was largely put aside, at least with respect to issues affecting the rights and aspirations of minority groups and the poor. Moreover, alliances with other groups, once relatively unusual, now became commonplace as council leaders became more aware of the interconnectedness of social problems and the tactical advantages of coalitions.

It is an interesting question whether the growth in political self-consciousness in the NCC parallels in any way the experience of other reform-minded groups in American society. To find an answer, the author examined the behavior of three, randomly selected national groups: the American Civil Liberties Union (ACLU); the National Association for the Advancement of Colored People (NAACP); and the American Federation of Labor (AFL), currently the American Federation of Labor & Congress of Industrial Organizations (AFL-CIO).

Early Stage of Social Concern. Large voluntary organizations do not typically come into existence for the explicit purpose of exerting political pressure, even though almost all do eventually become politically active to some degree. Sharing the Lockean conviction as to the urgency of keeping governmental powers limited in scope, voluntary groups that formed in the late nineteenth and early twentieth centuries generally did not endeavor to enlist government as an ally. This was as much true of those on the American left as on the right. Samuel Gompers, founder of the American Federation of Labor, expressed the sentiments of more than his own trade unions when he insisted that the federal courts and Congress should adhere to a hands-off policy in disputes in the private sector.

The AFL, NAACP, and ACLU all went through an initial stage, lasting 20 years or more, during which they attempted not to enlarge but to restrict the powers vested in governmental officials, local, state, and national. For many years following its founding in 1886, the AFL fought for legislation designed to limit the use of federal court injunctions in labor disputes. The NAACP from its founding in 1909 struggled to overturn Jim Crow statutes in the South and to protect southern blacks from lynch mobs, whose activities presupposed the acquiescence of local law-enforcement officers, who occasionally blatantly encouraged lynchers. Similarly, the ACLU from its inception in 1920 fought to place a constitutional barrier between persons holding unpopular views and officials who would punish them for expressing them. The organization's early years were taken up with intervening in behalf of persons charged with such crimes as advocating avoidance of the draft laws and the over-throw of the government.

The initial bias of all three reform organizations, then, was in favor of small government. The notion that the national government might have a positive role to play in achieving re-form goals either was not considered or else was considered but rejected. Samuel Gompers opposed governmentally adminis-tered social insurance during his tenure as AFL president (1886–1924) in the belief that it would put a straight jacket on labor, which could achieve all the security it needed, Gompers thought, through collective bargaining. The AFL was equally unwilling to accept federal old-age pensions, unemployment compensation, and governmentally assisted medical care. Simi-larly, many of those attracted to leadership positions in the ACLU in its early days were philosophical anarchists or Lockean liberals. Even the socialists and Communists on the ACLU board were inclined to side with proponents of small government because they opposed a capitalist government. The bias against "positive government" in the NAACP was so pronounced that even in the depths of the depression it refused to endorse governmental measures to correct the economic ills of society. Though the association did crusade in favor of a federal antilynching statute, the statute was really a black defense measure, broadly analogous to the AFL's support of laws prohibiting injunctions in labor disputes, not an espousal of "positive government."

In contrast, the initial stage of social activism for the FCC was not characterized by any marked degree of defensiveness or by strategies explicitly designed to foster the status aspira-tions of rank-and-file constitutents, a point that will receive attention later in this chapter.

Stage of Crisis and Doubt about Strategy. Although certain of the activists in each of the organizations had for some time advocated that the national government be regarded as a potential ally rather than as an alien force, a change in strategy came about not in response to the reasoned objections of the critics, but to the "logic of events" and a dramatic adverse alter-ation of external and internal conditions.

In the case of the AFL, external changes occurred in the

middle and late 1930s. In 1935 a dissident faction within the AFL, led by John L. Lewis, Sidney Hillman, and others, took issue with the policies long adhered to by the entrenched leadership. Calling itself the Committee on Industrial Organization, the dissident group primarily advocated two things: first, that the AFL's time-honored opposition to industrial unionism, involving a refusal to recruit among the emergent mass production industries, was inimical to the interests of the labor movement; second, that the federation had heedlessly limited its involvement in politics and had refused to endorse needed federal programs, even in the face of four years of unprecedented hardship for American workers. The CIO leaders were thus intent not simply on organizing workers in the mass production industries, but on mobilizing laborers in order to exert political pressure. So important was the CIO's emphasis on *political* strategies that for the first two years after its official constitution in 1936, it was more active in seeking to maximize labor's influence on the Roosevelt administration than in organizing strikes.[1] In April 1936 the CIO leaders established an agency known as Labor's Non-Partisan League (LNPL), which amounted to an abandonment of labor's traditional policies of independent, bipartisan political action (though CIO leaders were reluctant to admit it), adopting instead an alliance with the Democratic party.

The initial response among AFL leaders to this threat was to play for time by making token concessions to the insurgents, although they remained adamant on fundamental points. The concessions came partly in the form of public policy proposals: in 1935 the federation resolved in favor of federally financed slum clearance and urban rehousing programs and appointed a committee on housing from among its own members; it endorsed the Wagner-Steagall bill to provide housing accommodations for millions of workers; in 1936 it supported in principle federal aid to education and appointed a committee to fight any reductions in federal unemployment compensation. At the same time, however, federation leaders sought to undermine the CIO. Its industrial unionists were accused of turning their backs on "bread-and-butter" union issues and of becoming "too political." In 1938 the AFL repudiated both the CIO-sponsored

Labor's Non-Partisan League and the CIO's New York state affiliate, the American Labor Party, charging that the latter was "no longer a labor organization but a purely political one." The federation also reaffirmed its long-standing tradition of not endorsing major party presidential candidates.

A comparable crisis confronted the NAACP early in the 1940s. For many years the association had monopolized the struggle to achieve civil rights, at least in the black community. External events jeopardized this monopoly by provoking the organization of rival groups. Beginning in the 1940s, previously unemployed white workers returned to the factories to produce munitions for the war effort, while many black workers remained jobless. The NAACP was slow to respond, and a host of new black protest organizations sprang up to contest its supremacy. In the face of challenges from groups like the Congress of Racial Equality (CORE), founded in 1942, and A. Philip Randolph's March on Washington Movement (MOWM), initiated in 1942, the NAACP's very survival appeared in question around the beginning of World War II. At first it responded to these threats by endorsing legislation in areas heretofore regarded as outside its province, such as federal aid to education and increased federal funding of public health programs. However, it did not as yet depart from its essentially apolitical strategy.

A comparable crisis did not occur in the life of the ACLU until the late 1940s and early '50s. Though agitated by the establishment of the House Un-American Activities Committee (HUAC) in the late 1930s, the ACLU did not become profoundly distressed until 1947, at which time the ACLU, viewing the committee as a grave threat to civil liberties and due process of law, voiced its opinion that HUAC ought to be abolished. HUAC did not let this affront pass unnoticed. It issued a subpoena demanding (though without success) that the ACLU produce all its records for committee scrutiny. Yet it did not accuse the ACLU of "un-American" activities, a fact that added to the belief that the subpoena was a purely retaliatory gesture.

The ACLU was equally distressed by the implications of President Truman's 1947 loyalty-security order, under which federal civilian employees were to be investigated to determine possible "security risks." By 1949 roughly 2.5 million federal workers had been investigated, even though the great majority were in "non-sensitive" posts. The ACLU pointed with alarm to the fact that decisions involving an employee's whole subsequent career could be made by loyalty-security boards as a result of hearings that denied the accused such elementary procedural rights as the right to cross-examine accusers or to be apprised of evidence introduced against him. This was viewed as the most insidious far-reaching threat to Bill of Rights guarantees since the ACLU's founding 30 years previous. Initially the ACLU intensified the use of traditional strategies, seeking federal court orders to curb the loyalty-security "witch-hunters." It was dismayed to discover, however, that the courts were in no mood to intervene decisively in this area, as witnessed by the unsympathetic action taken on the ACLU's 1947 suit against HUAC.

Stage of Reconsolidation and Reform Group Alliances. In each of the three organizations, the period of crisis was associated in time with a decision either to reorganize or to drastically increase executive posts. The most dramatic revamping occurred in the case of the AFL, which faced a serious threat to its stability from both internal and external sources; but change in the other two groups was only somewhat less dramatic.

For many years the combined salaries in the AFL's administrative personnel (i.e., other than general office employees) was $22,000. By 1940, however, top officer salaries totaled $48,800. Though some of the increase was doubtlessly due to raises given persons already on the staff, the larger portion was apparently assigned to holders of new posts. Ten years later the administrative salary figure had reached $121,000. Salaries for office employees showed a parallel growth: $112,000 in 1930, $198,000 in 1940, and $339,000 in 1950. In the cases of the NAACP and ACLU, the data on staff executives show the number of positions filled rather than salary expenditures. Prior to its early 1940s crisis period, the NAACP's national office employed between 5 and 8 salaried executives. In 1942, however, the number increased to 12, and by 1947 it had reached 23. The number continued to increase in the 1950s, reaching 42 by 1960. The

ACLU's national office staff varied in size between 5 and 6 executives from the mid-1920s to the middle of World War II. By 1951, however, the total was up to 9; and as the organization mobilized to meet the McCarthy era challenge, its headquarters personnel rose still more, numbering 12 by 1959.

What appears to have happened in each of these organizations was that the crisis atmosphere forced the top leaders to recognize the need for highly skilled professionals, who could cope with an increasingly complex and threatening environment. Herbert Wilensky has shown that in the case of labor unions the types of men hired were those intellectuals whose skills enabled them to fill the roles of "contact men," "internal relations specialists," and "facts and figures men"; possibly these same skills were sought after by other types of reform groups facing similar problems.

It is probably no mere coincidence that this period of staff enlargement roughly coincided with a fundamental reorientation in the AFL's, NAACP's, and ACLU's political outlooks, since staff skills would be vitally important in the successful implementation of the new approach. As the following discussion will suggest, the basic redefinition was most apparent in the case of the AFL, somewhat less so with the NAACP, and least of all with the ACLU. But in all cases the crisis period marked a turning point from which there was no return to older ways.

All of those whom the author has interviewed in the ACLU have stressed the basic continuity between the organization's work in the 1960s and in the 1920s. One ACLU executive put it this way:

> The ACLU has traditionally been concerned with three kinds of problems: first, freedom of speech; second, freedom of association and third, due process of law. There never has been a period in which cases in all three of these areas have not been before us, though it is true that the relative emphasis changes from time to time. Today [the 1960s] it is the due process area where many of the cases tend to cluster.[2]

Now, as in the past, the ACLU places heavy emphasis on seeking redress through the courts; the union has avoided alliances

with political parties and has never sought to influence the outcome of elections.

Yet despite this basic continuity in goals and strategy, important changes in approach to social issues are apparent for
the periods since the early 1950s. The ACLU in recent years
has come to define civil liberties as having a wide measure of
substantive, not merely procedural, content. Though still much
concerned with protecting individuals whose rights have been
jeopardized by overzealous officials, it has become more and
more interested in broad issues affecting large numbers of individuals.

The beginning of this more broadly defined domain can
best be dated from the year 1952, when the ACLU opened its
permanent Washington office, initially having one, presently
having three, full-time staff executives. Though the Washington office does not make policy decisions, its very existence has
presumably been a factor in the advocacy the organization has
increasingly given on Capitol Hill to social welfare proposals.
Without limiting themselves to narrowly defined civil liberties'
aspects, ACLU witnesses have testified in support of the Johnson administration's 1966 civil rights bill, the 1967 open-occupancy housing bill, and other similar measures. In what is to
date perhaps the ACLU's boldest entry into the sphere of partisan politics, the southern regional director, Charles Morgan,
served in September 1969 as ACLU spokesman in presenting a
200-page brief before the Democratic National Committee.
The brief supported the candidacy of an Alabama black for a
position on the Democratic National Committee and opposed
the candidacy of two whites who enjoyed the backing of the
"regular" Alabama Democratic party.

Though the national ACLU has avoided becoming actively
involved in dealing with social problems, certain of its spin-off
organizations have not been so constrained. The Lawyers Constitutional Defense Committee (founded in 1964 by the ACLU
and several other liberal groups) has helped extend civil liberties protections to individuals (especially indigent blacks) at
the *trial* stage, instead of waiting until the *appellate* stage.
Though cases on appeal may be adequate vehicles for clarify-
ing constitutional law, the appeals process per se does not fully

insure the rights of the individual. In the same way the Roger Baldwin Foundation (founded in 1967 and named for the ACLU's nationally prominent first executive secretary) has devoted its energies to issues concerning social welfare, mental health, and poverty.

In view of certain pressures now being exerted on the national leaders, it is conceivable that ACLU involvement in broad substantive issues will increase still further, at least if the New York City affiliate and various state affiliates have their way. One very vocal faction maintains that the current definition of civil liberties is entirely too legalistic.[3] It is worth noting in this connection that coalitions between the ACLU and other liberal reform organizations, once relatively infrequent, have recently become much more common. It participates, along with other groups, in such coalitions as the National Committee against Discrimination in Housing, the Leadership Conference on Civil Rights, the National Civil Liberties Clearing House, and the Lawyers Constitutional Defense Committee. As a result, its perspective may become polyvalent.

A development closely related to this expansion in social and political interests is the substantial increase in recent years in the ACLU's dues-paying membership. The decision to make the ACLU into a mass membership organization was a self-conscious one aimed at providing the national organization with greater grass roots backup for its efforts during the McCarthy era. Membership was further amplified by the national board's decision, in 1950, after many years during which the total membership remained under 10,000, to build a network of state and local affiliates that would address themselves to local civil liberties needs. Consequently, the total membership in 1961 was 65,000. While the initial decision to enlarge the membership base was a defensive move designed by ACLU to counter the actions taken against the union and other civil liberties groups, it is evident that the long-term result has been to enhance the ACLU's political leverage in behalf of reform causes.

The NAACP and the AFL have witnessed roughly comparable developments in recent years. The NAACP's legislative interests in the 1920s and '30s were concentrated on seeking a federal antilynching statute. Beginning in the late 1940s, how-ever, the association came to recognize a deep and sustained stake in the legislative process as it began to address itself to a host of legislative proposals. In an action that was to have substantial long-range significance, it took the initiative, to-gether with a number of reform organizations, in forming in 1949 the National Emergency Civil Rights Mobilization to fight for passage of President Truman's civil rights package. The mobilization soon matured into a permanent body, the Leadership Conference on Civil Rights, which has remained closely tied to the NAACP but which is sufficiently autonomous to permit joint action on civil rights matters by a number of liberal organizations. Scarcely less significant are the NAACP's increasingly close ties with the headquarters staff of the AFL-CIO.

Among the three groups being discussed, the most exten-sive change in strategy and tactics occurred in the case of the AFL. As noted above, the federation modified its traditional bipartisan, narrowly defensive political stance in the 1930s, but only to the degree considered necessary to forestall further in-roads into its membership by the CIO. This conservative re-sponse came to appear inadequate, however, as the CIO grew despite the AFL's best efforts and as labor's enemies took ad-vantage of its internal squabbles to seize the upper hand in Congress. Though distressed by passage of the antistrike Smith-Connally Act of 1943, the federation was inclined to shrug off this setback, attributing it to the wartime emergency. But the passage of the 1947 Taft-Hartley Act, regarded by AFL leaders as antilabor legislation of the worst sort, could not be so easily dismissed; indeed, it came as a profound shock.

In 1948 the AFL junked its long-standing apolitical orienta-tion and authorized the establishment of the Labor League for Political Education, with the objectives of winning support both for the repeal of Taft-Hartley and for the reelection of President Truman, over whose veto the measure had been passed. Presumably, the AFL's greatly expanded staff resources were a factor in the alliances forged in the late '40s and early '50s with other reform organizations. A redefinition of its stake in national politics was testified to by the organization's beginning to support measures in which labor's interests were more than just defensive: civil rights, housing, welfare, tax policy, medical aid and so forth. In 1952 it formally endorsed the Democratic candidate for president and thus became, along with the CIO and certain other groups, an official part of the Democratic coalition. The merger between the CIO and the AFL in 1955 may thus be attributed in part to the resolving of former differences on the politics issue. Since the role of congressional lobbyist had long been recognized as one of the important responsibilities of a national labor federation, the merger would not in all likelihood have taken place without substantial agreement between the two self-proclaimed representatives of labor.[4]

COMPARISON WITH THE NCC

Comparing these three groups with the council suggests an essential similarity in behavior, but also one or two important points of difference. In all four cases the present stage of political self-consciousness was preceded by one in which leaders believed in the efficacy of private channels in resolving social issues and thus stressed the need to circumscribe government intervention (local and state, as well as national). Early interventions in the political process were normally confined to issues on which group members had an obvious vested interest; only gradually was the scope of concern broadened to include larger political issues. In this latter stage, especially, the national staff became important, since it was these persons who often were most acutely aware of the need to broaden the definition of group self-interest and to enter into mutual relations with other, similarly inclined groups. Though there are limits in the degree to which staff professionals can mold policy in an organization, a point emphasized in Harold Wilensky's 1955 work, *Intellectuals in Labor Unions*, they do nevertheless wield influence out of proportion to their number.

Having said all this, however, it is important not to neglect areas in which the council's behavior has been discrepant with that of the other three groups. Whereas there was a marked political defensiveness in the early activities of the NAACP, ACLU, and AFL, this was not true of the council's initial behavior and even in the 1930s, '40s, and '50s, when the council intervened occasionally to ward off social and political threats, it is clear that the NCC never became a "defense group" in quite the same way that the NAACP, for example, became one. The explanation for this difference probably lies in Protestantism's relatively high status in American life, which gave this interdenominational organization a confidence and security that the other bodies, with their more embattled constituents, did not have. The contrast should not be overdrawn, of course, since in one sense the very existence of the council owed something to Protestant anxiety over the apparent inability of traditional evangelism to reach the urban masses and to the fact that in an increasingly urbanized America even white Protestant churchmen had to relegitimate their values and institutions. But granting these qualifications, the point still seems a valid one.

Another interesting contrast, also probably related to the higher differential prestige of Protestantism, is that the council's interventions in the political process have mostly been successful (if success is measured by administrative rulings, acts of Congress, and so forth). On such diverse questions as civil rights, national educational policy, a U.S. ambassador to the Vatican, and the loyalty of Protestant churchmen, strong council actions have generally not gone unheeded. With the other three groups, however, it has not been uncommon for their legislative crusades to go on for many years, encountering repeated rebuffs and ultimately enjoying only partial success. This contrast calls attention to the fact that the NCC has not found itself locked in combat with other groups that have instantly mobilized against it whenever it has ventured into the public realm. While it is true that from time to time the council has had to contend with the animosity of rival bodies, such as the American Council of Christian Churches founded by Carl McIntyre in 1941, these rivalries have not basically conditioned its behavior in the way, for example, that probusiness groups affect the actions of the AFL-CIO.

Yet if high prestige offers some unique advantages to a group, it also has its drawbacks. Unlike the other three reform bodies, council lobbyists do not enjoy the support of a large,

consistently attentive audience, whose support can be galva-
nized at crucial moments in the legislative struggle, a deficiency
only partially compensated for by the activity of local and state
councils of churches analyzed in chapter 7. In the 1960s the
circulation of *MEMO*, the NCC Washington Office newsletter,
was at its peak, only 7,000, a minuscule number considering the
organization's enormously inclusive membership. A rank-and-
file membership that is aroused against an outgroup is more
likely to heed leadership requests for letters, telegrams, and
personal visitations; the NCC obviously lacks these media of
grass roots communication. With considerations like these in
mind, one observer, William C. McLoughlin, recently wrote in
a respected journal that the NCC may be dismissed as a political force: "The Protestant churches lack sufficient units to act
with their old confident vigor. They seem querulous and con-
fused. While the voice of the National Council of Churches
still speaks for reform and change, it has no way of implement-
ing its policies." [5]

One would be loath to accept McLoughlin's statement as it
stands. No group capable of delivering 40,000 white churchmen for a March on Washington, of leading the sophisticated
lobbying effort for the 1964 Civil Rights Act, or of reversing, in
collaboration with a handful of other groups, the tide of congressional mail on an issue as important as the Becker Amendment is to be altogether discounted as a political force.

There is, however, a germ of truth in McLoughlin's remark.
The council's capacity to implement its policies is indeed se-
verely constrained. Yet a somewhat more qualified assessment,
stressing the great contingency of its influence on national
policy, would be more accurate. On issues on which Protestantism's views have had a chance to mature over a period of years
(for example, the matter of civil rights in the years prior to
1963), a substantial show of strength, including back-up support from local councils of churches and local denominational
officials, is possible.

If the NCC is accorded a reputation for limited influence on
Capitol Hill, this may be so because of its tendency (common
among liberal Protestant organizations) to address a vast array
of issues, including many on which there is little internal con-

sensus and on which grass roots support is unlikely to be mobilized to any degree. Though a few stands may enjoy substantial grass roots support, these are overshadowed by the greater number that do not, thus detracting from the political prestige of the organization. Also, even on those issues in which the NCC has been quite active, congressmen do not attribute victory as being even in part the result of its efforts.

In light of this, NCC leaders might well consider reducing the variety of issues on which it takes a stand in the name of the churches and might concentrate instead on efforts to stimulate grass roots sentiment on a few issues of compelling moral significance. This would not, of course, offer any absolute assurance of success; but it might make it more difficult for federal lawmakers and bureaucrats to brush aside its claims. It is tempting for assemblies of churchmen to issue pronouncements on a great variety of subjects, since this fosters a feeling of being socially relevant, entails little risk, and generally prompts a fair amount of publicity in the press. A situation like the Birmingham crisis does not come along every day to galvanize churchmen on an issue; yet the NCC is generally passive, allowing external events to order its priorities. As the NCC staff personnel in Washington reported in interviews with the author, they were able in the Birmingham crisis to subordinate other matters to a single overriding priority, thus enhancing their political effectiveness. A more carefully thought out set of legislative priorities, like those that have strengthened the long-term effectiveness of the NAACP, AFL-CIO, and ACLU, might have a highly beneficial effect on council prestige in Washington.

One of the most difficult questions to answer about the council as it enters the decade of the 1970s is whether it can continue to serve as an effective vehicle for focusing Protestant-Orthodox concern about social issues. Will the animosities generated over the "Black Manifesto" and struggles within churches between black caucuses and denominational leaders diminish the organization's capacity to act? Will a way be found to involve the Eastern Orthodox churches significantly in the council's affairs, or will the existing Protestant-Orthodox rift widen into a genuine cleavage? Can ways be found to recoup recent substantial declines in NCC income, ways that do not involve giving "hostages" to the most conservative and reactionary elements in the constituency? These are hard questions, and the data at hand do not provide conclusive answers, especially since the NCC is continually changing. While it is impossible to foresee the future, present trends suggest that the organization may have already embarked upon a new phase of its life, an era of confrontation.

Notes

Several works have been relied upon repeatedly as sources for the present study. Valuable for historical materials relating to church involvement in social issues were John A. Hutchinson, *We Are Not Divided: A Critical and Historical Study of the Federal Council of the Churches of Christ in America* (1941); Samuel McCrea Cavert, *The American Churches in the Ecumenical Movement, 1900–1968* (1968); and Paul A. Carter, *The Decline and Revival of the Social Gospel: Social and Political Liberalism in American Protestant Churches, 1920–1940* (1956). Other broadly comprehensive works found useful in preparing various chapters were Donald B. Meyer, *The Protestant Search for Political Realism, 1919–1940* (1961); Charles H. Hopkins, *The Rise of the Social Gospel in American Protestantism, 1865–1915* (1940); and Robert H. Miller, *American Protestantism and Social Issues, 1919–1939* (1958). Newspapers and periodicals were an indispensable source, especially in connection with developments in the 1950s, '60s, and early '70s. Materials drawn from the *Christian Century* and from the *New York Times* proved valuable in researching virtually every chapter. Other useful periodical sources were *Christianity Today*, *Christianity and Crisis*, and the official house organ of the council, varying from time to time in title and format, the *Federal Council Bulletin*, *Interchurch News*, and *Tempo*.

Chapter 1

All the works listed in the selected bibliography ("Protestant Relations with the Existing Social Order") are worthwhile from the standpoint of the issues raised in this introductory chapter. For their theoretical insights J. Milton Yinger's *Religion and the Struggle for Power* (1946) and Gerhard Lenski's *The Religious Factor* (1961) should be especially noted.

1. Leslie W. Dunbar, *A Republic of Equals* (Ann Arbor: University of Michigan Press, 1966), p. 57. Dunbar mentions a fifth point in the liberal outlook, namely, lack of religious commitment, which is obviously absent in the council's case.

2. John A. Hutchinson, *We Are Not Divided: A Critical and Historical Study of the Federal Council of the Churches of Christ in America* (New York: Round Table Press, 1941), pp. 308–9, 44.

3. Ibid., p. 306.

4. Samuel McCrea Cavert, *The American Churches in the Ecumenical Movement, 1900–1968* (New York: Association Press, 1968), p. 142.

5. Hutchinson, p. 303.

6. Peter Day, "The National Council of Churches: An Evaluation," *Christianity and Crisis,* 16 May 1960, p. 67.

7. Ibid., p. 71.

8. Martin E. Marty, *The New Shape of American Religion* (New York: Harper & Row Publishers, 1959), p. 63.

9. Ibid., p. 77.

10. Peter L. Berger, *The Noise of Solemn Assemblies* (Garden City, N. Y.: Doubleday & Co., 1961), p. 38.

11. Ibid., pp. 46–47.

12. Ibid., pp. 60, 72.

13. Lawrence H. Fuchs, *The Political Behavior of American Jews* (Glencoe, Ill.: Free Press, 1956), chap. 11.

14. Philip E. Hammond, *The Campus Clergyman* (New York: Basic Books, 1966), pp. 43–44; J. Milton Yinger, *Religion and the Struggle for Power* (Durham, N.C.: Duke University Press, 1946, p. 157.

15. Gerhard Lenski, *The Religious Factor* (Garden City, N. Y.: Doubleday & Co., 1961), p. 275. Lenski's findings on this point are not wholly consistent with the results of other studies of ministers' attitudes. See: Charles Y. Glock and Benjamin B. Ringer, "Church Policy and the Attitudes of Ministers and Parishioners on Social Issues," *American Sociological Review* (Apr. 1956): 154, 156; Benton Johnson, "Ascetic Protestantism and Political Preferences," *Public Opinion Quarterly* 26, no. 1 (Spring 1962); 35–36. These studies found that parish clergy in main line Protestant churches are more liberal than their parishioners.

16. Marion K. Sanders, "A Professional Radical Moves in on Rochester," *Harper's,* July 1965, p. 52.

Chapter 2

Material for the opening section of this chapter having to do with the events leading up to and including the merger was drawn mainly from the works by Hutchinson listed in the introductory paragraph to these annotations. The later sections, pertaining to the larger significance of the merger, were based essentially on primary sources: *City Church* and *Town and Country Church* magazines, the *Interchurch News,* and interviews with several informants in the NCC Division of Christian Life and Mission. The writings of Amitai Etzioni, especially his *Modern Organizations* (1964), proved valuable in interpreting internal developments.

1. Hutchinson, *We Are Not Divided,* p. 82.

2. Quoted in Cavert, *American Churches,* pp. 195–96.

3. Charles H. Hopkins, *The Rise of the Social Gospel in American Protestantism, 1865–1915* (New Haven, Conn.: Yale University Press, 1940), pp. 318–19.

4. Amitai Etzioni, *Modern Organizations* (Englewood Cliffs, N. J.: Prentice Hall, 1964), p. 15.
5. *Christian Century*, 26 Nov. 1952, p. 1,374.
6. Quoted in *Town and Country Church*, Jan. 1960, p. 32.
7. *Newsweek*, 21 Dec. 1964, p. 45.
8. Interview with Rev. Dean M. Kelley, July 1967.
9. Ibid.
10. Interview with Rev. Jon Regier, Aug. 1967.

Chapter 3

The importance of "active minorities" in the internal leadership of large organizations is discussed at length in David B. Truman, *The Governmental Process* (1951), which also contains footnote references to the then-existing body of literature on this subject. On the matter of declining social distance between Protestant denominations and the related increase in support for inter-denominational organizations such as the council, see Robert E. Lee, *The Social Sources of Church Unity* (1960). Denominational attendance figures and data on involvement in leadership were derived from the FCC *Annual Reports* (available in the National Council of Churches archives, 475 Riverside Drive, New York City) and from the NCC *Biennial Report* (prior to 1960) and *Triennial Report* (also available there). Useful material was also found in the *Yearbook of American Churches* (annually, 1951–67) and in *Who's Who in America*. The 1950 NCC Constitution, relied on for the section dealing with the formal decision-making process, is reprinted as an appendix to the 1951 NCC *Biennial Report*.

1. David B. Truman, *The Governmental Process* (New York: Alfred A. Knopf, 1951), pp. 139–55.
2. Hutchinson, *We Are Not Divided*, p. 310.
3. Ibid., p. 73.

Chapter 4

A number of works were consulted in the preparation of this chapter, and for a complete listing the reader should see the selected bibliography ("Liberal and Conservative Tendencies among Member Churches" and "Staff Liberalism"). Especially valuable in interpreting trends among the more liberal-activist churches were the works by Carter, Meyer, and Miller. For data on liberal-church behavior subsequent to the information in these works, the author relied heavily on the *New York Times*.

Among the numerous volumes consulted with respect to the more conservative churches, a few were found to be especially useful: John Meyendorff, *The Orthodox Church, Its Past and Its Role in the World Today* (1960); Robert G. Torbet, *A History of the Baptists* (1963); and Paul M. Harrison, *Authority and Power in the Free Church Tradition* (1959). On the (conservative) black churches, see St. Clair Drake and Horace R. Cayton, *Black Metropolis* (1945); and Joseph R. Washington, *The Politics of God* (1967). *Newsweek* magazine also proved a useful source.

1. Donald B. Meyer, *The Protestant Search for Political Realism, 1919–1940* (Berkeley: University of California Press, 1961), pp. 44–45, 345.

2. Yinger, *Religion*, p. 139.

3. Robert H. Miller, *American Protestantism and Social Issues, 1919–1939* (Chapel Hill: University of North Carolina Press, 1958), pp. 74, 85–86; Paul A. Carter, *The Decline and Revival of the Social Gospel: Social and Political Liberalism in American Protestant Churches, 1920–1940* (Ithaca, N. Y.: Cornell University Press, 1956), pp. 82, 172, 175–76.

4. Miller, chap. 8; Carter, pp. 82, 172–76.

5. Robert G. Torbet, *A History of the Baptists* rev. ed. (Valley Forge, Pa.: Judson Press, 1963), p. 501.

6. Quoted in David M. Reimers, *White Protestantism and the Negro* (New York: Oxford University Press, 1965), p. 112.

7. "NCC Acts on Racial Crisis," *Christian Century*, 19 June 1963, p. 793.

8. *Christian Century*, 20 Nov. 1957, p. 1,374.

9. John Meyendorff, *The Orthodox Church, Its Past and Its Role in the World Today;* transl. from the French by John Chapin (New York: Pantheon Books, 1960), p. 224. See also: Alexander Schmemann, "Orthodox Agony and the World Council of Churches," *Christianity Today*, 8 Jan. 1958, pp. 3–4.

10. *Newsweek*, 9 Feb. 1970, p. 78.

11. Ibid.

12. U.S., Congress, House, *Congressional Record*, 89th Cong., 2d sess. 7 Apr. 1966, p. 8,043.

13. Paul M. Harrison, *Authority and Power in the Free Church Tradition* (Princeton, N. J.: Princeton University Press, 1959), pp. 152, 140.

14. Ibid., pp. 125, 135.

15. Ibid., p. 152.

16. "Fundamentalists' Nose Grip on A.B.C.," *Christian Century*, 5 June 1946, p. 725.

17. Willis H. Porter, associate general secretary, ABC, *The American Baptists and the Wider Fellowship*, rev. ed. (Valley Forge, Pa.: Division of Cooperative Christianity, ABC, 1967), p. 6.

18. *Newsweek*, 20 June 1960, p. 67.

19. ABC, *Yearbook of the American Baptist Convention* (Valley Forge, Pa., 1960), pp. 46–47.

20. Torbet, p. 477.

21. E. Franklin Frazier, *Black Bourgeoisie* (Glencoe, Ill.: Free Press, 1957), p. 88. See also: Gunnar Myrdal, *An American Dilemma*, vol. 2 (New York: Harper & Row Publishers, 1944), pp. 861–62, 877.

22. Horace A. White, "Who Owns the Negro Church," *Christian Century*, 9 Feb. 1938, p. 176; St. Clair Drake and Horace R. Cayton, *Black Metropolis* (New York: Harcourt, Brace & Co., 1945), chap. 15; Frazier, p. 129.

23. James M. Gustafson, "The Clergy in the United States," *Daedalus* 92, no. 4 (Fall 1963): 740–41. See also: Gustafson, "The Theological Education of Negro Ministers," in *The Advancement of Theological Education*, eds. H. R. Hiebuhr, D. D. Williams, and J. M. Gustafson (New York: Harper & Row Publishers, 1957), pp. 226–36.

24. Theodore M. Newcomb, *Persistence and Change: Bennington College and Its Students After Twenty-Five Years* (New York: John Wiley & Sons, 1967); Nevitt Sanford, *The American College* (New York: John Wiley & Sons, 1962), and *Where Colleges Fail* (San Francisco: Jossey-Bass, 1967); Liston Pope, *The Kingdom Beyond Caste* (New York: Friendship Press, 1957), p.

118; James Q. Wilson, *Negro Politics: The Search for Leadership* (Glencoe, Ill.: Free Press, 1960), p. 298.

25. Drake and Cayton, pp. 412–29, 613; W. Seward Salisbury, *Religion in American Culture* (Homewood, Ill.: Dorsey Press, 1964), pp. 128–29; Wilson, op. cit., pp. 128–30.

26. Quoted in "A Black Schism," *Newsweek,* 4 Mar. 1968, p. 190.

27. Joseph R. Washington, *The Politics of God* (Boston: Beacon Press, 1967), p. 211, chap. 7.

Chapter 5

Though somewhat biased because it was intended in part to justify his own position in the struggle, J. Howard Pew's *The Chairman's Final Report to the National Lay Committee* (1955) is an indispensable source on this topic. Pew provides not only a narrative of the events that transpired, but includes appendices containing verbatim transcripts of certain key meetings. The work is available in the NCC Research Library, 475 Riverside Drive, New York City. Articles appearing in the *Christian Century* and *Christianity and Crisis,* as well as interviews with informants in the NCC Office of Budget and Programming, provided useful supplementary information. For a glimpse into how the National Lay Committee was viewed by high-level NCC officials, Cavert, *American Churches,* should be consulted.

1. *Fortune,* Nov. 1957, p. 177.
2. Cavert, *American Churches,* p. 221.

Pew did make a gesture toward obtaining denominational validation of the people he chose to serve on the committee. The names of all perspective members were submitted to their respective denominational headquarters for approval (J. Howard Pew, *The Chairman's Final Report to the National Lay Committee* [New York: NCC, 1955], p. 2). There is no evidence of any denomination having refused to go along with his nominees.

3. John Kenneth Galbraith, " 'The Affluent Society' After Ten Years," *Atlantic* 223, no. 5 (May 1969): 37, 39.

4. Quoted in J. Howard Pew, *The Chairman's Final Report to the National Lay Committee* (New York: NCC, 1955), p. 10. See also: *Christian Century,* 13 Dec. 1950, pp. 1,475–76.

5. Pew, p. 11. So that the Lay Committee could enjoy some official administrative home, it was voted to make it a division of the yet-to-be-created Department of United Church Men. The General Board resolution also authorized creation of a parallel body, the "National Laywomen's Committee," to be situated in the Department of United Church Women.

6. From the minutes of the General Board, 28 Nov. 1951, reprinted in Pew, p. 15.

7. Ibid., p. 15.
8. *Christianity and Crisis,* 12 May 1952, p. 63.
9. Pew, pp. 32–33.
10. Ibid., pp. 128–36.
11. *Christianity and Crisis,* 7 Jan. 1952, p. 177.
12. Pew, pp. 186–88.
13. Ibid., pp. 43.

14. Ibid., p. 223.

15. Ibid., pp. 237–38.

16. Ibid., pp. 247–48, 250–51.

17. Interview with Eugene Carson Blake, Mar. 1969.

18. Letters in *Christianity and Crisis,* 12 May 1952, pp. 62–63. Blake's statement was viewed as a sufficiently serious challenge to liberals to require a response from the president of Union Theological Seminary, Henry P. Van Dusen (ibid., 7 July 1952, p. 89).

19. *Christian Century,* 21 Dec. 1960, p. 767; ibid., 25 Oct. 1961, p. 1,286.

Chapter 6

Among the books and articles cited in the notes and selected bibliography ("Staff Liberalism"), none stands out as being especially crucial. The importance of the NCC staff as an influence on NCC policy has not been properly appreciated in the literature, although Harvey G. Cox's article "The 'New Breed' in American Churches" (1967) is broadly applicable to the NCC and other church bureaucracies.

1. J. Milton Yinger, *A Sociologist Looks at Religion* (New York: Macmillan Company, 1963), p. 172.

2. Harrison, *Authority and Power,* pp. 136–42.

3. *Christianity Today,* 17 Mar. 1967, p. 42.

4. Harvey G. Cox, "The 'New Breed' in American Churches," *Daedalus* 96, no. 1. (Winter 1967): 141.

5. Ibid., pp. 141–42.

6. Franklin H. Littell, "Protestant Seminary Education in a Time of Change," in *Seminary Education in a Time of Change,* eds. James M. Lee and Louis J. Putz (Notre Dame, Ind.: Fides Publishers, 1965), p. 545.

7. Meyer, *Protestant Search,* p. 451, n. 53.

8. Herman Reissig, "Homeless Religious Radicals," *Christian Century,* 4 Aug. 1937, p. 972, background data obtained from *Who's Who in America.*

9. Meyer, p. 241.

10. Charles P. Taylor, *Ministry for Tomorrow: Report of the Special Committee on Theological Education of the Protestant Episcopal Church* (Greenwich, Conn.: Seabury Press, 1967), p. 62.

11. Background data obtained from *Who's Who in America.*

12. Reinhold Niebuhr, "The Radical Minister and His Church," *Radical Religion* 2 (Winter 1936): 25–27.

13. Lenski, *Religious Factor,* p. 139.

14. Ibid., p. 148.

15. Ibid., pp. 158, 168.

16. Ibid., p. 276.

Chapter 7

The most comprehensive work to date on state and local councils of churches is Ross W. Sanderson's *Church Cooperation in the United States: The Nation-Wide Backgrounds and Ecumenical Significance of State and Local Councils of Churches in Their Historical Perspective* (1960). The importance of local councils is also stressed in works by church council secretaries, including Forrest L. Knapp, *Church Cooperation: Dead-End Street or Highway to*

Unity? (1966); and William B. Cate, "Institutionalism and Ecumenical Co-operation in the Local Community" (1963).

1. Murray S. Stedman, *Religion and Politics in America* (New York: Harcourt, Brace & Co., 1961), p. 95. Stedman remarks that the NCC Washington Office is "not in a position to give the kind of detailed and expert counsel in legislative and administrative matters which the National Catholic Welfare Conference [roughly equivalent to the NCC Washington Office] is accustomed to giving."

2. Glock and Ringer, "Church Policy," pp. 154–55.

3. Anna Arnold Hedgeman, *The Trumpet Sounds: A Memoir of Negro Leadership* (New York: Holt, Rinehart and Winston, 1964), pp. 177, 194.

4. Interview with the NCC Office for Councils of Churches, 1967. The increasing interpenetration of the work of the OCC and that of councils of churches' secretaries is alluded to in Ross W. Sanderson, *Church Cooperation in the United States: The Nation-Wide Backgrounds and Ecumenical Significance of State and Local Councils of Churches in Their Historical Perspective* (New York: Association of Council Secretaries, 1960), pp. 228–29, 239. One should also take note of the work of the Association of Council Secretaries (founded in 1940), comprised of secretaries from councils at all levels. ACS annual meetings provide a forum for exchange of information and policy views.

5. William B. Cate, "Institutionalism and Ecumenical Cooperation in the Local Community," in *Institutionalism and Church Unity: A Symposium,* eds. Nils Ehrenstrom and Walter G. Muelder (New York: Association Press, 1963), p. 360.

Chapter 8

Constraints affecting NCC political activity are enumerated in James Allen Nash's doctoral dissertation, "Church Lobbying in the Federal Government" (1967). Luke E. Ebersole's *Church Lobbying in the Nation's Capital* (1951) and Dayton D. McKean's essay "State, Church and the Lobby" (1961) provide useful insights into the council's defensive posture in the 1935 to 1963 era, including the Vatican ambassador controversy. The discussion of the 1961 Air Force training manual controversy draws on R. Morton Darrow's "The Church and Techniques of Political Action" (1961), Cavert's *American Churches,* and the *Interchurch News* (Mar., Apr. 1960). Interdenominational Protestantism's initial response to the race issue is discussed in David M. Reimers's *White Protestantism and the Negro* (1965) and Robert W. Spike's *The Freedom Revolution and the Churches* (1965). An earlier work is also valuable: Frank S. Loescher's *The Protestant Church and the Negro: A Pattern of Segregation* (1948).

1. James Allen Nash, "Church Lobbying in the Federal Government" (Ph.D. diss., Boston University, 1967), p. 4.

2. "Consultation on Christian Witness in the Nation's Capital, Interim Report," mimeo, Division of Christian Life and Mission, NCC, 19 Dec. 1966, pp. 1–4.

3. *Annual Report* (New York: National Offices, FCC, 1935), pp. 108–9.

4. FCC, *Annual Report* (New York, National Offices, FCC, 1946).

5. Luke E. Ebersole, *Church Lobbying in the Nation's Capital* (New York: Macmillan Co., 1951), pp. 97–98.

6. *Time,* 12 Nov. 1951, p. 21.

7. Quoted in Hutchinson, *We Are Not Divided,* p. 135.

8. Robert Lewis Zangrando, "The Efforts of the National Association for the Advancement of Colored People to Secure Passage of a Federal Anti-Lynching Law, 1920–1940" (Ph.D. diss., University of Pennsylvania, 1963).

9. Robert W. Spike, *The Freedom Revolution and the Churches* (New York: Association Press, 1965), p. 86.

10. Louis C. Kesselman, *The Social Politics of FEPC: A Study in Reform Pressure Movements* (Chapel Hill: University of North Carolina Press, 1948), pp. 134–35.

11. J. Oscar Lee, letter to the author, Sept. 1967.

12. Espy's talk is reported in *Information Service,* 17 Feb. 1962, pp. 2–3.

Chapter 9

The basic source on the NCC Commission on Religion and Race is the commission's own publication, *Report* (published quarterly, 1964–67), available from the NCC Department of Social Justice. Useful interpretations by CORR staff personnel may be found in Spike's *Freedom Revolution* and Anna Arnold Hedgeman's *The Trumpet Sounds: A Memoir of Negro Leadership* (1964). For the section dealing with CORR during the directorship of Benjamin F. Payton, the author relied on Lee Rainwater and William L. Yancey, *The Moynihan Report and the Politics of Controversy* (1967), accounts in the *New York Times,* and interviews with NCC staff. The account of the legislative struggle involved in the passage of the 1964 and 1965 civil rights acts is based primarily on Congressional Quarterly Service, *A Revolution in Civil Rights* (1968).

1. Interview with Samuel McCrea Cavert, former general secretary of the NCC, July 1967.

2. *New York Times,* 26 May 1963, p. 1.

3. Interview with Eugene Carson Blake, Mar. 1969.

4. *Interchurch News,* June–July 1963, pp. 6–7.

5. *Christian Century,* 19 June 1963, p. 797.

6. Hedgeman, *Trumpet Sounds,* pp. 177–78.

7. U.S., Congress, House, *Congressional Record, Appendix,* 88th Cong., 1st sess., 3 Dec. 1963, p. A7448.

8. Quoted in Congressional Quarterly Service, *A Revolution in Civil Rights,* 4th ed. (Washington, D.C.: U.S. Government Printing Office, 1968), p. 59.

9. U.S., Congress, Senate, *Congressional Record,* 88th Cong., 2nd sess., 18 June 1964, p. 14,322.

10. Ibid., pp. 14,323–24.

11. Claude Sitton, "South Girds for Crisis," *New York Times,* 14 June 1964, p. 6.

12. Eric C. Blanchard, "The Delta Ministry," *Christian Century,* 17 Mar. 1965, p. 338.

13. Daniel P. Moynihan, "The President and the Negro," *Commentary* 43, no. 2 (Feb. 1967): 40, 41.

14. Lee Rainwater and William L. Yancey, *The Moynihan Report and the Politics of Controversy* (Cambridge, Mass.: M.I.T. Press, 1967), p. 237.

15. *New York Times*, 24 Feb. 1966, p. 74.

16. Benjamin F. Payton, "Civil Rights and the Future of American Cities," *Social Action* 33, no. 4 (Dec. 1966): 11.

Chapter 10

The official NCC publication *Tempo* and accounts appearing in the *New York Times* were the sources for the narrative. Two works dealing with the "Black Manifesto" have recently appeared: Arnold Schuchter, *Reparations: The Black Manifesto and Its Challenge to White America* (Philadelphia: Lippincott & Co., 1970); and Robert S. Lecky and H. Elliott Wright, *Black Manifesto: Religion, Racism and Reparations* (New York: Sheed and Ward, 1969). Neither work adequately treats the role of the NCC in the "Black Manifesto" issue.

1. *Tempo*, 1 July 1969, pp. 3, 9.

2. Stephen C. Rose, "Putting It to the Churches," *New Republic*, 21 June 1969, p. 19.

3. For the full text of the speech, see *Tempo*, 15 July 1969, p. 9.

4. *New York Times*, 27 July 1969, p. 54.

5. *Tempo*, 1 June 1969, p. 8.

6. *New York Times*, 27 July 1969, p. 54.

7. *Tempo*, 2 June 1969, p. 10.

8. *New York Times*, 27 July 1969, p. 54.

9. *Tempo*, 15 Aug. 1969, p. 10.

10. *Tempo*, 5 June 1969, p. 3.

11. *Tempo*, 15 July 1969, p. 3.

12. *New York Times*, 27 July 1969, p. 54.

13. Rose, "Putting It to the Churches," p. 21.

14. *New York Times*, 27 July 1969, p. 54.

15. *Christianity Today*, 22 May 1970, p. 37.

16. Sherman S. Roddy, "Black Manifesto—A Reappraisal," *Church and Society*, May–June 1970, pp. 40–41.

17. Ibid., pp. 48–49.

18. *Church and Society*, Sept.–Oct. 1970, p. 15; *Christianity Today*, 22 May 1970, p. 37.

Chapter 11

Three works served as the basis for the discussion of church involvement in the general federal school aid fight. These were Frank J. Munger and Richard F. Fenno, *National Politics and Federal Aid to Education* (1962); Eugene Eidenberg and Roy D. Morey, *An Act of Congress: The Legislative Process and the Making of Education Policy* (1969); and Dean M. Kelley and George R. LaNoue, "The Church-State Settlement in the Federal Aid to Education Act" (1966). The section on theological viewpoints relating to Protestant concern with public education was based largely on Thomas G. Sanders, *Protestant Concepts of Church and State: Historical Backgrounds and Approaches for the Future* (1964). The main source for the section dealing with the Becker Amendment controversy was William M. Beaney and Edward N. Beiser, "Prayer and Politics: The Impact of 'Engle' and 'Schempp' on the Political Process" (1964).

1. "Church and State in Religion and Public Education," a pronouncement passed by the NCC General Board, 20 May, 1953 (available from the NCC Office of Information).

2. "Public Funds for Public Schools," a pronouncement passed by the NCC General Board, 22 Feb. 1961 (available from the NCC Office of Information).

3. Frank J. Munger and Richard F. Fenno, *National Politics and Federal Aid to Education*, The Economics and Politics of Public Education Series, no. 3 (Syracuse N. Y.: Syracuse University Press, 1962), p. 9.

4. Thomas G. Sanders, *Protestant Concepts of Church and State: Historical Backgrounds and Approaches for the Future* (New York: Holt, Rinehart and Winston, 1964), p. 257.

5. Paul Blanshard, *American Freedom and Catholic Power* (Boston: Beacon Press), 1949.

6. Sanders, pp. 20–21, 277.

7. Ibid., p. 271.

8. Cavert, *American Churches*, p. 235.

9. Munger and Fenno, p. 173.

10. Dean M. Kelley and George R. LaNoue, "The Church-State Settlement in the Federal Aid to Education Act," in *Religion and the Public Order: An Annual Review of Church and State and of Religion*, ed. Donald A. Giannella (Chicago: University of Chicago Press, 1966), pp. 116–17.

11. U.S., Congress, House, Committee on Education and Labor, General Subcommittee on Education, *Hearings on H. R. 2361 and H. R. 2362*, 89th Cong., 1st sess., p. 737.

12. George R. LaNoue, "Protestants and Politics," mimeo (New York: Teachers College, Columbia University, n.d.), p. 2.

13. Kelley and LaNoue, *Church-State Settlement*, pp. 126–28.

14. Eugene Eidenberg and Roy D. Morey, *An Act of Congress: The Legislative Process and the Making of Education Policy* (New York: W. W. Norton and Company), 1969, p. 108 n.

15. Ibid., p. 62.

Chapter 12

The basic theoretical perspective underlying the argument in this chapter is to be found in Mancur Olson, Jr., *The Logic of Collective Action: Public Goods and the Theory of Groups* (1965), which stresses the importance of "selective" incentives to group cohesion. Also, theoretically valuable for the internal cohesion of interest groups is Truman's *Governmental Process*. Several instances of the NCC's modification of tactics so as to forestall internal strife are cited in Nash, "Church Lobbying." The conservative publication *Christianity Today* was used extensively to discover internal dissent vis-à-vis NCC political activism and to determine the response of the NCC leaders to such dissent.

1. Truman, *Governmental Process*, p. 116.

2. V. O. Key, *Politics, Parties and Pressure Groups,* 5th ed. (New York: Crowell, 1964), pp. 85–88.

3. U.S., Congress, Senate, Committee on the Judiciary, Subcommittee on Constitutional Rights, *Hearings on S. 3296 and other bills,* 89th Cong., 2d sess., 28 July 1966, pp. 1,498–99.

4. The figure 56.7 million differs somewhat from other published information on the council's aggregate membership. The figure 42.5 million members is the total appearing in the *Yearbook of American Churches* (1967). The reason for the discrepancy is not immediately apparent. U.S., Congress, Senate, Subcommittee on Constitutional Amendments of the Committee on the Judiciary, *Hearings on Senate Joint Resolution 148,* 89th Cong., 2d sess., 5 Aug. 1966, pp. 44–45, 47–48.

5. U.S., Congress, House, Special Subcommittee on Labor of the Committees on Education and Labor, *Hearings on H R 77 and H R 4350 and similar bills* (to repeal sec. 14(b) of Taft-Hartley), 89th Cong., 1st sess., 4 June 1965, pp. 652–53.

6. *New York Times,* 19 Sept. 1966.

7. Ibid.; U.S., Congress, Senate, *Congressional Record,* 89th Cong., 2d sess., 20 Sept. 1966, pp. 23, 121–22. For the NCC rebuttal see: Lauris Whitman and Glen Trimble, "Proof and Daniel Poling," *Information Service,* 19 Nov. 1966, pp. 1–4.

8. U.S., Congress, Senate, Committee on the Judiciary, Subcommittee on Constitutional Rights, *Hearings on S. 3296 and other bills,* 89th Cong., 2d sess., 28 July 1966, pp. 1,498–1,500.

9. U.S., Congress, House, Committees on Education and Labor, Special Subcommittee on Labor, *Hearings on H. R. 77 and H. R. 4350,* 89th Cong., 1st sess., 4 June 1965, pp. 654–57.

10. *Christianity Today,* 26 Mar. 1965, p. 45; *New York Times,* 6 Mar. 1965, p. 13.

11. *Christianity Today,* 14 Nov. 1964, p. 154.

12. *Christianity Today,* 1 Jan. 1965, p. 362.

13. *New York Times,* 4 Dec. 1964, p. 19.

14. Ibid.

15. Ibid. See also *Christianity Today,* 1 January 1965, p. 362.

16. Nash, "Church Lobbying," p. 311.

17. *New York Times,* 10 Aug. 1967, p. 16.

18. Quoted in *Christianity Today,* 10 Nov. 1967, p. 152.

19. James Y. Holloway, "Violence and Snopes," *Katallagate* (official publication of the Committee of Southern Churchmen, Nashville, Tennessee), Winter 1967–68, p. 4.

20. *Christianity Today,* 5 July 1968, pp. 43–44.

21. Mancur Olson, Jr., *The Logic of Collective Action: Public Goods and the Theory of Groups* (Cambridge, Mass.: Harvard University Press, 1965), pp. 50–51.

22. Ibid., p. 61.

23. Ibid., p. 63.

24. Ibid., p. 132.

25. Ibid., p. 135.

26. Ibid., p. 160.

27. Samuel McCrea Cavert, *Church Cooperation and Unity in America: A Historical Review, 1900–1970* (New York: Association Press, 1970), p. 31.

Chapter 13

The selected bibliography ("ACLU, NAACP, and AFL-CIO") offers a complete list of the works consulted for the comparative section of this chapter. Of special importance in understanding the internal dynamics of these three groups were Philip Taft, *The A. F. of L. from the Death of Gompers to Merger* (1959); Charles M. Markman, *The Noblest Cry: A History of the American Civil Liberties Union* (1964); Bean Barton, "Pressure for Freedom: The American Civil Liberties Union" (1955); and Clement Vose, *Caucasians Only: The Supreme Court, the NAACP and the Restrictive Covenant Cases* (1959).

1. Art Preis, *Labor's Giant Step: Twenty Years of the CIO* (New York: Pioneer Press, 1964), p. 46.

2. Interview with Allen Wrightman, ACLU national office, Aug. 1967.

3. Robert J. Christen, "A Major Conflict in the ACLU," *Dissent*, Sept.–Oct. 1969, pp. 375–79.

4. Sidney Lens, "Labor Unity is No Panacea," *Antioch Review* 15, 2 (June 1955): 187.

5. William C. McLoughlin, "Is There a Third Force in Christendom?" *Daedalus* 96, no. 1 (Winter 1967): 63.

Bibliography

Protestant Relations with the Existing Social Order

Berger, Peter L. *The Noise of Solemn Assemblies*. Garden City, N. Y.: Doubleday & Company, 1961.

Cavert, Samuel McCrea. *The American Churches in the Ecumenical Movement, 1900–1968*. New York: Association Press, 1968.

Day, Peter. "The National Council of Churches: An Evaluation." *Christianity and Crisis*, 16 May 1960, pp. 67–71.

Dunbar, Leslie W. *A Republic of Equals*. Ann Arbor: The University of Michigan Press, 1966.

Fuchs, Lawrence H. *The Political Behavior of American Jews*. Glencoe, Ill.: Free Press, 1956.

Hammond, Philip E. *The Campus Clergyman*. New York: Basic Books, 1966.

Hutchinson, John A. *We Are Not Divided: A Critical and Historical Study of the Federal Council of the Churches of Christ in America*. New York: Round Table Press, 1941.

Lenski, Gerhard. *The Religious Factor*. Garden City, N. Y.: Doubleday & Company, 1961.

Marty, Martin E. *The New Shape of American Religion*. New York: Harper & Row Publishers, 1959.

Salisbury, W. Seward. *Religion in American Culture*. Homewood, Ill.: Dorsey Press, 1964.

Yinger, J. Milton. *Religion and the Struggle for Power*. Durham, N. C.: Duke University Press, 1946.

The 1950 Merger and Member-Church Involvement

Carter, Paul A. *The Decline and Revival of the Social Gospel: Social and Political Liberalism in American Protestant Churches, 1920–1940*. Ithaca, N. Y.: Cornell University Press, 1968.

Cavert, Samuel McCrea. *The American Churches in the Ecumenical Movement, 1900–1968*. New York: Association Press, 1968.

Christian Century, 13 Dec. 1950.

Douglas, H. Paul, and Bruner, Edmund. *The Protestant Church as a Social Institution.* New York: Institute for Social and Religious Research, 1935.

Etzioni, Amitai. *Modern Organizations.* Englewood Cliffs, N. J.: Prentice Hall, 1964.

Hopkins, Charles H. *The Rise of the Social Gospel in American Protestantism, 1865–1915.* New Haven, Conn.: Yale University Press, 1940.

Hutchinson, John A. *We Are Not Divided: A Critical and Historical Study of the Federal Council of the Churches of Christ in America.* New York: Round Table Press, 1940.

Lee, Robert E. *The Social Sources of Church Unity.* New York: Abington Press, 1960.

Meyer, Donald B. *The Protestant Search for Political Realism, 1919–1940.* Berkeley: University of California Press, 1961.

Truman, David B. *The Governmental Process.* New York: Alfred A. Knopf, 1951.

U.S. Bureau of the Census. *Census of Religious Bodies.* Washington, D. C.: United States Government Printing Office, 1926 and 1936.

Liberal and Conservative Tendencies among Member Churches

ABC. American Baptist Convention Yearbook, 1948 and 1960.

Berger, Peter L. "A Market Model for the Analysis of Ecumenicity." *Social Research* 30, no. 1 (Spring 1963): 77–90.

Carter, Paul A. *The Decline and Revival of the Social Gospel: Social and Political Liberalism in American Protestant Churches, 1920–1940.* Ithaca, N. Y.: Cornell University Press, 1956.

Drake, St. Clair, and Cayton, Horace R. *Black Metropolis.* New York: Harcourt, Brace and Co., 1945.

Encyclopedia of the African Methodist Episcopal Church. 2d ed. Compiled by Bishop Richard R. Wright. Philadelphia: Book Concern of the AME Church, 1948.

Frazier, E. Franklin. *Black Bourgeoisie.* Glencoe, Ill.: Free Press, 1957.

————. *The Negro Church in America.* New York: Shocken Books, 1964.

Gustafson, James M. "The Theological Education of Negro Ministers." In *The Advancement of Theological Education,* edited by H. R. Niebuhr, D. D. Williams, and J. M. Gustafson. New York: Harper & Row Publishers, 1957.

Harrison, Paul M. *Authority and Power in the Free Church Tradition.* Princeton, N. J.: Princeton University Press, 1959.

Hopkins, Charles H. *The Rise of the Social Gospel in American Protestantism, 1865–1915.* New Haven, Conn.: Yale University Press, 1940.

Loescher, Frank S. *The Protestant Church and the Negro: A Pattern of Segregation.* New York: Association Press, 1948.

Meyendorff, John. *The Orthodox Church: Its Past and Its Role in the World Today.* Translated from the French by John Chapin. New York: Pantheon Books, 1960.

Meyer, Donald B. *The Protestant Search for Political Realism, 1919–1940.* Berkeley: University of California Press, 1961.

Miller, Robert H. *American Protestantism and Social Issues, 1919–1939.* Chapel Hill: University of North Carolina Press, 1958.

Myrdal, Gunnar. *An American Dilemma,* vol. 2. New York: Harper & Row Publishers, 1944.

Pope, Liston. *The Kingdom Beyond Caste.* New York: Friendship Press, 1957.
Reimers, David M. *White Protestantism and the Negro.* New York: Oxford University Press, 1965.
Smith, Charles S. *A History of the African Methodist Episcopal Church.* Philadelphia: Book Concern of the AME Church, 1922.
Torbet, Robert G. *A History of the Baptists.* Rev. ed. Valley Forge, Pennsylvania: Judson Press, 1963.
Washington, Joseph R. *The Politics of God.* Boston: Beacon Press, 1967.
Wilson, James Q. *Negro Politics: The Search for Leadership.* Glencoe, Ill.: Free Press, 1960.
Yinger, J. Milton. *Religion and the Struggle for Power.* Durham, N. C.: Duke University Press, 1946.

The National Lay Committee Controversy

Blake, Eugene Carson. Letter to the Editor. *Christianity and Crisis,* 12 May 1952, pp. 62–63.
Cavert, Samuel McCrea. *The American Churches in the Ecumenical Movement, 1900–1968.* New York: Association Press, 1968.
FCC. *Annual Report.* New York: National Offices, NCC, 1950.
Galbraith, John Kenneth. " 'The Affluent Society' After Ten Years." *Atlantic* 223, no. 5 (May 1969): 37–44.
Lundberg, Ferdinand. *The Rich and the Super-Rich: A Study of Power and Money in America.* New York: Bantam Books, 1969.
NCC. *First Biennial Report.* New York: National Offices, NCC, 1953.
Pew, J. Howard. *The Chairman's Final Report to the National Lay Committee.* New York: National Offices, NCC, 1955.
"What Happened at Cleveland." *Christian Century,* 13 Dec. 1950, pp. 1,481–82, 1,500. [Concerns the NCC founding convention.]

Staff Liberalism

Cox, Harvey G. "The 'New Breed' in American Churches." *Daedalus* 96, no. 1 (Winter 1967): 135–50.
Harrison, Paul M. *Authority and Power in the Free Church Tradition.* Princeton, N. J.: Princeton University Press, 1959.
Lenski, Gerhard. *The Religious Factor.* Garden City, N. Y.: Doubleday & Company, 1961.
Littell, Franklin H. "Protestant Seminary Education in a Time of Change." In *Seminary Education in a Time of Change,* edited by James M. Lee and Louis J. Putz. Notre Dame, Ind.: Fides Publishers, 1965.
Newcomb, Theodore M. *Persistence and Change: Bennington College and Its Students After Twenty-Five Years.* New York: John Wiley & Sons, 1967.
Niebuhr, Reinhold. "The Radical Minister and His Church." *Radical Religion* 2 (Winter 1936): 25–27.
———. "Religion as a Source of Radicalism." *Christian Century,* 11 Apr. 1934, pp. 491–94.
Reissig, Herman. "Homeless Religious Radicals." *Christian Century,* 4 Aug. 1937, pp. 971–73.
Sanford, Nevitt. *The American College.* New York: John Wiley & Sons, 1962.
———. *Where Colleges Fail.* San Francisco: Jossey-Bass, 1967.
Taylor, Charles P. *Ministry for Tomorrow: Report of the Special Committee on*

Theological Education of the Protestant Episcopal Church. Greenwich, Conn.: Seabury Press, 1967.

Yinger, J. Milton. *A Sociologist Looks at Religion.* New York: Macmillan Company, 1963.

Local Church Councils

Cate, William B. "Institutionalism and Ecumenical Cooperation in the Local Community." In *Institutionalism and Church Unity: A Symposium,* edited by Nils Ehrenstrom and Walter G. Muelder. New York: Association Press, 1963.

Glock, Charles Y., and Ringer, Benjamin B. "Church Policy and the Attitudes of Ministers and Parishioners on Social Issues." *American Sociological Review* 21, no. 2 (Apr. 1956): 148–56.

Johnson, Benton. "Ascetic Protestantism and Political Preferences." *Public Opinion Quarterly* 26, no. 1 (Spring 1962): 35–45.

Knapp, Forrest L. *Church Cooperation: Dead-End Street or Highway to Unity?* Garden City, N. Y.: Doubleday & Company, 1966.

Lee, Robert E. *The Social Sources of Church Unity.* New York: Abington Press, 1960.

Pratt, Henry J. "The Protestant Council of the City of New York as a Political Interest Group." Ph.D. diss., Columbia University, 1962.

Sanderson, Ross W. *Church Cooperation in the United States: The Nation-Wide Backgrounds and Ecumenical Significance of State and Local Councils of Churches in Their Historical Perspective.* New York: Association of Council Secretaries, 1960.

U.S. Congress. House. *H. R. 3198,* Union Calendar no. 1085, 81st Cong., 2d sess., created pursuant to *H. R. 298.* Washington, D. C.: U.S. Government Printing Office, 1950. Reprinted in *Public Opinion and Propaganda,* edited by Daniel Katz et. al. New York: Dryden Press, 1954.

Civil Rights Involvement and CORR

Blanchard, Eric C. "The Delta Ministry." *Christian Century,* 17 Mar. 1965, pp. 337–38.

Congressional Quarterly Service. *A Revolution in Civil Rights.* 4th ed. Washington, D.C.: U.S. Government Printing Office, 1968.

CORR. *Reports.* New York: National Offices, NCC, 1963–66. [Issued quarterly, 1963–66.]

FCC. *Annual Reports.* New York: National Offices, NCC, section dealing with Department of Race Relations.

Hasledon, Kyle. "11 A.M. Is Our Most Segregated Hour." *New York Times Magazine,* 2 Aug. 1964, pp. 24–25.

Hedgeman, Anna Arnold. *The Trumpet Sounds: A Memoir of Negro Leadership.* New York: Holt, Rinehart and Winston, 1964.

Hilton, Bruce. *The Delta Ministry.* New York: Macmillan Company, 1969.

Hutchinson, John A. *We Are Not Divided: A Critical and Historical Study of the Federal Council of the Churches of Christ in America.* New York: Round Table Press, 1941.

Interchurch News, June–July 1963, Aug.–Sept. 1963. [*Interchurch News* is published by the NCC.]

Kesselman, Louis C. *The Social Politics of FEPC: A Study in Reform Pressure Movements.* Chapel Hill: University of North Carolina Press, 1948.

"Mississippi—An Ecumenical Ministry." *Social Action* 21, no. 3 (Nov. 1964): 16–19. [*Social Action* is published by the United Church of Christ.]

Moynihan, Daniel P. "The President and the Negro." *Commentary* 43, no. 2 (Feb. 1967): 31–45.

Payton, Benjamin F. "Civil Rights and the Future of American Cities." *Social Action* 33, no. 4 (Dec. 1966): 1–6.

Rainwater, Lee, and Yancey, William L. *The Moynihan Report and the Politics of Controversy.* Cambridge, Mass.: M.I.T. Press, 1967.

Reimers, David M. *White Protestantism and the Negro.* New York: Oxford University Press, 1965.

"The Role of the National Council of Churches in the Mississippi Summer Protest." *Social Action* 31, no. 3 (Nov. 1964): 10–15.

Schaller, Lyle. *The Churches' War Against Poverty.* Nashville: Abington Press, 1967.

Spike, Robert W. *The Freedom Revolution and the Churches.* New York: Association Press, 1965.

Vose, Clement. *Caucasians Only: The Supreme Court, the NAACP, and the Restrictive Covenant Cases.* Berkeley: University of California Press, 1959.

Zangrando, Robert Lewis. "The Efforts of the National Association for the Advancement of Colored People to Secure Passage of a Federal Anti-Lynching Law, 1920–1940." Ph.D. diss., University of Pennsylvania, 1963.

NCC Educational Policy

Beaney, William M., and Beiser, Edward N. "Prayer and Politics: The Impact of 'Engle' and 'Schempp' on the Political Process." *Journal of Public Law* 13, no. 2 (1964): 475–98.

Eidenberg, Eugene, and Morey, Roy D. *An Act of Congress: The Legislative Process and the Making of Education Policy.* New York: W. W. Norton & Company, 1969.

Hunt, R. L. "Why Bus Transportation." *Phi Delta Kappan* 42, no. 8 (May 1961): 356–60.

Kelley, Dean M., and LaNoue, George R. "The Church-State Settlement in the Federal Aid to Education Act." In *Religion and the Public Order: An Annual Review of Church and State and of Religion, 1965,* edited by Donald A. Giannella. Chicago: University of Chicago Press, 1966.

Munger, Frank J., and Fenno, Richard F. *National Politics and Federal Aid to Education.* The Economics and Politics of Public Education Series, no. 3. Syracuse, N. Y.: Syracuse University Press, 1962.

Sanders, Thomas G. *Protestant Concepts of Church and State: Historical Backgrounds and Approaches for the Future.* New York: Holt, Rinehart and Winston, 1964.

Stedman, Murray S. *Religion and Politics in America.* New York: Harcourt, Brace and Co., 1961.

The Effect of Activism on NCC Cohesion

"Address by Edwin Espy." *Information Service,* 17 Feb. 1962, p. 2.

Cavert, Samuel McCrea. *Church Cooperation and Unity in America: A Historical Review, 1900–1970.* New York: Association Press, 1970.

Darrow, R. Morton. "The Church and Techniques of Political Action." In *Religious Perspectives in American Life,* vol. 2, edited by James W. Smith and A. Leland Jamison. Princeton, N. J.: Princeton University Press, 1961, pp. 161–94.

Ebersole, Luke E. *Church Lobbying in the Nation's Capital.* New York: Macmillan Company, 1951.

FCC. *Annual Report.* New York: National Offices, FCC, 1935 and 1946.

Hubbard, Howard. "Five Long Hot Summers and How They Grew." *Public Interest,* no. 12 (Summer 1968): 16–20.

Interchurch News, Mar. and Apr. 1960.

Key, V. O. *Politics, Parties and Pressure Groups.* 5th ed. New York: Crowell, 1964.

LaNoue, George R. "Protestants and Politics." Mimeographed. New York: Teachers College, Columbia University, n.d.

McKean, Dayton D. "State, Church and the Lobby." In *Religious Perspectives in American Life,* vol. 2, edited by James W. Smith and A. Leland Jamison. Princeton, N. J.: Princeton University Press, 1961, pp. 119–60.

Nash, James Allen. "Church Lobbying in the Federal Government." Ph.D. diss., Boston University, 1967.

NCC. "Consultation on Christian Witness in the Nation's Capital, Interim Report." Mimeographed, 19 Dec. 1966.

Olson, Jr., Mancur. *The Logic of Collective Action: Public Goods and the Theory of Groups.* Cambridge, Mass.: Harvard University Press, 1965.

Whitman, Lauris, and Trimble, Glen. "Proof and Daniel Poling." *Information Service,* 19 Nov. 1966, pp. 1–4.

ACLU, NAACP, and AFL-CIO

ACLU. *Annual Report.* New York: ACLU, selected years.

AFL-CIO. *Report of the Proceedings of the Annual Convention.* New York: ACLU, Washington, D. C.: AFL-CIO, selected years.

Barton, Bean. "Pressure for Freedom: The American Civil Liberties Union." Ph.D. diss., Cornell University, 1955.

Christen, Robert J. "A Major Conflict in the ACLU." *Dissent,* Sept.–Oct. 1969, pp. 375–79.

DuBois, W. E. B. *Dusk of Dawn.* New York: Harcourt, Brace & Co., 1940.

Johnson, Guy. "Negro Racial Movements and Leadership in the United States." *American Journal of Sociology* 43, no. 1 (July 1937): 57–71.

Kroll, Jack. "Labor's Political Role." *Annals of the American Academy of Political and Social Sciences* 274 (Mar. 1951): 118–23.

Lens, Sidney. "Labor Unity is No Panacea." *Antioch Review* 15, no. 2 (June 1955): 180–94.

NAACP. *Annual Report.* New York: NAACP, selected years.

Odegard, Peter. *American Politics: A Study in Political Dynamics.* New York: Harper & Row Publishers, 1951.

Preis, Art. *Labor's Giant Step: Twenty Years of the CIO.* New York: Pioneer Press, 1964.

Taft, Philip. *The A. F. of L. from the Death of Gompers to Merger.* New York: Harper & Row Publishers, 1959.

———. "Internal Characteristics of American Unionism." *Annals of the American Academy of Political and Social Sciences* 274 (Mar. 1951): 94–101.

Vose, Clement. *Caucasians Only: The Supreme Court, the NAACP, and the Restrictive Covenant Cases.* Berkeley: University of California Press, 1959.

Wilensky, Herbert. *Intellectuals in Labor Unions.* Glencoe, Ill.: Free Press, 1955.

Zangrando, Robert Lewis. "The Efforts of the National Association for the Advancement of Colored People to Secure Passage of a Federal Anti-Lynching Law, 1920–1940." Ph.D. diss., University of Pennsylvania, 1963.

Index

African Methodist Episcopal Church, 80–82. *See also* Black demoninations

Air Force training manual controversy, 147–48

American Baptist Convention, 69; participation in council, leadership, 52, 53, 54, 55, 62; conservative tendencies, 73–78; effect on council policy, 82; as Baptist church North, 49, 66; reaction to Forman manifesto, 196; selective benefits as factor in council involvement, 256–57; Washington staff, 143, 224; stand on education issues, 230

American Civil Liberties Union, 149, 267–76 passim; in 1965 education struggle, 223, 225

American Council of Christian Churches, 277

American Federation of Labor, 267–76 passim

Association of Council Secretaries, 167, 168

Becker, Frank (congressman), 228, 229

Black denominations: participation in council leadership, 49, 52, 54, 55, 56, 62; conservative tendencies, 78–82; involvement in Black Manifesto issue, 195, 198; *see also* National Baptist Convention, African Methodist Episcopal Church

Blake, Eugene Carson, 57, 230, 264; in National Lay Committee controversy, 99–103; as NCC civil rights leader, 158–87 passim

Carothers, J. Edward, 237–38

Cavert, Samuel McCrea, 27, 89; quoted, 158, 256

Child benefit theory, 212, 221, 222, 225, 226

Christian Life and Work, NCC Division of, 39, 41; merger with Division of Home Missions, 42–44

Christianity Today, 102, 110, 127, 247

Church and Economic Life, NCC Department of, 18, 39; in National Lay Committee controversy, 93–94, 98

Church of the Brethren, 54, 62, 144

Cleveland conferences (leading to formation of NCC), 30–31, 87–89

Congregational Church. *See* United Church of Christ

Conservatives (response to NCC), 234–48. *See also* American Baptist Convention, Eastern Orthodox churches, Black denominations

Council of Churches of New York City, 126, 134, 179

Cultural and Racial Relations, NCC Department of. *See* Race Relations

Dahlberg, Edwin T., 58, 75, 77

Day, Peter, 18–19, 251

Decision making process (in NCC), 58–61, 159–66, 193–98, 210–18, 232

Delta Ministry, 54, 173–77

Denominational involvement in council, 46–58, 61–62, 252–59. *See also* Individual denominations

Disciples of Christ: participation in council leadership, 49, 52, 53, 54, 58, 62; evolving political attitudes

(1900–1960), 64–68; involvement in Black Manifesto issue, 195

Eastern Orthodox churches: participation in council leadership, 52, 53, 54, 56, 62; conservative tendencies, 69–73, 251; effect on council policy, 82

Elementary and Secondary School Act of 1965, 218–27, 264

Elliott, Willis E., quoted, 250

Episcopal Church: participation in council leadership, 52, 53, 54, 55, 56, 57, 61; evolving political attitudes (1900–1960), 64–68; overrepresented on National Lay Committee, 87; Washington staff, 144; involvement in Black Manifesto issue, 190, 194, 203; internal strife related to civil rights, 245; early tenuous involvement in council, 255

Espy, R. H. Edwin, 110–11, 198, 247; role in NCC shift toward activism, 155–56, 162

Etzioni, Amitai, 35, 41, 44

Evangelical United Brethren Church: participation in council leadership, 52, 53, 54, 55, 56, 57, 61

Fiers, A. Dale, 177, 195

Flemming, Arthur, as NCC president, 58, 248, 264; as NCC spokesman on education, 223–25

Foreign policy involvement (of NCC), 1, 2, 239–40

Foreign Missions Conference of North America, 31, 34

Forman, James, 188–206 passim

Founding convention (of FCC, 1908), 14–15

Frazier, E. Franklin, 79

Freedom Budget for All Americans, 183–84

Great Depression, 116, 263; effect on council, 27–28; effect on constituent churches, 65–67

Hall, Cameron P., 18, 39

Hedgeman, Anna Arnold, 167, 185

Holloway, James Y., quoted, 250–51

Home Missions, NCC Division on, 35–41; origins as Home Missions Conference of North America, 34

Hunter, J. David, quoted, 236–37

Hutchinson, B. E., 96–97, 99–102

Internal Revenue Code as constraint on churches, 143

Interchurch Center, 42, 190–91, 198

Interreligious Federation for Community Organization (IFCO), 187; role in Black Manifesto issue, 191–95, 202

Johnson, F. Ernest, 17, 26

Johnson, President Lyndon B., 168, 178, 219–20

Kelley, Dean M.: comments on change in NCC social action strategy, 41–42; leadership in church-state redefinition, 217; role in education struggles, 220, 230–31

King, Martin Luther, Jr., 160, 161, 167, 172, 205, 264

Laity, political attitudes of, 18–21, 123–24, 134

Lee, J. Oscar: role in 1949 civil rights mobilization, 152; in 1963–67 era, 162, 164–65, 185

Lenski, Gerhard, 20–21, 119

Lewis, John (of SNCC), 166–67, 249

Liberal activism (in NCC), 13, 21–22, 141–233 passim

Lichtenberger, Arthur, 165, 230

Lutheran Church in America: participation in council leadership, 52, 53, 54, 55, 56, 61; evolving political attitudes (1900–1960), 64–68; attitudes on education matters, 209, 224, 230

Marshall, Calvin, 193, 202–3

Martin, William T., 58, 95, 99

Methodist Church. *See* United Methodist Church

Miller, J. Irwin, 58, 103–4, 264; role in 1954 council statement on economic principles, 97; civil rights role, 151, 161

Moynihan, Daniel P., 179–80
Mueller, Reuben, 57, 58, 246–47

National Association for the Advancement of Colored People, 149, 182, 267–76 passim
National Association of Evangelicals, 213, 224
National Baptist Convention, 53, 195, 198. *See also* Black denominations
National Black Economic Development Conference (NBEDC), 181, 191–98, 201–4
National Catholic Conference. *See* Roman Catholic Church
National Committee of Black Churchmen, 187, 195, 201
National Education Association, 220, 226–27
National Lay Committee, 18, 84–104 passim, 263
National Preaching Mission (in FCC), 27–29
Niebuhr, Reinhold: attack on social gospel assumptions, 17; member of Union Seminary faculty, 116; confronts problem of middle class parish, 119; criticizes *Engel V. Vitale* decision, 228

Office for Councils of Churches (of NCC), 125, 126, 135
Olson, Mancur, Jr., 252–59
Oxnam, G. Bromley, 89, 152

Payton, Benjamin F., 177–87, 240–41
Pew, J. Howard, 18, 84–104 passim, 263
Poling, Daniel A., 239–40
Protestant conciliar movement, 125, 127, 136
Presbyterian Church in the U. S. (Southern Presbyterian): participation in council leadership, 49, 52, 53, 54, 56, 62; evolving political attitudes (1900–1960), 64–68; involvement in Black Manifesto issue, 196, 203; internal strife related to civil rights, 246, 248; early tenuous involvement in council, 255
Presbyterian Church, United; Presby-

terian Church in the U. S. A. *See* United Presbyterian Church

Quakers (Religious Society of Friends), 54, 61; Washington staff, 143

Race Relations, FCC Commission on, 148–50; NCC Department on Cultural and Racial Relations, 152, 162. *See also* Religion and Race; J. Oscar Lee
Reformed Church in America: participation in council leadership, 49, 53, 54, 62; involvement in Black Manifesto issue, 190
Regier, Jon: an organizational leader, 37–41, 44; role in civil rights, 162, 164
Religion and Public Education, NCC Committee on, 212, 215
Religion and Race, NCC Commission on (CORR), 42, 158–87 passim. *See also* Race Relations
Revised Social Ideals. *See* Social Creed
Roman Catholic Church: basis for forming separate school system, 209; position on federal aid to education, 210, 211, 212; opposed by some Protestant groups on school issue, 214; church-state doctrines arouse Protestant concern, 216–18; National Catholic Conference role in 1965 school bill, 220, 225, 226, 227; liberal Catholics' role in defeat of Becker amendment, 230–31; growing liberal Catholic coalition with NCC, 263, 265
Roosevelt, President Franklin D., 27, 144, 146, 150, 262

School prayer struggle, 227–32
Sherrill, Henry Knox, 57; role in National Lay Committee issue, 90–91, 99; civil rights role in 1940's, 152
Smith, B. Julian, 165, 170
Social Creed, "Social Ideals of the Churches" (1908), 15–16; "Revised Social Ideals" (1932), 17, 26, 88, 149
Social Gospel Movement: as embodied

in early council, 15, 33, 34, 262; defended against criticism from Niebuhr, 17; movement activists as denominational delegates to council, 48; declining force in 1930's and '40's, 50–51; effect of movement on constituent council bodies, 64–65; as factor in activity of National Lay Committee, 92, 104, 263
Spike, Robert W., 165–79, 180, 184

Taft, Charles P., 18, 39, 86, 97
Transformationism (as a premise in revised liberal Protestant stands on church-state issues), 216–17
Tuller, Edwin H., 196, 230

Union Theological Seminary: as source of NCC staff, 113–16; and basic church-state issues, 216
Unitarian-Universalist Church, 129, 224
United Church of Christ (also Congregational and Evangelical and Reformed churches), participation in leadership, 49, 52, 53, 54, 55, 61; evolving political attitudes, 64–68; involvement in Black Manifesto issue, 198; policy proposals related to civil disobedience, 251
United Methodist Church (also Meth-

odist Church), participation in council leadership, 49, 52, 53, 54, 55, 56, 57, 61; evolving political attitudes (1900–1960), 64–68; Washington staff, 143; involvement in Black Manifesto Issue, 190, 194; stand on education issues, 230
United Presbyterian Church (also Northern Presbyterian, Presbyterian Church in the U.S.A.), participation in council leadership, 49, 52, 53, 54, 55, 57, 61; evolving political attitudes (1900–1960), 64–68; overrepresented on National Lay Committee, 87; Washington staff, 144; response to Birmingham, 161; involvement in Black Manifesto issue, 190, 194, 203
Unity of the Brethren Church, 245, 258

Vatican ambassador controversy, 146–47, 277

Washington Office (of NCC), 145–46, 248
Wedel, Cynthia O., 57

Yale Divinity School, as source of NCC staff, 113–15; and basic church-state issues, 216

Henry J. Pratt, currently Assistant Professor of the Department of Political Science at Wayne State University, received an A.B. from Dartmouth College (1956), an M.P.A. from the University of Michigan (1959), and a Ph.D. in political science from Columbia University (1962). He has published studies of ethnic minority group interest, churches and urban renewal, and urban planning. His continuing research interests are in the areas of ethnic-religious and urban politics.

This manuscript was edited by Aletta Biersack. The book was designed by Joanne Kinney. The type face for the text is Linotype Caslon, and the display face is Caslon Old Style. Both were designed by William Caslon about 1725.

The text is printed on Nashoba paper and the book is bound in Columbia Mills' Llamique cloth over binders' board. Manufactured in the United States of America.